# interchange

## English for international communication

## Jack C. Richards

### with Jonathan Hull and Susan Proctor

**1**

## Teacher's Manual

The right of the
University of Cambridge
to print and publish
all kinds of books
was granted by law
in 1534.
The University has printed
and published continuously
since 1584.

## Cambridge University Press

Cambridge • New York • Port Chester • Melbourne • Sydney

Published by the Press Syndicate of the University of Cambridge
The Pitt Building, Trumpington Street, Cambridge CB2 1RP
40 West 20th Street, New York, NY 10011, USA
10 Stamford Road, Oakleigh, Melbourne 3166, Australia

First published 1990

Printed in the United States of America

ISBN 0 521 35989 9 Teacher's Manual One
ISBN 0 521 35988 0 Student's Book One
ISBN 0 521 35990 2 Workbook One
ISBN 0 521 35203 7 Class Cassette Set One
ISBN 0 521 35204 5 Student Cassette One

Book design: Circa 86, Inc.
Cover design: Tom Wharton


Illustrators
Jack DeGraffenried
Craig Hanna


*British Library Cataloguing in Publication Data*
Richards, Jack C.
    Interchange : English for international communication .
    Teacher's manual 1.
    1. English language. Usage
    I. Title   II. Hull, Jonathan   III. Proctor, Susan
    428
    ISBN 0-521-35989-9

# Contents

# Plan of Student's Book 1

| | Topics | Functions | Grammar/Pronunciation |
|---|---|---|---|
| **UNIT 1** | **Topics** Greetings; names; occupations; countries; nationalities; spelling | **Functions** Introducing oneself; asking for personal information; greeting people; saying goodbye | **Grammar** Present tense statements with *be*; Wh- and Yes/No questions with *be* |
| **UNIT 2** | **Topics** Greetings; occupations and workplaces; numbers; names; addresses | **Functions** Greeting people; describing occupations; describing work | **Grammar** Wh-questions with *do*; prepositions: *for, at, in, to*; present tense statements <br> **Pronunciation** Word stress |
| **UNIT 3** | **Topics** Money; prices; expenses; shopping | **Functions** Asking about prices; selling and buying things | **Grammar** Possessive pronouns; demonstrative adjectives and pronouns (singular, plural); Wh-questions with *be* <br> **Pronunciation** Plural *s* |

## Review of Units 1–3

| | | | |
|---|---|---|---|
| **UNIT 4** | **Topics** Music, movies, and TV programs; entertainers; invitations; dates and times | **Functions** Describing likes and dislikes; making invitations | **Grammar** Object pronouns; Yes/No questions with *do*; *there is*; prepositions: *at, on* <br> **Pronunciation** Question intonation |
| **UNIT 5** | **Topics** Families; interesting people | **Functions** Asking about and describing families; describing people; making small talk; ending a conversation | **Grammar** Wh- and Yes/No questions with *do/does* (3rd person) <br> **Pronunciation** Third-person *s* |
| **UNIT 6** | **Topics** Leisure and recreation; sports and exercise | **Functions** Describing routines and activities; talking about frequency; asking about and describing exercises | **Grammar** Adverbs of frequency <br> **Pronunciation** Reduced form of *do* |

## Review of Units 4–6

| | | | |
|---|---|---|---|
| **UNIT 7** | **Topics** Greetings; weekend activities; vacations | **Functions** Talking about past events; asking for information; narrating | **Grammar** Past tense; Wh- and Yes/No questions in past tense <br> **Pronunciation** Past tense *-ed* |
| **UNIT 8** | **Topics** Cities and places; neighborhoods; houses and apartments | **Functions** Asking about and describing locations of places; asking about and describing a neighborhood | **Grammar** *There is, there are*; *one, any, some* <br> **Pronunciation** Vowel contrast /ey/ and /ɛ/ |

| Listening | Reading/Writing | Interchange Activity | |
|---|---|---|---|
| **Listening** Listening to sounds and identifying what people are doing; listening to a description of a missing person | **Writing** Writing a description of someone<br><br>**Reading** Fashion firsts; dating customs | **Interchange** Describing people in a picture | UNIT **9** |

### Review of Units 7–9

| | | | |
|---|---|---|---|
| **Listening** Listening to descriptions of events; listening for order of events | **Writing** Writing a story in the past tense<br><br>**Reading** Car facts; article about catching a thief | **Interchange** Narrating a story based on pictures | UNIT **10** |
| **Listening** Listening to descriptions of hometowns; listening for correct and incorrect information | **Writing** Describing a country<br><br>**Reading** City living; famous cities | **Interchange** Planning a "perfect" vacation | UNIT **11** |
| **Listening** Listening to complaints and advice; listening to questions | **Writing** Writing about a home remedy<br><br>**Reading** Facts about colds; home remedies | **Interchange** Taking an exercise class in English | UNIT **12** |

### Review of Units 10–12

| | | | |
|---|---|---|---|
| **Listening** Listening to someone making restaurant reservations; listening to restaurant orders | **Writing** Writing a restaurant review<br><br>**Reading** Food facts; when and how much to tip | **Interchange** Ordering a meal in a restaurant | UNIT **13** |
| **Listening** Listening to a radio quiz show; listening for correct and incorrect information about places | **Writing** Writing a comparison of two cities<br><br>**Reading** World geography; nations of the world | **Interchange** A quiz that tests general knowledge | UNIT **14** |
| **Listening** Listening to and receiving telephone messages; identifying invitations | **Writing** Writing invitations and excuses<br><br>**Reading** Free time; how to make an invitation | **Interchange** Giving and receiving phone messages | UNIT **15** |

### Review of Units 13–15

### Interchange Activities

vii

## Spelling Differences between American and British English

Words in Book 1 that have different spelling in British English:

| American spelling | British spelling |
|---|---|
| center | centre |
| check (noun) | cheque (noun) |
| color | colour |
| disk jockey | disc jockey |
| favorite | favourite |
| flavor | flavour |
| glamorous | glamourous |
| harbor | harbour |
| humor | humour |
| jail | gaol |
| jewelry | jewellery |
| kilometer | kilometre |
| labor | labour |
| liter | litre |
| neighbor | neighbour |
| neighborhood | neighbourhood |
| program | programme |
| theater | theatre |

## Phonetic Symbols

| | | | |
|---|---|---|---|
| iy | (sheep) | k | (key) |
| ɪ | (ship) | g | (girl) |
| ɛ | (yes) | s | (sun) |
| ey | (train) | z | (zoo) |
| æ | (hat) | ʃ | (shoe) |
| ʌ | (cup) | ʒ | (television) |
| ə | (a banana) | tʃ | (chair) |
| ər | (letter) | dʒ | (joke) |
| ɑ | (father) | f | (fan) |
| ɔ | (ball) | v | (van) |
| ow | (no) | w | (window) |
| ʊ | (book) | y | (yellow) |
| uw | (boot) | h | (how) |
| ay | (fine) | θ | (think) |
| ɔy | (boy) | ð | (the feather) |
| aw | (house) | m | (mouth) |
| ə | (a camera) | n | (nose) |
| ɜr | (word) | ŋ | (ring) |
| p | (pen) | l | (letter) |
| b | (baby) | l | (ball) |
| t | (tie) | r | (rain) |
| d | (door) | r | (here) |

# Introduction

*Interchange* is a three-level course in English as a second or foreign language for young adults and adults. The course covers the skills of listening, speaking, reading, and writing, with particular emphasis on listening and speaking. The primary goal of the course is to teach communicative competence, that is, the ability to communicate in English according to the situation, purpose, and roles of the participants. The language used in *Interchange* is American English; however, *Interchange* reflects the fact that English is the world's major language of international communication and is not limited to any one country, region, or culture. Level One is for beginners and takes students from beginner or false beginner to low-intermediate level.

## COURSE LENGTH

*Interchange* is a self-contained course covering all four language skills. Each level covers between 60 and 90 hours of class instruction time. Depending on how the book is used, however, more or less time may be utilized. The Teacher's Manual gives detailed suggestions for optional activities to extend each unit. Where less time is available, the course can be taught in approximately 60 hours by reducing the amount of time spent on communication activities, reading, writing, optional activities, and the Workbook.

## COURSE COMPONENTS

The course consists of a Student's Book, Teacher's Manual, Workbook, Class Cassettes, and Student's Cassette. Here is a summary of what each component includes:

**Student's Book**  The Student's Book contains fifteen six-page units, with a two-page review unit after every three units; there are five review units in all. Following Unit 15 is a set of communication activities called Interchange Activities, one for each unit of the book. Unit Summaries, at the end of the Student's Book, contain lists of the key

vocabulary and expressions used in each unit as well as additional grammar explanations.

**Teacher's Manual**  The Teacher's Manual contains detailed suggestions on how to teach the course, an extensive set of optional follow-up activities, complete answer keys to the Student's Book and Workbook exercises, tests for use in class and test answer keys, and transcripts of those listening activities not printed in the Student's Book and in the tests.

**Workbook**  The Workbook contains stimulating and varied exercises that provide additional practice on the teaching points presented in the Student's Book. A variety of exercise types is used to develop students' skills in grammar, reading, writing, spelling, vocabulary, and pronunciation. The Workbook can be used both for classwork and for homework.

**Class Cassettes**  There is a set of two cassettes for class use to accompany the Student's Book. They contain recordings of conversations, grammar summaries, pronunciation exercises, and listening activities, as well as recordings of the listening exercises used in the tests. A number of different native-speaker voices and accents are used, as well as some nonnative accents. There are native-speaker voices when the tape is used to model language; nonnative accents are used in some of the listening exercises to remind students that many people who speak English use it as a second or foreign language. Exercises that are recorded on the cassettes are indicated with the symbol ▭

**Student Cassette**  A cassette is also available for students to use for self-study. The Student Cassette contains selected recordings of conversations, grammar, and pronunciation exercises from the Student's Book.

## APPROACH AND METHODOLOGY

*Interchange* is based on the following methodological principles.

## Integration of form and function

In *Interchange,* grammar is seen as an important component of communicative competence. However, grammar is always presented communicatively, with exercises focusing on both accuracy and fluency. In this way, there is a link between grammatical form and communicative function. Fluency is achieved through information-gap tasks, pair work, group work, and role plays.

## Emphasis on meaningful communicative practice

Throughout the course, students have the opportunity to personalize the language they learn, to make use of their own world knowledge, and to express their ideas and opinions. Information-sharing activities allow for a maximum amount of student-generated communication.

## Focus on productive and receptive skills

In *Interchange,* both production and comprehension form the basis of language learning. Students' productive skills are developed through speaking and writing tasks, and their receptive skills are developed through listening and reading. The course teaches students to understand language that is at a higher level than they can produce, and this prepares them to make the transition from the classroom to the real world.

## Variety of learning modes

A number of different kinds of learning activities are used throughout the course. These include whole class activities and tasks done in small groups, pairs, or individually. This variation allows for a change of pace within lessons. The extensive use of pair work and group work activities in *Interchange* makes the course ideal in both large and small classes and gives students a greater amount of individual practice and interaction with others in the classroom.

## Teacher's and learners' roles

The teacher's role in *Interchange* is to present and model new learning items; however, during pair work, group work, and role play activities, the teacher's role is that of a facilitator. Here the teacher's primary function is to prepare students for an activity and then let them complete it using their own resources. During this phase, the teacher gives informal feedback to students and encourages maximum student participation.

The learners' role in *Interchange* is to participate actively and creatively in learning, using both the materials they study in the course and their own knowledge and language resources. Students are treated as intelligent adults with ideas and opinions of their own. Students learn through interacting with others in pair or group activities and draw both on previous learning as well as their own communicative skills.

## Teacher-friendly and student-friendly presentation

*Interchange* is easy to follow, with clearly identified teaching points, carefully organized and sequenced units, comfortable pacing, and a variety of stimulating and enjoyable learning tasks.

---

# SYLLABUS

*Interchange* has an integrated, multi-skills syllabus that links grammar, communicative functions, and topics. (See Plan of Book One on pp. iv–vii.) The syllabus also contains the four skills of listening, speaking, reading, and writing, as well as pronunciation and vocabulary. It is carefully graded, with a gradual progression of teaching items and frequent reviews.

**Grammar**    The course has a graded grammar syllabus that contains the essential grammar, tenses, and structures needed for a basic level of language proficiency. The grammar points are introduced in communicative contexts and through grammar summaries that illustrate the meaning and usage of each item.

**Functions**    A functional syllabus parallels the grammar syllabus in the course. Each unit presents several key functions (e.g., introducing oneself, asking for personal information, greeting people) that are linked to the grammar points and topic of the unit. Student's Book One presents about 45 essential functions, which provide a communicative base for beginner students and enable them to participate in simple communication on a wide variety of topics.

**Topics**    The course deals with contemporary and adult topics that are of interest and relevance to learners of different cultural backgrounds. Information is presented that can serve as a basis for cross-cultural comparison and that both students and teachers will find stimulating and enjoyable. The topics have been selected for their interest to both homogeneous and heterogeneous classes.

**Listening**   The course reflects current understanding of the nature of listening comprehension in second and foreign language learning. Two kinds of listening skills are taught. *Top-down processing skills* require students to use background knowledge, the situation, context, and topic to arrive at comprehension through using key words and predicting; *bottom-up processing skills* require students to decode individual words in the message to derive meaning. Both of these skills are used in listening for gist, listening for details, and inferring meaning from context. The recordings on the Class Cassettes contain both scripted and unscripted conversations with the natural pauses, hesitations, and interruptions that occur in real speech.

**Speaking**   Speaking skills are a central focus of *Interchange.* Many elements in the syllabus (e.g., grammar, functions, topics, listening, pronunciation, vocabulary) provide support for oral communication. Speaking activities in the course focus on conversational fluency, such as the ability to open and close conversations, introduce and develop conversational topics, take turns in conversations, use communication strategies and clarification requests, and understand and use idiomatic expressions. In addition, a range of useful conversational expressions is taught.

**Reading**   The course treats reading as an important way of developing receptive language and vocabulary. At the same time, the reading passages provide stimulating adult content that both students and teachers will enjoy. The readings demonstrate a variety of text types (e.g., newspaper and magazine articles, surveys, letters) and develop the reading skills of guessing words from context, reading for main ideas, skimming, scanning, and making inferences, as well as reading for pleasure and for information. This approach also develops both top-down and bottom-up processing skills in reading.

**Writing**   Writing activities in *Interchange* focus on different forms of writing (e.g., descriptions,

narratives, postcards, advertisements, reviews). Writing is sometimes used as a basis for other activities, such as games and information-sharing activities. The teaching notes for each unit give detailed suggestions on how to present writing activities to focus on the process of writing (i.e., through collecting information about a topic, planning, writing a draft, revising, and editing).

**Pronunciation**   Level One treats pronunciation as an integral part of oral proficiency. The pronunciation exercises focus on important features of spoken English, including stress, rhythm, intonation, reductions, linking sounds, and sound contrasts. Suprasegmental features of pronunciation receive particular attention because of their important role in producing natural-sounding speech.

**Vocabulary**   Vocabulary plays a key role in *Interchange.* The course teaches a productive vocabulary of about 850 words. Vocabulary is introduced in two main ways. Productive vocabulary is presented through a wide variety of vocabulary exercises and through speaking and grammar activities. Receptive vocabulary is introduced through reading and listening exercises. Vocabulary learning is often enhanced through presenting words in semantically related sets or categories.

# UNIT STRUCTURE AND ORGANIZATION

Although the sequencing of exercise types varies throughout *Interchange,* a typical unit presents two main topics or functions, with related exercises. The exercises in each unit are grouped into two or three sections; these are referred to as "cycles" in the teaching notes. A cycle is a self-contained sequence of exercises that usually consists of the introduction of a new topic through a Snapshot or Word Power exercise; a Conversation that introduces the new grammar; a Grammar Focus that provides controlled and communicative grammar practice; Pronunciation; Pair Work, Group Work, or Role Play exercises that provide fluency practice of the teaching point; follow-up Listening and Writing activities; and a Reading.

The following exercise types are used throughout the course:

| Exercise Title | Purpose |
|---|---|
| Snapshot | These exercises contain interesting, real-world information that introduces the topic of a unit or part of a unit. They also build receptive vocabulary. The information in the Snapshot is presented in a graphic form, which makes it easy to read. |
| Word Power | These vocabulary exercises present key words related to the topic of the unit that can be used throughout the unit. |
| Conversation | Conversation exercises introduce new grammar points and functions. They present the grammar in a situational context and also serve as models for speaking tasks. |
| Grammar Focus | These exercises present summaries of new grammar items followed by controlled and freer communicative practice of the grammar. |
| Pair Work Group Work Role Play | These oral exercises provide freer and more personalized practice of the new teaching points and increase the opportunity for individual student practice. |
| Pronunciation | These exercises practice pronunciation points usually found in the Conversation or Grammar Focus exercises. |
| Listening | These exercises provide listening practice related to the topic of the unit and develop students' receptive skills. |
| Writing | Writing exercises provide follow-up written practice based on the topic and grammar of the unit. These exercises are often task-based (e.g., writing a postcard). |
| Reading | Reading exercises develop reading skills as well as receptive language and vocabulary. |
| Interchange Activities | These activities provide a communicative extension to the unit. They allow students to use the language and skills in the unit creatively. These activities are a key part of each unit. |

# REVIEW UNITS, UNIT SUMMARIES, AND TESTS

**Review Units** These occur after every three units and contain exercises that review the teaching points from the three preceding units. They are mainly speaking and listening exercises that review grammar, vocabulary, conversational expressions, and listening. They can also be used as informal tests of students' oral production and listening.

**Unit Summaries** These are at the end of the Student's Book and contain a summary of the key productive vocabulary used in each unit, together with conversational expressions and additional grammatical information. The key vocabulary lists the productive vocabulary used in the Conversation, Grammar Focus, Word Power, Pair Work, and Group Work exercises.

**Tests** There are five tests, one for use after every three units of the Student's Book. The tests enable the teacher to evaluate students' progress in the course and to decide if any areas of the course need further review. The tests are on pages 152–169 in the Teacher's Manual and may be photocopied for class use. Complete information on administering and scoring the tests, as well as answer keys, is located at the back of the Teacher's Manual.

# GENERAL GUIDELINES FOR TEACHING *INTERCHANGE*

The philosophy underlying *Interchange* is that learning a second or foreign language is more meaningful and effective when the language is used for real communication instead of being studied as an end in itself. *Interchange* follows a multi-skills syllabus in which each component of the course is linked. For example, a vocabulary-building exercise can serve as the basis for a speaking task, a role play activity may lead into a listening task, or a grammar exercise may often prepare students for a functional activity.

The following general guidelines can be used when teaching the course.

## Teaching vocabulary

Vocabulary is a key element in *Interchange* because a wide productive vocabulary is essential in learning a second or foreign language. Before presenting any exercise, it is helpful to see which words are needed in order to complete the task and which are not essential – not all new vocabulary needs presentation in advance. Students should recognize that in most language-learning situations they will encounter vocabulary they do not know; however, they do not need to understand every word. In addition, students need to understand that when they encounter an unknown word, they can often guess its meaning from the situation or context.

Where it is necessary to pre-teach new vocabulary, use the following strategies:

■ Ask students to look at the context in which a word is used and to try to find any clues to its meaning. Encourage students to guess meanings of new words.

■ Where necessary, provide the meanings of words through definitions, mime, synonyms, examples, or translation. It is not necessary to give long explanations.

■ In general, discourage the use of dictionaries during class time, except where it is suggested within an exercise.

■ After teaching a unit, ask students to review the Unit Summary to see how many of the words they can remember.

■ Encourage students to keep a vocabulary notebook and to write down new words as they learn them.

## Teaching grammar

Correct use of grammar is an essential aspect of communicative competence. In *Interchange*, grammatical accuracy is an integral part of proficiency, but it is always a means to an end rather than an end in itself. It is important to remember that second language learners do not develop grammatical proficiency by studying rules. They acquire new grammar by using the language in situations where it is needed. This means that

grammar should always be practiced communicatively. However, language learning also involves testing out hypotheses about how the language works. In developing these hypotheses, some students will rely more on grammatical explanations than others.

In the Grammar Focus exercises, the information in the color panels should be used to explain new grammar points. Give additional examples and explanations if necessary to clarify the grammar, but avoid turning any lesson into a grammar class. Lead students into the practice activities for the new grammar points as quickly as possible. Then use the students' performance on these activities to decide if further clarification or grammar work is needed. There are many additional grammar exercises in the Workbook that can be used as a follow-up.

## Teaching listening skills

The Listening exercises are designed to bridge the gap between the classroom and the real world. While most of the Listening exercises have the heading "Listening," there are also some that act as an extension of the Conversations.

When teaching listening, it is important to remind students that in most listening situations the aim is *not* to remember the specific words or phrases used but to extract the main ideas or information. To help students do this, the Listening exercises usually contain a task that helps students identify a purpose for listening, which encourages them to ignore language that is not related to this purpose. When presenting an exercise, it is also important to prepare students for the task through pre-listening activities. These include asking questions about the topic, asking students to make predictions, and making use of the context provided by the pictures and the situation.

## Teaching speaking skills

A number of different kinds of activities focus on speaking skills in the course: Conversations, Pair Work, Group Work, Class Activities, Role Plays, and Interchange Activities. Each of these activities involves different learning arrangements in the class.

**Conversations**   These exercises can be used for both listening and speaking practice. They usually require students to work with one or two partners. Since the Conversation exercises model conversational expressions and pronunciation and present new teaching items, accurate repetition of the Conversations on the tape is important. However, students should not be asked to memorize them.

When students practice Conversations, teach them to use the "Look Up and Say" technique. For this technique, students look at the page and then look up and say their line while maintaining eye contact with their partner. This encourages students to avoid a "reading" pronunciation and intonation when practicing Conversation exercises together.

**Pair Work**   The course makes extensive use of pair work activities. These give students a chance for individual practice and maximize the amount of speaking practice they get in each class. Some students may be unfamiliar with pair work tasks and may not think that they can learn from their classmates. If so, remind students that practicing with a partner is a useful way of improving their fluency in English and gives them more opportunity to speak English in class.

**Group Work and Class Activities**   The course also makes frequent use of group work and whole class activities. In the group work activities, students usually work in groups of three to five. Often one student is the group secretary and takes notes to report back to the class later. In the class activities, the whole class is involved (e.g., completing a survey or gathering information).

**Role Plays and Interchange Activities**   These exercises are important for developing fluency and are also fun. They focus on the creative use of language and require students to draw on their own language resources to complete a task or to improvise and keep a conversation going.

In doing these types of speaking activities, the following guidelines are important:

■ Make sure students fully understand the task and have the information they need. Assign roles and model the task where necessary.

■ Set up pairs or groups so that students of different ability levels and different first languages can work together. This arrangement will encourage students to help and learn from each other.

■ Vary the pair or group arrangements so that students do not always work with the same classmates.

■ Discourage use of the students' native languages when doing an activity, and get them to use as much English as possible in class.

**Giving Feedback**   It is important to give clear feedback on students' performance, but feedback should not inhibit students' attempts to communicate. Accuracy in speaking a new language takes a long time to accomplish in second language

learning, and both student and teacher need to realize this. Some aspects of language will be more difficult than others, depending on the students' levels of proficiency or native tongues. Immediate results are not always apparent. The teacher will need to assess which aspects of the students' performance are worth drawing attention to at any particular time in their language development.

It is better to give occasional but focused feedback on one thing at a time than to overwhelm a student with too much information. The teacher will have many opportunities to give individual feedback when students are working in pairs or groups. During these activities, the teacher can move around the class giving feedback on grammar, pronunciation, and vocabulary when needed. This is also an opportunity to determine if additional practice work is needed. Students often prefer this type of private or personalized feedback to feedback given in front of the whole class.

## Teaching reading skills

The approach to the teaching of reading in *Interchange* is similar to that used for teaching listening. The purpose for reading determines the strategy the students should use, such as reading the passage for main ideas (i.e., skimming), looking quickly for specific information in the passage (i.e., scanning), reading more slowly for detailed understanding, reading for the author's attitude, or reading to identify a sequence of events. It is important not to present each reading exercise as if it always requires the same approach (e.g., 100 percent comprehension of the passage). When students are doing a reading exercise, check that they are using appropriate reading strategies. For example:

■ Students should read silently and not subvocalize (i.e., pronounce words or move their lips while reading).

■ Students should read only with their eyes and not use a pencil or finger to follow the sentence they are reading.

■ Students should not use their dictionaries to look up every new word they encounter in a reading passage.

To encourage student interaction in the class, many reading passages can be done as pair work. Sometimes reading activities can be assigned for homework if class time is short.

## Teaching writing skills

The Writing exercises present models of different kinds of writing, but it is important to use these models simply as a springboard for the students' writing rather than as a basis for copying. Most of the writing tasks can be completed by a sequence of activities that focus on the following writing processes:

*Pre-writing phase:* Through discussion of the topic, reading of the model composition, or brainstorming, students generate ideas and collect information related to the topic, and then make notes.

*Planning:* Students use their ideas, information, and notes to plan their compositions. During this phase, they should make rough outlines and quickly write a first draft using phrases but without writing complete sentences. The focus here is on ideas that might be useful for the writing assignment, not on grammar and spelling.

*Drafting:* Students now write a second draft in sentence form, again without worrying about spelling, grammar, or punctuation.

*Revising:* Students read their own or a classmate's composition and ask questions for clarification or give suggestions for further information to include. Then they reorganize, revise, and rewrite their compositions.

*Editing:* Students check their compositions for accuracy, by concentrating on both clarifying their ideas and correcting grammar, spelling, and punctuation.

---

# TESTING STUDENTS' PROGRESS

The following testing procedures are suggested for use with *Interchange.*

## Using the tests in the Teacher's Manual

Five tests are contained in the Teacher's Manual to assess students' learning (see pages 152–169). There is one test to be used after every three units. These are progress tests that assess students' learning of grammar, conversational expressions, vocabulary, and listening. (For testing students' oral performance, see the following section.) The tests draw on each set of three units as a whole and are not linked to specific exercises in each unit. Only items actively presented and practiced in the Student's Book are tested. Each test takes approximately 45 minutes to complete in class. A satisfactory rate of learning should lead to 80 percent and above accuracy. If students score lower than this, the teacher may wish to reteach some sections of the book, give additional supplementary exercises, or assign extra homework

exercises to do. In addition to using these tests, the teacher can also informally check students' oral and written progress at the end of each unit.

## Using tests prepared by the teacher

It is also possible to check students' progress at the end of each unit using teacher-prepared tests. When developing these tests, it is important to keep the following principles in mind:

■ The principal goal of *Interchange* is communicative competence. Test items should reflect use of language in communicative contexts rather than in isolation.

■ Test items should reflect the kind of practice activities used in a unit (i.e., test what has been taught and test it in a format similar to that in which it was presented in the unit).

■ Distinguish between items that were presented receptively and those that were presented productively. Test productively only the language that students have practiced productively.

Here are some examples of possible test items:

1. Keeping a conversation going on a topic by asking follow-up questions
2. Completing missing parts of a conversation focusing on the grammar, vocabulary, or expressions in the unit
3. Providing suitable conversational expressions for different purposes (e.g., opening a conversation, expressing apologies)
4. Selecting an item from two or three choices, such as choosing an appropriate pronoun or adverb in a sentence
5. Completing a sentence with the suitable form of a verb or the correct word
6. Reordering scrambled sentences using the correct word order
7. Choosing the correct lexical item to complete a sentence
8. Supplying missing words in a passage, either by selecting from words given or using the cloze technique
9. Completing a short writing task similar to one presented in the unit
10. Answering questions or supplying information following a model provided in the unit
11. Reading a sentence aloud with correct pronunciation
12. Reading a passage similar to one in the unit and completing questions or a task based on it

Other useful information on oral testing techniques can be found in *Testing Spoken Language* by Nic Underhill (Cambridge University Press, 1987).

# HOW TO TEACH A TYPICAL UNIT IN *INTERCHANGE*

The unit-by-unit notes give detailed suggestions for teaching each unit. However, on a general basis, the following procedures can be used to teach *Interchange*.

Introduce the topic of the unit by asking questions and eliciting information from the students related to the theme or topic. Then explain what the students will study in the unit (i.e., mention the main topics, functions, and grammar as presented in the Plan of Book One on pp. iv–vii). Next present the exercises, using the following guidelines.

## Snapshot

■ Books closed. Introduce the topic by asking questions about it. Use these questions to elicit or present the key vocabulary of the Snapshot and to ask for students' opinions on the topic they are going to read about.

■ Books open. Lead the students through the information in the Snapshot. Go over any problems of comprehension as they arise.

■ Students complete the task individually or in pairs.

■ Students compare answers with a partner or around the class.

■ As an alternative, ask students to read the Snapshot for homework and complete the task, using a dictionary. Then students can compare answers with a partner in class.

## Word Power

■ Introduce and model the pronunciation of the words in the exercise.

■ Explain the task.

■ Students complete the task individually or in pairs, without using a dictionary if possible.

■ Students compare answers.

■ Check students' answers.

## Conversation

■ Optional: Books open. Students cover the conversation. Use the picture to set the scene.

■ Books closed. Before presenting the conversation, explain the situation. Write questions on the board based on the conversation for students to answer later.

■ Play the conversation on the tape or read it aloud. Students listen for answers to the questions. Check students' answers.

■ Books open. Play the tape again. Students listen only.

■ Present the conversation line by line using the tape. Present new vocabulary, model pronunciation, and explain idiomatic expressions.

■ Students practice the conversation in pairs. Use the "Look Up and Say" technique.

## Grammar Focus

■ Use the tape to present the sentences in the color panel (see p. 6).

■ Give students additional examples to illustrate the grammar point where necessary. If appropriate, practice the sentences in the color panel as in a drill.

■ Students complete the task. This can often be completed orally as a whole class activity before students complete it individually or in pairs. If necessary, students can write the answers on a separate piece of paper.

■ Students compare answers in pairs.

■ Call on students to read their answers aloud. Check and give feedback.

## Pair Work

■ Divide the class into pairs. If there is an odd number of students, form one set of three.

■ Explain the task and model it with one or two students. Call on a pair of students to do the task as a further model if necessary.

■ Set a time limit.

■ Students practice in pairs. Move around the class and give help as needed.

■ Optional: Students change partners and do the task again.

■ Call on pairs of students to do the activity in front of the class.

## Group Work

■ Divide the class into groups of three to five.

■ Explain the task and model it with some of the students.

■ Set a time limit.

■ Students practice in groups. Move around the class and give help as needed.

■ Optional: Students form new groups and do the task again.

## Role Play

- Assign roles to the students.
- Explain each role and clarify the cues.
- Model each role with students in the class and show how to use the cues. Encourage students to be creative and use their own language resources. They should not look at each other's cues or information.
- Set a time limit.
- Students do the role play. Go around the class and give help as needed.
- Students change roles and do the role play again.
- Call on students to do the role play in front of the class.

## Pronunciation

- Use the tape to introduce the teaching point.
- Play the tape again. Students practice.
- Give additional examples for students to practice if necessary.

Remind students of the pronunciation point when appropriate (i.e., during the Conversation and pair work or group work tasks).

## Listening

- Optional: Books open. Use the picture to set the scene.
- Books closed. Set the scene and explain the situation.
- Play the tape. Students listen for general comprehension. Point out any key vocabulary that is essential for the task.
- Books open. Explain the task. Remind students that they don't have to understand everything on the tape.
- Play the tape again once or twice. Students listen and complete the task.
- Students compare answers in pairs.
- Check students' answers.

## Writing

- Explain the task and go over the model composition.
- Elicit key vocabulary and language students might need.
- Students write rough drafts of their compositions. They should not worry about grammar, spelling, or punctuation at this stage.

- Students get feedback on the content and organization of their drafts from other classmates and from the teacher. Students then revise their drafts.
- Students prepare a final version (for homework if necessary). At this time, students check for organization, grammar, vocabulary, and spelling.
- Optional: Students exchange and read each other's compositions.

## Reading

- Before students read the passage, use questions to introduce the topic of the passage and to help establish background knowledge.
- Preview the vocabulary and pre-teach only key words that students might not be able to infer from context. Encourage students to guess the meanings of words using context clues.
- Explain the task.
- Students read the passage silently. Discourage students from using a pencil or finger to point at the text or from subvocalizing (i.e., pronouncing words silently) while reading.
- Students compare answers in pairs.
- Check students' answers.
- Optional: Ask follow-up discussion questions.

## Interchange Activities

These activities are found at the back of the book. There is one Interchange Activity for each unit in the book. Sometimes pairs of students will use different pages for role play or information-gap tasks.

- Where necessary, assign the students roles (A, B, C, etc.) and their page numbers for the task.
- Model the activity. Encourage students to be creative. They should focus on communication, not on grammar. They should not refer back to the unit once they have begun the activity.
- Students do the task. Go around the class and give help as needed.
- Where appropriate, call on pairs of students to do the activity in front of the class.
- Optional: Use a tape or video recorder to record the students' performances. Then play them back to the class and discuss their merits.

## Unit Summaries

Students can study the Unit Summary for homework, before the teacher presents a unit in class, in order to familiarize themselves with the vocabulary and expressions used in the unit; alternatively, students can use the Unit Summary as a review activity after each unit has been taught (e.g., for homework).

## Workbook

Preview each unit of Workbook exercises before introducing the unit in class. Note that the Workbook exercises do not present teaching points in exactly the same sequence as the exercises in the Student's Book. Rather, the Workbook exercises are more integrative, often combining vocabulary and teaching points from two or more Student's Book exercises into one activity. The Workbook can be used in a number of ways:

■ After students complete a Student's Book exercise, assign a Workbook exercise with the same teaching point, to be completed in class or as homework.

■ After several Student's Book exercises have been completed, assign appropriate Workbook exercises to be done as homework.

■ At the end of a unit, have students do all the Workbook exercises as a review or for homework.

## From the authors

We hope you enjoy teaching *Interchange*. We have tried to write a course that is interesting, innovative, and useful, and that both teachers and students will enjoy using. We would be happy to hear from you!

Jack C. Richards
Jonathan Hull
Susan Proctor

# 1 Please call me Dave

This unit has two cycles and presents the language needed for names, greetings, and introductions. It focuses on questions and statements with the verb *be*. There are no Reading or Pronunciation exercises in this unit.

## UNIT PLAN

### Cycle 1

**1** Conversation: *A warm-up activity for the class members to get to know one another*

**2** Names in English: *Cultural information on how names are used in English*

**3** Word Power: *Vocabulary needed to talk about jobs*

**4** Conversation: *Presents Wh-questions and verb* be

**5** Grammar Focus – Wh-questions with *be*: *Grammar summary followed by practice exercises*

**6** Countries and Nationalities: *A vocabulary-building exercise*

**7** Spelling: *A review of the alphabet and spelling*

### Cycle 2

**8** Snapshot: *Introduces the topic of the use of English around the world*

**9** Conversation: *Presents Yes/No questions and the verb* be

**10** Grammar Focus – Yes/No questions with *be*: *Grammar summary followed by practice exercises*

Interchange 1: *A role play to review the teaching points of the unit*

**11** Conversation: *Practices saying goodbye and introduces the days of the week*

# 1 CONVERSATION: Introductions

This exercise presents conversational expressions used for self-introductions and introduces the verb *be*.

## 1

■ Books open. Play the tape several times. Ss listen only; they do not practice these sentences.

■ Go over the introductions line by line.

## 2 Class activity

■ Introduce yourself to the class as in 1 above.

■ Present the "Useful expressions." Explain that "Sorry" and "Excuse me" can both be used to ask for repetition or clarification. Model the correct pronunciation of "Excuse me."

■ Ss take turns introducing themselves to the class.

## Optional activity: *Game – The Name Game*

Ss may enjoy this game as an ice-breaker. Decide if you want Ss to use only first names or both first and last names while playing the game.

■ Ss form a circle.

■ Use something small, like a tennis ball or a ball of paper. Say your name and throw the ball to a S.

■ This S quickly says his or her name and throws the ball to another S.

■ Continue around the class.

■ Optional: You could play the game again with the Ss saying the name of the person they are throwing the ball to.

# 2 NAMES IN ENGLISH

This exercise clarifies the use of titles and names in English and anticipates a common problem where Ss sometimes misuse a title and first name (e.g., "Mr. Dave").

## 1

■ Write your own first and last name on the board with the correct title. Tell the Ss whether they should call you by your first name or by title and family name by using the expression "Please call me . . ."

■ Ss read the information. Point out that a title is used only with a full name or family name. Explain the titles:

Mr. /ˈmɪstər/ = for both single and married men
Mrs. /ˈmɪsɪz/ = for married women only
Miss /mɪs/ = for unmarried women only
Ms. /mɪz/ = for both single and married women (This title is becoming increasingly popular and is replacing "Mrs." and "Miss," especially in business.)

■ Optional: Explain the titles "Dr." /ˈdɑktər/ and "Professor" /prəˈfɛsər/.

■ Point to Ss in the class and give their full names with a title (e.g., "She's Ms. Vera de Cruz," "He's Mr. Kenji Sato") and with first names only (e.g., "She's Vera," "He's Kenji").

■ Explain that in the U.S. and Canada, people use first names more often than titles and family names. In situations where people see each other regularly (e.g., at work, in an English class), people usually use first names with each other.

■ Ss identify some of their classmates using first names or titles and last names, depending on which Ss choose to be called.

■ Optional: In a homogeneous class, compare how titles and names are used in English with the Ss' native language.

## 2

■ Play the tape several times. Ss check if the names and titles are correct or incorrect and then compare answers with a partner. Check Ss' answers.

Answers:

a) I    b) C    c) I    d) C    e) C    f) I

# 3 WORD POWER: Jobs

This exercise presents names of common jobs.

## 1 Pair work

■ Present each word. Check that Ss know the meanings. If not, give a simple definition (e.g., "A bank president is the top person in a bank").

■ Ss repeat each word. Correct pronunciation and stress.

■ Ss complete the task in pairs. Check Ss' answers.

Answers:

*Office work*
typist
clerk
receptionist
secretary

*Management & business*
supervisor
bank president
company director
sales manager

*Professions*
architect
doctor
engineer
lawyer

## 2

■ Ss add two more jobs to each category, using their dictionaries if necessary. Compare answers around the class.

Possible answers:

*Office work*
custodian
file clerk
telephone operator
word processor

*Management & business*
administrative assistant
department manager
section head
vice president

*Professions*
accountant
dentist
teacher
writer

## Optional activity

■ Scramble the letters of ten additional jobs and write them on the board. To make it easier, give Ss the first letter:

d t i e t s n  (d___)     t e r e c a h  (t___)
p t o i l     (p___)     n r s u e     (n___)
a r o c t     (a___)     w e r r i t    (w___)
m e l o d     (m___)     s o r i a l     (s___)

■ Pairs rearrange the letters to find the jobs. Check Ss' answers.

Answers:

| | |
|---|---|
| dentist | teacher |
| pilot | nurse |
| actor | writer |
| model | sailor |

---

## 4 CONVERSATION: Meeting someone

This conversation presents the grammar points in Exercise 5. ("What do you do?" and "Hey, Noriko, can I join your class?" are presented here only as expressions.)

## 1

■ Books open. Play the tape. Ss listen.

■ Present the conversation line by line. Explain that "By the way, . . ." is used when we want to change the topic.

■ Ss practice the conversation in pairs. Make sure Ss use reduced forms and correct word stress.

■ Encourage Ss to use the "Look Up and Say" technique when practicing the conversation (i.e., Ss briefly look at a sentence in the conversation and then look up at their partner and say the sentence from memory).

■ Present the "Useful expressions" and any other useful vocabulary that may be needed for Ss to personalize the language in the conversation. Ask questions from the conversation around the class (e.g., "Where are you from, Mrs. Lee?", "What do you do, Angela?"). Help Ss use the correct word in their answers and model the correct pronunciation for each S's job.

## 2 Class activity

■ Ask two Ss to model the task by introducing themselves to each other as in the conversation. Ss don't need to use the last line of the conversation in this activity.

■ Optional: Explain that adults often shake hands when meeting each other for the first time. Demonstrate how to shake hands properly with several Ss. Point out that a handshake should be firm and that it should not be held for more than a few seconds.

■ Ss get up and go around the class and meet four classmates. (Optional: Ss can practice shaking hands with each other during the activity.)

## 5 GRAMMAR FOCUS: Wh-questions with *be*

The Grammar Focus shows how Wh-questions and statements are formed with the verb *be*.

■ Use the tape to present the questions and statements in the box. Ss repeat.

■ Point out the differences between personal pronouns as subjects (*I, you,* etc.) and as adjectives (*my, your,* etc.). Give examples (e.g., "I am Mary," "My name is Mary").

■ Write on the board other statements using the verb *be* and elicit Wh-questions from the Ss:

| *Statement* | *Question* |
| --- | --- |
| We are from Canada. | Where are we from? |
| My first name is Ken. | What is my first name? |
| Their last name is Jackson. | What is their last name? |

### 1

■ Ss complete the missing words individually and then compare with a partner. Check Ss' answers.

Answers:

A: What is his name?
B: His name is Seiji Ozawa.
   He is a conductor.
A: Where is he from?
B: He is from Japan.

A: What is her name?
B: Her name is Catherine Deneuve.
   She is an actress.
A: Where is she from?
B: She is from France.

A: What are their names?
B: Their names are Barbra Streisand and Michael Jackson. They are singers.
A: Where are they from?
B: They are from the United States.

### 2

■ Model the reduced forms of *be* (e.g., *what's, where's, his name's, she's*). Ss repeat. Explain that reduced forms are commonly used in conversation and full forms are often used in writing.

■ Ss practice the conversations using the contractions *what's, where's, he's, she's, they're.*

### 3 Pair work

■ Ss cover the Grammar Focus, parts 1 and 2.

■ Ask questions about the first picture. Encourage Ss to come up with any responses they can.

Who's this? (The names of the famous people are in the box.)
Where's she from?
What is she?

■ Ss work in pairs and talk about the people. Go around the class and give help as needed.

■ Check Ss' answers.

Answers (left to right):

Dolly Parton = American country and western singer
Charles and Diana = Prince and Princess of Wales
Desmond Tutu = Archbishop of Cape Town, South Africa
Yoko Ono = Japanese artist and rock singer (John Lennon's widow)
Sylvester Stallone = American actor

### Optional activity

*Preparation:* Bring pictures of well-known people and personalities from magazines, about five for each group of Ss.

■ Ss work in groups. Give each group a set of about five pictures. Explain the task: Groups identify as many people in the pictures as possible. Tell Ss to keep a tally. Set a time limit of about five minutes.

■ Groups exchange pictures and repeat the task.

■ Compare groups' tallies around the class.

## 6 COUNTRIES AND NATIONALITIES

This exercise introduces the vocabulary of countries and nationalities. Many nationalities can be described with either an adjective or a noun. However, there's no simple rule to determine which nationality can take the same word as an adjective and a noun (e.g., "He's Brazilian." "He's a Brazilian.") or which nationality has an adjective and a noun in different forms ("She's Spanish." "She's a Spaniard."). In this exercise, only the adjective form is taught. People from the U.S. are often called "Americans"; people from

Canada, the U.S., and Mexico are sometimes called "North Americans."

■ Explain the words *country* and *nationality*. Model how to use them in sentences:

T: I am from (name of country). I am (nationality).
*(Pointing to S)* She is from Japan. She is Japanese.
*(Pointing to another S)* He's from Brazil. He's Brazilian.

## 1 Pair work

■ Explain the task. Ss work in pairs and complete the chart. Ss can use a dictionary or the Unit Summary in the Student's Book to check their answers.

Answers:

(The stressed syllables are underlined here for the optional task that follows.)

| *Country* | *Nationality* |
|---|---|
| Australia | Australian |
| Brazil | Brazilian |
| Britain | British |
| Canada | Canadian |
| China | Chinese |
| Germany | German |
| Italy | Italian |
| Japan | Japanese |
| Mexico | Mexican |
| Portugal | Portuguese |
| Spain | Spanish |
| the U.S. | American |
| *(or)* the United States | |

■ Model the pronunciation of the countries and nationalities. Make sure Ss stress the correct syllable in each word.

■ Optional: Ss underline the stressed syllables in their books (e.g., "Australia").

## 2

■ Ss continue to work in pairs and add five more sets of countries and nationalities. Ss can use their dictionaries if necessary. Go around the class and give help as needed.

## 3

■ Elicit some names of countries and model the task:

T: Give me the name of a country.
S1: France.

T: What's someone from France called?
S1: I don't know.
S2: French, I think.

■ Ss take turns asking questions in pairs, groups, or around the class.

---

## 7 SPELLING

This exercise focuses on recognizing spelling.

■ Check that Ss can say the alphabet correctly in English. If they have any difficulty with it, check their pronunciation, particularly of sounds that may be difficult for them (e.g., the difference between *r/l*, *b/v*, *m/n*).

■ Model how to ask questions about people's names:

T: Maria, how do you spell your last name?
S1: M-O-R-E-N-O.
T: OK, thanks. And José, how do you spell your first name?
S2: J-O-S-E.
T: Thank you. Now it's your turn, Yutaka.
S3: OK. Heidi, how do you spell your first name?

■ Ss take turns asking about each other's names around the class.

## 1

■ Play the tape once or twice. Ss check the correct answers.

Answers:

a) Louis
b) Helen
c) Roger
d) Kathryn

## 2 Group work: *Spelling contest*

■ Ss form groups of four. Groups choose ten words from the unit and make a list.

■ Now two groups work together and do the task. Go over the model dialog and tell groups to keep score (e.g., one correct answer = one point). The group with the most points is the winner.

■ Find out who the group winners are.

---

## 8 SNAPSHOT: English today

This exercise presents interesting information about the role of English around the world.

■ Books closed. To present the topic, ask questions about the languages used in the Ss' countries and introduce these terms:

first language = native language or mother tongue
second language = a language, not a first
  language, that is widely used in a country (e.g.,
  English in India)
foreign language = a language studied in school as
  a subject, but not widely used in a country (e.g.,
  English in Japan or France)
USSR = Union of Soviet Socialist Republics, or
  the Soviet Union
4 million = 4,000,000

■ Ss read the Snapshot and complete the task. Ss should be able to do this task without a dictionary. Ss compare answers with a partner.

Answers:

India       = second
the USSR    = foreign
New Zealand = first
France      = foreign

## Optional activity

In a heterogeneous class:

■ Find out how many different first languages there are in the class. Ask questions like these and write the information on the board:

T: What's your first language, Celia?
S: Spanish.
T: How many speak Spanish as a first language?

In a homogeneous class:

■ Find out how many different foreign languages Ss can speak or are studying. Ask questions like these and write the information on the board:

T:  Who is studying another foreign language?
S1: I'm studying Chinese.
S2: I'm studying French.
T:  Who speaks another foreign language?
S2: I speak German.

---

## 9 CONVERSATION

This conversation contains the grammar points presented in Exercise 10. The present continuous in "I'm studying English" is presented as an expression here.

**1**

■ Books open. Play the first part of the tape. Ss listen.

■ Present the conversation. Explain that "Excuse me" has several functions in English (e.g., to get someone's attention, to ask for repetition, to close a conversation). Here, it is used to ask for clarification. "Oh, really?" shows the listener's interest in what someone has said. Model the correct intonation of "Oh, really?":

Oh, really?

and the correct stress in "va**ca**tion."

■ Optional: Ss practice the conversation.

**2**

■ Books closed. Tell Ss not to worry about understanding every word; they only need to understand the gist of what is said.

■ Play the second part of the tape once or twice.

■ Books open. Play the tape again. Ss complete the task and compare answers. Check Ss' answers.

Answers:

V  I'm not married.
V  I'm staying with friends.
G  I'm here with my sister.
V  I'm not free tonight.
G  How about tomorrow?

---

## 10 GRAMMAR FOCUS:
### Yes/No questions with *be*

This exercise shows how Yes/No statements and questions are formed with the verb *be*.

■ Play the tape to present the questions and statements in the box. Ss repeat. Model the stress in "No, I'm **not**," "Yes, I **am**," "Yes, he **is**," "No, she **isn**'t." Explain that the verb in the response "Yes, I am" cannot be reduced to "I'm." (The same is true for the responses "Yes, he/she is" and "Yes, they are.")

■ Show how Yes/No questions are formed from statements by writing some examples on the board:

| *Statement* | | *Question* |
|---|---|---|
| She is a student. | = | Is she a student? |
| They are my classmates. | = | Are they my classmates? |

■ Ask similar Yes/No questions with *be* around the class about the Ss.

■ Then call on Ss to ask questions to other Ss.

## 1

■ Ss complete the missing words and then compare with a partner.

Answers:

A: <u>Are</u> you from the United States?
B: <u>Yes</u>, I <u>am</u>. I'm from Chicago.

A: <u>Is</u> Rosa from Chile?
B: <u>No</u>, she <u>isn't</u>. She's from Argentina.

A: Is George Michael an actor?
B: No, he <u>isn't</u>. He <u>is</u> a singer.

A: Are <u>you</u> in English 101?
B: No, <u>I'm</u> <u>not</u>. I'm in English 102.

■ Write some names of Ss (e.g., "Pedro," "Susan and Maria") or famous people on the board and ask Ss to make up Yes/No questions about them. Write the questions on the board:

| *Pedro* | *Susan and Maria* |
|---|---|
| Is Pedro from Peru? | Are Susan and Maria sisters? |
| Is Pedro a teacher? | Are Susan and Maria Italian? |

■ Call on Ss to answer the questions.

## 2

■ Ss work individually and write five questions. Move around the class and check their questions.

■ Ss form groups and take turns asking some of their questions.

## INTERCHANGE 1:
## Press conference

This is a role play activity that involves interviews. It recycles much of the language of the unit. The emphasis is on communication rather than on accuracy; Ss should use any strategies they can to get the information they need. This is an information-gap activity. Ss in Group A look at page 102 and Ss in Group B look at page 104. (They should not look at each other's page.)

*Preparation:* Make name tags: Ss in Group A need name tags with "Reporter" and Ss in Group B need name tags with "Movie Star."

For this activity, there are two groups – Group A (reporters) and Group B (actors and actresses). Group B consists of 11 students (if you play the game exactly as written); Group A consists of the rest of the class. If the cues for Group B are not all suitable for your class (e.g., because your class is all male or all female, or a different size), write different cues using the names of other actors and actresses, and give them suitable roles in the movie. (In this situation, use blank forms to replace Group A's cues.)

■ Explain the situation: A film company has just made a new James Bond movie. The company is telling reporters at a press conference about it.

■ Present the names of the actors and actresses. Write their names on the board and have Ss practice them. Present any new vocabulary (e.g., movie role, secret agent, spy, the CIA = the U.S. Central Intelligence Agency, the KGB = the Soviet intelligence agency).

■ Divide the class into two groups. Explain Group A's and Group B's tasks and model some of Group A's questions with a S from Group B:

T: Is your first name Clint?
S: Yes, it is.
T: What's your nationality?
S: I'm American.

■ Set a time limit of 10 or 15 minutes for the activity. Ss do the activity. Go around the class and give help as needed.

■ After the time is up, Ss in Group A check their information with Ss in Group B.

---

## [11] CONVERSATION:
## Saying goodbye

This exercise introduces expressions for saying goodbye and the days of the week. It should be presented at the end of a lesson.

■ Review the days of the week if necessary.

## 1

■ Books open. Play the tape once or twice. Ss listen.

■ Present each dialog. Substitute the appropriate day of the week for the third dialog (e.g., "See you on Monday"). Explain that "Have a nice evening" is used in the late afternoon and early evening. People in the U.S. and Canada also say "Have a nice day" when saying goodbye in the morning or early afternoon.

## 2 Class activity

■ Books closed. Ss get up and move around the class and practice saying goodbye to each other.

## Optional activity: *Game – Word Bingo*

This activity reviews vocabulary and spelling.
Time: 10–15 minutes.

- Make up a list of 24 words from the unit.
- Show Ss how to make a Bingo card on a piece of paper (see Figure 1.1).

| B | I | N | G | O |
|---|---|---|---|---|
| T | R | R |  |  |
| S | a | D |  |  |
| B |  | FREE SPACE |  |  |
| gh |  | T | w |  |
| C |  | B |  | R |

Figure 1.1

- Dictate the words from your list – first say the word, spell it, and then use it in a sentence:

T: "Name." N-A-M-E. My name is John.
T: "Teacher." T-E-A-C-H-E-R. I'm a teacher.

Ss listen and write down each word inside a box in random order on their cards.

- Now call out a word in a random order from your list. Ss find it on their cards and circle it. (You should check off the word on your list so that you don't repeat any words and so you can later check a S's card after he or she gets "Bingo.")

- Ss do not write in the "free space" – the free space counts as a word. (For example, in the "N" column, Ss would need only four other words to get "Bingo.")

- The first S to get five circled words in a row in any direction (including the "Free Space") shouts "Bingo!" Ask the S to read off the five circled words and check them against your list.

- Optional: Ss form groups and make their own lists. Then two groups, A and B, play Bingo together. Group A first dictates its list of words to Group B and then a S from Group A reads off the words in a random order until a S in Group B calls "Bingo." Then it is Group B's turn.

# 2 It's a great job!

This unit has two cycles and develops the themes of work and school while teaching Ss how to talk about work, jobs, addresses, and telephone numbers. It also introduces Wh-questions with *do,* present tense statements using regular verbs, and additional greetings.

## UNIT PLAN

### Cycle 1

**1** Conversation: *Practices greetings used at different times of the day*

**2** Listening: *A follow-up exercise on greetings*

**3** Pronunciation: *Introduces the notion of stress on different syllables in words in English*

**4** Snapshot: *Introduces the topics of education and jobs*

**5** Word Power: *Develops the vocabulary needed to talk about work*

**6** All in a Day's Work: *Follow-up listening activity on the vocabulary of jobs*

### Cycle 2

**7** Conversation: *Introduces Wh-questions with* do *and prepositions*

**8** Grammar Focus – Wh-questions with *do: Grammar summary followed by practice exercises*

**9** Writing: *A personalized writing practice on jobs*

**10** Listening: *A follow-up listening on the theme of jobs*

**11** Numbers: *A review of numbers 0 to 1,000*

**12** Conversation: *Practices giving names, addresses, and phone numbers*

Interchange 2: *An information-sharing activity that reviews questions and statements*

**13** Reading: *Scanning job advertisements for specific information*

## 1 CONVERSATION: Greetings

This exercise presents formulaic expressions for greetings in English.

### 1

■ Books open. Play the tape twice. Ss listen.

■ Explain that greetings in English differ from formulaic greetings in some other languages. Questions like "How are you?" are not always real questions about someone's health, but simply polite expressions.

■ Present each line of the conversation. Ss repeat. Model the reduction in "How are you doing?" /hɑwər jə 'duwɪŋ/.

■ Books closed. Greet Ss around the class and elicit the different responses practiced.

#### Alternative presentation

■ If your class meets in the afternoon or evening, write the first and third conversations on the board, substituting the appropriate greetings (e.g., "Good afternoon," "Good evening").

■ Present the conversations without the tape.

■ Greet Ss around the class and elicit the different responses practiced.

### 2

■ Ss practice greeting each other.

## 2 LISTENING

This exercise practices distinguishing different greetings.

■ Explain the task: Ss will hear a greeting on the tape. Tell Ss that only one of the responses is correct.

■ Optional: Before playing the tape, ask Ss to suggest greetings for each of the responses.

■ Play the tape several times. Ss check the correct responses. Check Ss' answers.

Answers:

a)  Hi! How are you?
b)  Oh, not bad, thanks.
c)  Fine, thanks.
d)  Pretty good, thanks. How about you?

## 3 PRONUNCIATION: Word stress

This exercise introduces the notion of stress on different syllables in words. A syllable is a word or part of a word that can receive stronger or weaker stress; it always includes a vowel.

### 1

■ Introduce the notion of stress by writing the words *morning* and *today* on the board. Explain that both words have two syllables. Underline the stressed syllables: <u>mor</u>ning, to<u>day</u>. Point out that stress in English is on different syllables in different words.

■ Play the tape. Ss practice.

### 2

■ Ss do the task and then compare answers. Play the tape to check Ss' answers.

Answers:

| *1st syllable* | *2nd syllable* | *3rd syllable* |
|---|---|---|
| **lan**guage | to**night** | univer**sity** |
| **Sat**urday | va**ca**tion | conver**sa**tion |

## 4 SNAPSHOT: Education and salary

This exercise introduces the major theme of the unit – jobs and work.

■ Books closed. Introduce the topic of jobs and salaries.

■ Either: (1) present any new vocabulary (e.g., salaries, fewer, graduate, postgraduate), and then Ss read the Snapshot; or (2) Ss read the Snapshot, using their dictionaries.

■ Elicit suggestions from Ss on how much people would earn in their native country after about three years of high school or secondary school, after three years of college, and after getting a postgraduate degree (e.g., master's, Ph.D.). Write the information on the board.

■ Ss do the task and compare answers with a partner.

■ Check Ss' answers around the class and write the most common jobs suggested for each category on the board.

## 5 WORD POWER:
### Workplaces and jobs

This exercise develops the vocabulary of workplaces and jobs.

**1**

■ Ask Ss to look through the vocabulary. Explain any new words.

■ Ss complete the task either individually or in pairs. Check Ss' answers.

Possible answers:

(Some jobs can be matched to several workplaces.)

a)  bank teller, cashier, clerk, manager, receptionist, secretary, supervisor, typist
b)  clerk, manager, receptionist, secretary, supervisor, typist
c)  cashier, chef, clerk, manager, receptionist, secretary, typist
d)  clerk, manager, receptionist, secretary, supervisor, typist
e)  cashier, manager, salesclerk, supervisor

**2**

■ Ss underline the stressed syllables and then compare with a partner. Check Ss' answers.

Answers:

<u>bank</u> teller
<u>cash</u>ier
<u>clerk</u>
<u>chef</u>
<u>man</u>ager
re<u>cep</u>tionist
<u>sales</u>clerk
<u>sec</u>retary
<u>super</u>visor
<u>typ</u>ist

**3 Group work**

■ Ss cover the jobs in part 1 and look only at the workplaces (a–e).

■ Model the task by reading the first question aloud:

T:  Who works in a bank?
S1: A bank teller.
S2: A clerk.

■ Ss work in groups and take turns asking questions about the workplaces.

■ Then Ss ask each other questions about the three other workplaces: a restaurant, a hospital, and a department store.

■ Check Ss' answers around the class.

Possible answers:

a restaurant = chef, waiter, waitress, host or hostess
a hospital = doctor, nurse, typist, secretary, office manager
a department store = cashier, manager, salesclerk, supervisor

## Optional activity

■ Bring pictures of people with unusual or interesting jobs, or ask Ss to bring pictures to class.

■ Ss work in pairs and try to identify each job.

## Optional activity

■ Bring photos or pictures of workplaces.

■ Ss identify as many jobs as possible for each workplace.

## 6 ALL IN A DAY'S WORK

Students will hear five people talk as they do their jobs.

■ Explain the situation and task.

■ Play the tape once or twice. Ss listen and write down what they think each job is.

■ Show how to use the model dialog for Ss to compare their answers.

■ Ss do the task either as a class activity or in groups. Check Ss' answers.

Possible answers:

1. receptionist
2. photographer
3. taxi driver
4. typist, secretary
5. teacher

## 7 CONVERSATION

This conversation introduces Wh-questions with *do* and prepositions.

■ Books closed. Set the scene.

■ Write these questions on the board:

What's the woman's job?
Is it an interesting job?
Is the man a teacher?
What's his part-time job?

■ Ask Ss to listen for answers to the questions.

■ Play the tape several times. Check Ss' answers. Ask what other information they heard.

■ Books open. Present the conversation line by line. If necessary, explain these words: "hamburger," a "Big Mac" = the biggest hamburger sold at McDonald's, and a "Whopper" = the biggest hamburger sold at Burger King.

■ Play the tape again, pausing after each line. Ss repeat. Model the stress in "Where do you **work**?" and "What do you **do**?"

■ Ss practice the conversation in pairs. Remind Ss to use the "Look Up and Say" technique to practice conversations. (See the teacher's notes in Unit 1, Exercise 4, for a description of the technique.)

■ Optional: Ss act out the conversation in front of the class, using their own words (i.e., it is not necessary to repeat the exact words or sentences in the book).

---

## 8 GRAMMAR FOCUS:  Wh-questions with *do;* prepositions

This exercise practices Wh-questions with the auxiliary verb *do.* It also shows how the prepositions *for, at, in,* and *to* are used. Prepositions are a difficult part of English grammar, and there are many exceptions to rules for prepositional usage. However, at this level, you can give these examples or ask Ss to look at the Unit Summary.

| | |
|---|---|
| I work *for* Toyota. | *for* + name of company |
| *for* Ms. Jones. | *for* + name of person |
| *for* a lawyer. | *for* + job |
| I work *in* a bank. | *in/at* + workplace |
| *at* a restaurant. | |
| I work *in* the sales department. | *in* + department/ section |
| *in* the front office. | |
| I go *to* Stanford. | *to* + name of school |

■ Use the tape to present the questions and statements in the box. Explain how *do* is used to form questions from full verbs. Model the reduced form of *do* in the questions (e.g., "Where 'dya' work?" /wɛr djə wɜrk/, "What 'dya' do?" /wɑt djə duw/).

Point out that prepositions and articles are unstressed.

■ Ask the Wh-questions from the box to Ss around the class. Ss should answer using real information about themselves.

### 1

■ Explain the task. Go over any new vocabulary.

■ Ss complete the task individually and then compare with a partner.

■ Call on Ss to read their answers to the class, as in the example sentences.

Answers:

I work in a store. I'm a salesclerk. I sell clothes.
I work at the Seafood Palace Restaurant. I'm a chef. I cook the meals.
I work for Pan Am. I'm a flight attendant. I serve passengers.
I work in a hospital. I'm a nurse. I help the patients.
I work in a factory. I'm a carpenter. I make furniture.
I work in an office. I'm a receptionist. I answer the phone.

### 2

■ Ss complete the task individually. Check Ss' answers.

Answers:

A: Where do you work?
B: I work for Japan Air Lines.
A: Oh, really? And what do you do?
B: I am a flight attendant.

A: Where do you work?
B: I work for the *Daily News.*
A: Oh, what do you do there?
B: I am a photographer.

A: What do you do?
B: I'm a student.
A: Where do you go to school?
B: I go to Jefferson College. I'm studying business.

■ Ss practice the conversations in pairs.

### 3

This could be a group work or class activity.

■ Books closed. Model the task or call on several Ss to talk about what they do. Encourage Ss to use greetings and expressions from Units 1 and 2 to start their conversations (e.g., "Oh hi, Bill," "Excuse me, Jean," "Good morning, Chen").

■ Ss work in groups or get up and walk around the class to do the task. Encourage Ss to keep talking and not to worry about grammar or pronunciation. Take notes on general problems Ss may have and then go over them with the class at the end of the activity.

## Optional activity: *Game – What's the Question?* ✓

This activity reviews Wh-questions. Time: 10–15 minutes.

Each S will need three blank cards.

■ Form groups of four or five, or divide the class into two teams – A and B. Give each S three blank cards.

■ Ss think of three statements that could be answers to Wh-questions (e.g., "I work in a zoo." "He is a Russian guide." "I study dancing at Harvard University."). Then Ss write one statement on each blank card.

■ Collect all of the Ss' cards and put them in a pile face down.

■ Group A starts. One S picks up a card and reads it aloud to a S from Group B. That S then tries to make a suitable Wh-question for it. Ss on both teams decide whether the question is correct or not. If it is, Group B wins a point; if it is not correct, a S from Group A tries to correct it. If the correction is acceptable, Group A gets the point instead. Keep a record of team scores on the board. The team with the most points wins.

---

## 9 WRITING

This exercise practices writing a short job description. Ss have been well prepared for this by the preceding activities, although spelling and grammar may still require attention. The first part of the activity could be assigned for homework; if it is, ask Ss not to write their names on their compositions.

### 1

■ Ss read the model compositions. Explain that Ss should write something similar about themselves. Encourage Ss to give additional information if they can.

■ Optional: For further clarification of the task, model the task by writing a composition about yourself or about a S in the class on the board.

■ Ss write their compositions. Tell Ss not to write their names on their compositions. Move around the class and help Ss wherever necessary. (For this classroom activity, it is not necessary to correct every error in the Ss' compositions.)

### 2

■ Collect the Ss' compositions, mix them up, and then pass them out randomly around the class.

■ Each S reads a composition and tries to guess who the writer is. Tell Ss to take the composition back to the person they think is the writer and ask "Is this your composition?" If the answer is "Yes," the writer keeps the composition.

### Alternative presentation

■ If you have a homogeneous class (e.g., all college Ss, all businesspeople in the same company) whose compositions might end up being rather similar, omit part 2 of the task and instead ask Ss to write as many sentences as possible about themselves in 10 minutes.

■ When Ss finish writing, ask them to count how many sentences they wrote. Then find out who wrote the most sentences and ask that S to read them to the class.

### Optional activity

Each group needs six blank cards.

■ Ss work in groups of four. Each group chooses six jobs to write about. Then the group writes a description of each job on a card without including the name of the job.

■ Groups exchange cards and Ss try to guess the names of the jobs.

---

## 10 LISTENING

This exercise practices listening for key words. Ss need to realize early on that they don't need to listen for every word when listening. Wherever possible, they should try to use key words to guess meaning.

■ Before playing the tape, Ss look at the pictures. Ask questions:

What's this man's job?
Is this man a salesman?
What's this woman's job?

■ Play the tape several times. Ss number only three of the pictures.

■ Ss compare answers. Check Ss' answers.

Answers:

1. doctor  2. businesswoman  3. office worker

■ Optional: Ss work in pairs. Ask Ss to listen for additional information about each person's job. Play the tape again. Ss take notes. Then find out how much additional information the Ss heard and write it on the board for the class.

## 11 NUMBERS

This exercise presents numbers from 0 to 1,000.

**1**

■ Present the numbers.

**2**

■ Play the first part of the tape. Ss listen and repeat. Model the contrasts in stress (e.g., thir**teen**/**thir**ty).

■ Play the second part of the tape. Ss write down numerals. Check Ss' answers.

Answers:

a) 16   b) 50   c) 30   d) 19   e) 90   f) 14   g) 17
h) 80

■ Ss practice the numbers.

### Optional activity: *Dictation*

■ Make a list of 10 or 15 random numbers from 0 to 1,000 and then read the numbers aloud to the class. Ss write down the numbers by using numerals (not by spelling the numbers). Check Ss' answers.

### Optional activity: *Countdown*

■ Choose a number and ask Ss to count backwards from it (e.g., 50, 49, 48, 47, 46, 45, etc.).

### Optional activity: *Math quiz*

■ Have a math quiz by asking one S to say two numbers and asking another S to add them as quickly as possible:

T:  Rosa, say two numbers, please.
S1: 19 and 60.
T:  Tina, please add them.
S2: 79.

## 12 CONVERSATION:
Names and addresses

This exercise introduces talking about addresses and phone numbers.

**1**

■ Books open or closed. Set the scene.

■ Play the tape. Ss listen.

■ Books open. Present the conversation line by line. Point out that in American English *address* is pronounced as either **ad**dress /'ædrɛs/ or ad**dress** /ə'drɛs/.

■ Explain that in North America people respond to the expression "Thank you very much" with "You're welcome." In other countries, different responses are used (e.g., in Britain, no response or other responses like "Don't mention it" or "Not at all").

■ Ss practice the conversation in pairs.

■ Books closed. Ss change partners and ask each other for their names, addresses, and phone numbers.

**2**

■ Play the tape. Ss complete the task and compare answers. Check Ss' answers.

Answers:

| Name | Street |
| --- | --- |
| John Foster | 1959 Bank Street |
| Pat Phillips | 2751 Cook Street |

| Apt. no. | City, state | Phone |
| --- | --- | --- |
| 811 | Miami, Florida | 468-3503 |
| 301 | Dallas, Texas | 524-3891 |

### Optional activity: *Class telephone list*

■ Tell Ss they are going to make a class phone list like this:

*English Class Telephone List*

| First name | Last name | Phone number |
| --- | --- | --- |
| Pedro | Garcia | 632-0573 |
| Yoko | Morita | 684-9921 |

■ Remind Ss of the kinds of questions they need to ask and write them on the board:

What's your first name?
How do you spell it?
And what's your last name?
What's your telephone number?

■ Ss go around the class and make their own class phone lists.

## INTERCHANGE 2: Who is it?

This is a good review of Yes/No and Wh-questions and practices identifying people from written information.

Each S needs a card to write his or her description on.

**1**

■ Explain that a zodiac sign is the name for a group of stars. Some people believe that your zodiac sign influenced events when you were born. Ask Ss to find their zodiac signs. Model how each sign is pronounced:

| | | | |
|---|---|---|---|
| Aries | /ˈɛriyz/ | Libra | /ˈliybrə/ |
| Taurus | /ˈtɔrəs/ | Scorpio | /ˈskɔrpiyow/ |
| Gemini | /ˈdʒɛmɪnɑy/ | Sagittarius | /sædʒəˈtɛriyəs/ |
| Cancer | /ˈkænsər/ | Capricorn | /ˈkæprɪkɔrn/ |
| Leo | /ˈliyow/ | Aquarius | /əˈkwɛriyəs/ |
| Virgo | /ˈvɜrgow/ | Pisces | /ˈpɑysiyz/ |

**2**

■ Give each S a card. Go over the written model. Tell Ss to write information about themselves on their cards. They should write five things about themselves – zodiac sign, hometown, job, favorite singer, favorite actor or actress – as in the example.

■ Collect the cards.

## 3 Class activity

■ Give each S a card and explain the task: Ss ask questions and try to find out who the card describes.

■ Before Ss begin, model the correct pronunciation and stress for the questions. Set a time limit of about 10 minutes.

■ Ss get up and do the task. Each time a S matches a card with a class member, the S returns the card to you and gets another one.

■ After the time is up, find out who matched the most cards.

## 13 READING: Job advertisements

This exercise practices skimming and scanning.

**1**

■ Check that Ss understand the jobs listed above the ads.

■ Explain the task: Ss read the ads and match the jobs to the ads. Point out that there are eight jobs but only six ads. Since Ss have learned all the vocabulary they need for this exercise, they do not need to use their dictionaries.

■ Ss do the task individually or in pairs. Check Ss' answers.

Answers:

| | | |
|---|---|---|
| English teacher | chef | sports instructor |
| receptionist | manager | guide |

**2**

■ Ss complete the task and then compare with a partner. Check Ss' answers.

Answers:

| | |
|---|---|
| college degree | = English teacher |
| good English | = English teacher, sports instructor, guide |
| foreign language | = sports instructor, guide |

## Optional activity: *Classified ads*

Make photocopies of job ads from an English newspaper.

■ Ss work in groups of four. Give copies of the job ads to each group. Explain the task: Ss classify the jobs in the ads into different categories. Write some examples on the board:

indoor or outdoor jobs
jobs that need English
exciting or boring jobs
white- or blue-collar jobs
safe or dangerous jobs

■ Groups do the task and then report their classifications to the class.

## Optional activity: *Game – Hangman*

This activity reviews vocabulary and spelling.
Time: 5–10 minutes.

■ Ss form groups of four or five. Each group chooses a word from the unit.

■ Class activity: On the board, one group draws a hangman diagram and blanks – one blank for each letter of the word (see Figure 2.1).

Figure 2.1

■ Other groups take turns guessing the letters in the word. If a group guesses a correct letter, write it in the correct blank on the board; if not, draw one part of the body (in this order: head, neck, left arm, right arm, body, left leg, right leg, left foot, right foot).

■ The object of the game is for a group to guess the correct word before the picture is completed.

■ The group guessing the correct word is the winner and gets to put its diagram and blanks on the board.

# 3 I'm just looking, thanks

This unit has three cycles and teaches Ss how to talk about possessions, money and expenses, and buying things. It presents singular and plural nouns, possessive pronouns, and demonstrative adjectives.

## UNIT PLAN

### Cycle 1

**1** Snapshot: *Introduces the theme of money and expenses*

**2** Expenses: *This activity personalizes the topic of the Snapshot and introduces "How much . . . ?"*

**3** Listening: *A listening task that involves comparing prices*

**4** Word Power: *Introduces the vocabulary of clothing and personal items*

**5** Yours or Mine?: *Introduces possessive pronouns*

### Cycle 2

**6** Pronunciation: *Presents the different ways plural s is pronounced*

**7** Conversation: *Introduces demonstrative adjectives and pronouns*

**8** Grammar Focus: *Practices demonstrative adjectives and pronouns*

**9** Role Play: *A fluency activity that extends the language practiced in this cycle*

### Cycle 3

**10** Conversation: *Introduces expressions used when buying things*

**11** Listening: *Listening for information about things for sale*

Interchange 3: *An open-ended class activity that reinforces the teaching points of the unit*

**12** Reading: *Reading ads for shopping information*

# 1 SNAPSHOT: The cost of living in the United States

This exercise introduces the theme of prices and expenses.

Prepare Ss for the exercise by comparing U.S. dollars with your own currency or your Ss' currencies by giving Ss equivalents of various amounts (e.g., $20,000, $1,666, $250). Model the pronunciation of dollar prices (e.g., $350 = "three hundred and fifty dollars"). Explain how figures written in dollars and cents are pronounced (e.g., $2.30 = "two dollars and thirty cents" or "two thirty"). Draw attention to the *s* at the end of the word "dollar*s*." Dictate some dollar amounts for Ss to calculate (e.g., $141 + $29 + $45 = . . . ).

■ Introduce the notion of expenses by listing some typical monthly expenses (e.g., rent, food, transportation). (You don't need to mention how much you personally pay for these things.)

■ Either present new vocabulary (e.g., salary, taxes, insurance) or ask Ss to use a dictionary. Model the pronunciation of each word.

■ Ss read the Snapshot individually and do the task. Ss compare with a partner.

■ Class activity: Find out what the class's biggest monthly expenses are and write them on the board.

■ Optional: Ask the class to suggest typical monthly expenses for an average person in your country (e.g., a married businessperson with two children). Do this as a whole class activity and list the items on the board with the amounts in your own currency.

# 2 EXPENSES

This exercise builds vocabulary and also introduces the question form "How much do you spend on . . . ?"

If you think any of the topics in this exercise are too personal, substitute other topics (e.g., movies, magazines, clothing).

## 1 Group work

■ Explain new words (e.g., rent).

■ Ss work in groups and complete the task. One S in each group is the secretary. He or she writes down the items.

## 2 Class activity

■ Groups calculate their averages and report them to the class. Write the averages on the board.

# 3 LISTENING

This exercise practices listening for prices.

■ Find out from Ss what each of the items on the chart costs in your city. Then ask Ss what they think prices are like in Honolulu, Mexico City, and Tokyo (e.g., "Is it cheap there? Is it expensive?").

■ Books closed. Play the tape. Ss listen.

■ Books open. Remind Ss of the information they should write down. Ss listen again and complete the task. Check Ss' answers.

Answers:

|  | *One gallon of gas* | *Bus fare* | *Dinner for two in a restaurant* |
|---|---|---|---|
| Honolulu | $1.30 | $0.60 | $50.00 |
| Mexico City | 0.70 | 0.01 | 12.00 |
| Tokyo | 3.70 | 1.30 | 80.00 |

# 4 WORD POWER: Possessions

This exercise teaches the names of common personal items in English.

## 1 Pair work

■ Present the new vocabulary by pointing out the items present in the classroom. Model the pronunciation of each word. You could also present items through mime or gesture (e.g., pretend to be using a calculator).

■ Ss do the task. Check answers around the class.

Answers:

| *Men's clothing* | *Women's clothing* | *School supplies* | *Jewelry* |
|---|---|---|---|
| trousers | slip | bag | necklace |
| tie | blouse | folder | bracelet |
| sport shirt | skirt | calculator | ring |

**Alternative presentation**

■ After modeling the pronunciation of the items, tell Ss to do as much of the task as they can. Then check answers around the class and explain any new vocabulary.

## 2

■ Ss do the task in pairs. Go around the class and give help as needed. Check Ss' answers and list them on the board.

Possible answers:

| *Men's clothing* | *Women's clothing* | *School supplies* | *Jewelry* |
|---|---|---|---|
| sport jacket | dress | briefcase | earrings |
| shorts | sweater | ballpoint pen | cuff links |
| T-shirt | pants | notebook paper | tie pin |
| trunks | bathing suit | backpack | pendant |

■ Optional: Ss work in groups. Ask Ss to look at each other and around the classroom for three minutes and find other words for the four categories. Ss can use their dictionaries if necessary. Find out which group has the most words.

## Optional activity: *Game – What's in the bag?*

This activity involves identifying names of objects. Time: 10–15 minutes.

*Preparation:* Each group needs a paper bag containing 15–20 different things. Write a letter on each bag (A, B, C, etc.) and number the items (#1, #2, #3, etc.). Choose objects that are familiar to the Ss, but ones they may not know the names of in English (e.g., button, stamp, piece of string, crayon, cap of a pen, paper clip, rubber band). The bags should not all contain the same items.

■ Explain the game to the class. Each group gets a bag and has to identify the items in it. Write these sentences on the board for Ss to use:

| | |
|---|---|
| Do you know what this is? | I think it's . . . |
| What's this called? | It might be called . . . |
| What's the name of this? | Gee, I have no idea. |

■ Ss form groups. Give each group a bag. One S in each group is the secretary. The group takes out one object at a time and tries to guess its name. The group secretary writes down the names:

#1 a paper clip
#2 a stamp
#3 . . .

■ Stop after about five minutes. Groups exchange bags.

■ After groups have looked at all the bags, stop the activity. Which group identified the most objects?

---

## 5  YOURS OR MINE?

This exercise presents possessive pronouns.

### Class activity

■ Collect a few items from Ss and place them on your desk. Model the task and the possessive pronouns by picking up each item and talking about it as in the example. Write additional sentences on the board if necessary. Present all the pronouns in this way. Ss practice.

■ Optional: Show Ss how to ask questions with possessive pronouns:

T:  Is this yours, John?
S1: No, it isn't mine.
T:  *(Pointing to two students)* Are these books yours?
S2: Yes, they're ours.
T:  I think this is Sue's. Sue, is this yours?
S3: No, I think it's Tina's.

■ Hand back the Ss' items.

■ Now ask each S to put an item on your desk. (If you have a small class, ask Ss to put several things on the desk.) Ss take turns choosing items and trying to identify them.

## Optional activity: *Whose is this?*

This exercise reviews pronouns.

*Preparation:* Tell each S to bring a small, interesting, or unusual item to class. Encourage Ss to bring things that tell something about themselves (e.g., stuffed animal, toy, badge, cap, souvenir).

■ Put all the objects in a box or bag in front of the class. Ss take turns taking an object out of the bag. Then they try to guess who it belongs to:

S1: I think this is Joan's.
T:  Why?
S1: Well, this is a . . . , and Joan collects . . .
T:  OK. Why don't you ask her?
S1: Joan, is this yours?
S2: Yes, it's mine. (No, it's not mine.)

## 6 PRONUNCIATION: Plural *s*

This exercise introduces the different ways of pronouncing plural *s*. The rules are:

#1 Plurals of words ending in the sounds /s/, /z/, /ʃ/, /tʃ/, /t/, and /d/ take an extra syllable /ɪz/ (e.g., dress – dresses).
#2 After words ending in a vowel sound and after other voiced consonants, *s* is pronounced /z/ (e.g., bag – bags).
#3 After other unvoiced final consonants, *s* is pronounced /s/ (e.g., clerk – clerks).

**1**

■ Use the tape to present each set of nouns. Ss practice.

**2**

This can be done either as a class activity, in pairs, or individually.

■ To make it easier to refer to the three sounds, write each sound on the board and number them:

| 1 | 2 | 3 |
|---|---|---|
| /z/ | /s/ | /ɪz/ |

■ Ss do the task.
■ Play the tape. Ss check their answers.

Answers:

| 1 | 2 | 3 |
|---|---|---|
| /z/ | /s/ | /ɪz/ |
| hotels | typists | classes |
| guides | books | nurses |
| cameras | belts | glasses |
| ties | | |

■ Optional: Write additional plural nouns on the board and ask Ss to pronounce them (e.g., nouns from Exercise 4).

## 7 CONVERSATION: Prices

This exercise introduces demonstrative adjectives and pronouns.

**1**

■ Books open. Set the scene. Sally and Carlos are in a department store.

■ Play the first part of the tape once. Ss listen only.

■ Present the conversation line by line. Go over new vocabulary. Explain the following expressions:

It's OK. They're all right. That's not bad = the item is neither good nor bad (i.e., "It's OK.")
on sale = the price is lower than the regular price
thanks, anyway = the speaker does not want to buy the item

■ Ss practice the conversation in groups of three.

**2**

■ Set the scene: Explain that Sally and Carlos look at three other items in the store.

■ Books closed. Play the second part of the tape. Ss listen only.

■ Books open. Play the tape again. Ss complete the task.

Answers:

| Item | Price | Do they buy it? |
|---|---|---|
| Jacket | $99 | No |
| Camera | $79.50 | No |
| Ballpoint pen | $1.58* | Yes |

*Including tax.

## 8 GRAMMAR FOCUS: Demonstrative adjectives and pronouns

This exercise presents demonstrative adjectives (this/that, these/those) and pronouns (it/they).

■ Use the tape to present the questions and statements in the box. Ss practice. Explain the difference between this/that and these/those by referring to objects in the classroom that are close to you and far away.

■ Call on Ss to make similar questions with "How much is/are . . . ?" and the appropriate responses.

■ Ss complete the task.

Answers:

A: Can I help you?
B: How much are these/those jeans?
A: They are $60.
B: Sixty or sixteen?
A: Sixty.
B: Sixty dollars! Are you kidding?

A: Good evening.
B: How much are these/those sunglasses?

A: They are $25.
B: Oh, really?
A: Would you like to buy them?
B: Yes, I'll take them. They are very nice.

A: Good afternoon.
B: Hi! How much is this/that backpack?
A: It is $35. Would you like to buy it?
B: Well, I'll think about it.

A: Good morning. Can I help you?
B: How much is this/that bicycle?
A: It is on sale. It is only $500.
B: Five hundred dollars! Well, I'm just looking, thanks.

Explain that "Are you kidding?" (in the first conversation) shows surprise at the high price; it also means "Are you joking?"

■ Ss practice in pairs.

## Optional activity

*Preparation:* Bring pictures of clothing and accessories from fashion or mail order catalogs. Remove the prices and keep a record of them. This activity works better if the items selected are rather expensive and/or overpriced. Either give a different set of pictures to each group, or photocopy one set for each group.

■ Ss form groups or pairs and try to guess the price of each item. Set a time limit of about 10 minutes.

■ When Ss have finished the task, give the actual prices.

---

## 9 ROLE PLAY:
### In a department store

This is a fluency exercise that reviews the language used in Exercises 6–8.

■ Explain the activity: The clerk (Student A) should start with "Good morning. Can I help you?" (or "Good afternoon" or "Good evening"). Encourage Ss to be as creative as possible and to extend the role play if they can. Model the task if necessary.

■ Ss do the task. Go around the class; do not explicitly correct errors, but give assistance if there is a communication breakdown. Ss change roles and do the activity again.

■ Ask one or two pairs to act out the role play in front of the class.

## 10 CONVERSATION

This exercise practices making a telephone call and talking about something for sale.

Use model telephones if your school has them; if not, have Ss sit back to back.

### 1

■ Books closed. Set the scene. Write these questions on the board:

What's for sale?
How old is it?
How much is it?

■ Play the tape several times. Ss listen and write down their answers.

■ Books open. Ss look over the conversation and check their answers.

■ Present the conversation line by line. Ss repeat. Model the stress in "**What** would you **like** to **know**?" and "**How much** do you **want** for it?"

■ Ss practice the conversation in pairs.

### 2 Pair work

■ Explain that when people in the U.S. and Canada want to sell used things, they hold a "garage sale." They either put an ad in the newspaper or a sign on the street announcing the sale.

■ Present the "Useful expressions." Give Ss other time phrases to substitute (e.g., "It's about two and a half years old"). Tell Ss to make up their own information on age, price, kind, and so forth.

■ Model the task with one S by following the conversation in part 1 – you are the seller (A) and the S is the caller (B).

■ Ss do the role play.

■ Ss change partners and roles and do the activity again.

■ Optional: Ask each S to make a list of two or three things (household or personal items) she or he would like to sell. Then Ss work in pairs and talk about the things:

S1: I'm selling a watch.
S2: What kind is it?
S1: . . .
S2: And how old is it?
S1: . . .
S2: Well, let me think about it.

## Optional activity: *Car for sale*

This activity practices writing a description of a car. Time: 10–15 minutes.

*Preparation:* Cut out color magazine pictures of cars or other vehicles. Each group needs one picture.

■ Explain the task: In groups, Ss write an ad for the car in their picture using their own information. Put these cues on the board and explain them:

Kind:                         Special features:
Age:                          Price:
Color:                        Person to contact:
Miles/kilometers:             Phone:
Condition: (excellent, good,
    fair, poor)

■ Groups use the cues to prepare their ads. Go around the class and give help as needed.

■ Groups take turns reading their ads to the class. Other Ss ask questions to get more information. Which car would Ss most like to buy? Why?

## 11 LISTENING

This exercise practices listening to telephone calls and writing down things for sale.

■ Set the scene.

■ Books closed. Play the tape several times. Ss listen only.

■ Books open. Play the tape again. Ss complete the information.

Answers:

| For sale | Kind | Age | Price |
|---|---|---|---|
| piano | Baldwin | about 50 years old | $900 |
| TV | RCA | about 15 years old | $50 |
| car | Volkswagen | about 20 years old | $3,600 |

■ Optional: Ss use the information to practice making telephone calls.

## INTERCHANGE 3:
## Swap meet

This exercise practices asking questions about things for sale and responding with short-answer descriptions.

Each S needs three blank cards.

## 1

■ Set the scene by explaining "swap meet": In many cities in the U.S. and Canada, people bring new and used things they want to sell to a designated public place (e.g., a supermarket or stadium parking lot), usually on weekends.

■ Ask Ss to think of three things (real or imaginary) that they would like to sell at a swap meet.

■ Go over the example description of a "Bicycle for Sale."

■ Ss write down a short description of each thing they want to sell on "For Sale" cards.

## 2 Class activity

■ Divide the class into two groups: sellers and buyers. The sellers put their "For Sale" cards on their desks or on the wall for the buyers to see easily. Remind the buyers that they have $300 to spend at the swap meet.

■ Model the task with one or two Ss by asking several sellers about their things. When you buy something, write down the item, price, and seller. Keep a list of items you want to buy.

■ Ss do the activity. Set a time limit of about 10 minutes.

## 3

■ Buyers report to the class what they want to buy.

## 4

■ Ss switch roles as buyers and sellers and do the activity again.

## 12 READING:
## Shopping advertisements

This exercise practices scanning for key words.

■ Ss should be able to do this task without using their dictionaries.

■ Books open. Explain these phrases:

save 25%  = items are marked down 25% from
              the regular price
              (e.g., a $10 item will cost $7.50)
30% off   = items are marked down 30% from
              the regular price
              (e.g., a $10 item will cost $7)

■ Ask Ss to read the ads without trying to understand every word. Tell Ss to guess what kind of stores they are. Check Ss' answers.

Answers:

Simpson's      = a department store
Fisher         = an office supply store
Sharper Image  = an electronics store

■ Ask other questions about these kinds of stores (e.g., "What's the name of a good department store around here?").

## 1 and 2

■ Ss complete the tasks individually or in pairs. Remind Ss not to use dictionaries.

Answers to part 1:

|                | *Simpson's* | *Fisher* | *Sharper Image* |
|----------------|:-----------:|:--------:|:---------------:|
| a briefcase    | X           |          |                 |
| pencils        |             | X        |                 |
| a bracelet     | X           |          |                 |
| a CD player    |             |          | X               |
| computer paper |             | X        |                 |
| headphones     |             |          | X               |

Answers to part 2:

a) T    b) F    c) F    d) T    e) T

# Review of Units 1–3

This unit reviews making personal introductions, Wh- and Yes/No questions, and asking about the cost of things.

> ## UNIT PLAN
>
> **1** Getting to know you: *Reviews questions with* be *and personal introductions*
>
> **2** Quiz: *Reviews Yes/No questions with* be, *countries and nationalities, and jobs*
>
> **3** What's the question?: *Reviews Wh- and Yes/No questions*
>
> **4** Listening: *Practices listening for questions*
>
> **5** The cost of living: *Reviews using "How much . . . ?" and subject-verb agreements with* be

## 1 GETTING TO KNOW YOU

This exercise reviews questions with *be* and self-introductions.

### Pair work

- Explain the situation.
- Model the task and show Ss how to elaborate:

A: Hi. How are you?
B: Fine, thanks.
A: By the way, my name is Mary Gibbs.
B: Hi. I'm Nobu Tanaka.
A: Nice to meet you, Nobu. Are you from Japan?
B: Yes, I am. I'm from Kobe.
A: Are you a student here?
B: Yes, I am. I go to Riverside Community College. And how about you, Mary? What do you do?
A: I work for an advertising agency. I'm a graphic artist.
B: Oh, really? And where are you from?
A: I'm from California.
B: Well, enjoy your lunch. Nice talking to you, Mary.
A: Nice talking to you, too, Nobu.
B: Bye.
A: Bye-bye.

- Ss practice the conversation in pairs. Remind Ss to use the "Look Up and Say" technique. Go around the class and give help as needed.

- Optional: Books closed. Ss perform the conversation in front of the class. Elicit comments on what was good in the conversations and what could be improved.

## 2 QUIZ

This exercise reviews Yes/No questions with *be,* countries and nationalities, and jobs.

### 1 Pair work

- Explain the task: Ss write five questions about famous people. Some of the questions should be answered with "Yes" and some with "No." Go over the example questions. Write additional questions on the board:

Is Olivia Newton-John Australian?
Are the Rolling Stones a jazz group?
Is Steven Spielberg a movie director?

- Ss do the task in pairs. Go around the class and give help as needed.

### 2 Group work

- Pairs work in groups of four and take turns asking their questions. Ss keep score of correct answers.
- Find out which Ss had the most correct answers.

■ Optional: Ss ask their questions to the rest of the class.

---

## 3 WHAT'S THE QUESTION?

This activity reviews Wh- and Yes/No questions.

### 1

■ Explain the task and say that there may be more than one correct question for each answer. Point out that answers with "Yes" or "No" need Yes/No questions, and that the others need Wh-questions.

■ Model the task:

T: *(Reads answer)* "No, my apartment isn't on Main Street. It's on River Street." What's the question?
S1: Is your apartment on Main Street?
T: That's right. Good. How about this one? *(Reads answer)* "I teach business English."
S2: What do you do?
T: Good. Can you ask another Wh-question?
S3: What do you teach?

■ Ss do the task individually and write down the questions. Go around the class and give help as needed.

### 2

■ Ss check with a partner. Check Ss' answers around the class.

Possible answers:

Is your apartment on Main Street?
Where are the Taylors from?
Is that one yours?
What do you do?   *(or)*   What do you teach?
Is this Sue's car?   *(or)*   Is that Sue's car?
Are you a student?
What do you do?   *(or)*   Where do you teach?
Is Carlos from Mexico?
Is your phone number 955-8821?

■ Optional: Ss write five statements like the ones in the book. Then Ss take turns reading their statements to the class and calling on other Ss to make the questions.

---

## 4 LISTENING

In this exercise students practice listening for questions.

■ Books closed. Set the scene and play the tape. Ss listen only.

■ Books open. Explain the task. Play the tape again, pausing after each cue. Ss check the correct answers.

■ Ss compare their answers. Check Ss' answers around the class.

Answers:

a) At Saxon's Department Store.
b) It's on Vine Street.
c) Yes, I'm in the electronics department.
d) Yes, we do.
e) They're on sale. About $65–$200.
f) Yes, I work on Saturdays.
g) OK. See you on Saturday.

---

## 5 THE COST OF LIVING

This activity reviews talking about prices with "How much . . . ?" and subject-verb agreement with *be.*

### 1 Pair work

■ Explain the task: Ss ask about the six items listed.

■ Model the task:

T: How much is a movie ticket?
S: It's five dollars.

■ Ss work in pairs and do the task. Go around the class and give help as needed.

### 2

■ Explain the task. If the class is heterogeneous, Ss could also ask about the cost of things in each other's countries (e.g., "How much is a cup of coffee in Brazil?" "How much are baseball tickets in Japan?").

■ Ss do the task in pairs.

■ Optional: Pairs take turns asking questions in small groups or to the rest of the class.

### Test 1

See page 151 for general instructions on using the tests. Test 1 covers Units 1–3. Photocopy the test (pp. 152–154) and distribute it in class. Allow 45–60 minutes for the test. Listening material for tests is on Side 4 of the Class Cassette, and the test answer key and tape transcripts are at the back of the Teacher's Manual.

# 4 What kind of music do you like?

This unit has two cycles. It teaches Ss how to talk about entertainment and about likes and dislikes. It also presents Yes/No questions with *do*, object pronouns, *there is*, and prepositions.

## UNIT PLAN

### Cycle 1

**1** Snapshot: *Introduces the theme of music*

**2** Word Power: *Presents vocabulary of entertainment*

**3** Conversation: *Introduces Yes/No questions with* do

**4** Grammar Focus: *Practices the grammar of questions and statements with* do *and introduces object pronouns*

**5** Pronunciation: *Contrasts intonation for Yes/No and Wh-questions*

**6** Entertainment Survey: *A fluency activity on the topic of entertainment*

### Cycle 2

**7** Listening: *Introduces the theme of likes and dislikes*

**8** Conversation: *Introduces making invitations and talking about times of events*

**9** Grammar Focus: *Controlled practice of* there is *and prepositions*

**10** Listening: *Practices listening for times and days*

**11** Invitations: *Practices writing about events with a follow-up fluency activity on invitations*

**12** Reading: *Practices reading for opinions and inferencing*

Interchange 4: *A role play task that practices asking for information about current events*

## 1 SNAPSHOT: Music sales in North America

This exercise introduces the theme of music and entertainment and presents the vocabulary of different kinds of music.

■ Books closed. Introduce the topic of music by asking Ss questions. Present the vocabulary of the Snapshot (e.g., rock, pop, country, favorite) through your questions:

Do you like rock music?
Do you like Bruce Springsteen?
Which pop groups do you like?
Who is your favorite rock star?

■ Explain these kinds of music:

country = country and western music
rhythm and blues = a kind of jazz
gospel = a kind of church music with a simple
   melody and harmony

### Alternative presentation

■ Books closed. To introduce the vocabulary in the Snapshot, play taped examples of different kinds of music (e.g., rock, classical, jazz).

■ Books open. Ss read the Snapshot, complete the task, and compare their answers with a partner. Encourage Ss to ask each other questions (e.g., "What is your favorite kind of music?" "Do you like jazz?").

■ As a follow-up, take a poll of the class favorites. Write the information on the board and then compare it with the Snapshot.

## 2 WORD POWER: Entertainment

This exercise presents vocabulary for various types of entertainment, which Ss will use throughout the unit.

### 1 Pair work

■ Ask Ss to cover the word chart so that they do not begin the task yet. Give definitions and examples of any new vocabulary (e.g., game shows, soap operas, thrillers, westerns).

■ Ss complete the task in pairs. Check Ss' answers.

Answers:

| *Music* | *Movies* | *TV programs* |
|---|---|---|
| jazz | horror films | game shows |
| classical | science fiction | news |
| pop | thrillers | soap operas |
| rock | westerns | talk shows |

■ Now check Ss' pronunciation of the words.

### 2

■ Ss complete the task individually or in pairs. Check Ss' answers and write them on the board.

Possible answers:

| *Music* | *Movies* | *TV programs* |
|---|---|---|
| country and | adventure | cartoons |
|   western | comedies | documentaries |
| disco | love stories | movies |
| folk | musicals | sports |
| reggae | | |

## 3 CONVERSATION: Likes and dislikes

This conversation introduces Yes/No questions with *do* and practices talking about likes and dislikes.

■ Books open. Set the scene.

■ Play the tape. Ss listen.

■ Present the conversation line by line. Explain these words and expressions:

U2 = a popular rock group (it takes the plural pronoun *them*)
I can't stand . . . = I hate or I strongly dislike something (e.g., "I can't stand rock music").

■ Model the blend in "Do you . . . ?" /dəjə/ and the pronunciation of *them* /ðəm/ in "Do you like them?" (which is unstressed here).

■ Ss practice the conversation in pairs.

■ Optional: Books closed. Ss practice the conversation using their own words.

## 4 GRAMMAR FOCUS: Yes/No questions with *do*; object pronouns

This exercise practices Yes/No questions with *do* and object pronouns.

■ Use the tape to present the questions and answers in the box. Point out that a singular noun (e.g., jazz) takes a singular object pronoun (e.g., it), and that a plural noun (e.g., U2, TV programs) takes a plural object pronoun (e.g., them).

■ Optional: Elicit from Ss other expressions to describe likes and dislikes (e.g., She's/He's/It's/They're terrific, all right, OK, awful, kind of cute/good/old, pretty stupid) and write them on the board.

■ Ss complete the conversations. Check Ss' answers.

Answers:

A: Do you like disco music?
B: Yes, I really like it. How about you?
A: I don't like it very much.

A: Who's your favorite actress?
B: Jane Fonda. I really like her.
A: Jane Fonda! I can't stand her!

A: Do you like Ann Murray?
B: No, I don't like her very much. But I like Whitney Houston. Do you?
A: Yes, I do. She's terrific!

A: What kind of TV programs do you like?
B: Game shows. I like them a lot. Do you like them?
A: No, I don't like them very much. I like music videos.

A: Do you like Sly Stallone?
B: He's OK. My favorite actor is Tom Cruise. Do you like him?
A: Yes. I do.

A: What do you think of the Rolling Stones?
B: Well, I don't like them very much.
A: Oh really? I like them a lot.

■ Ss practice the conversations.

■ Optional: Ss take turns practicing the conversations again – Student A with book open and Student B with book closed. This time Ss give their own answers and improvise where appropriate.

---

## ⑤ PRONUNCIATION: Question intonation

This exercise introduces intonation patterns used with Yes/No and Wh-questions.

**1**

■ Explain that "intonation" is the musical pitch of the voice, which rises and falls throughout a sentence in English.

■ Books open. Play the first part of the tape, or model the intonation patterns in the questions. Point out that Yes/No questions usually end with rising intonation, and Wh-questions usually end with falling intonation.

■ Play the tape again. Ss repeat.

**2**

■ Play the second part of the tape. Ss practice the questions.

■ Optional: Ss look at Exercise 3 on page 23 again and mark the intonation patterns with arrows over the questions in the conversation. Then Ss practice the conversation again, paying attention to question intonation.

## Optional activity: *Who am I?*

This activity practices Yes/No questions. Time: 10–15 minutes.

*Preparation:* Cut out magazine pictures, one for each S, of well-known people that your Ss are sure to know (e.g., entertainers, singers, musicians, actors, actresses, TV personalities, politicians).

■ Ask each S to come to the front of the class. Pin or tape a picture to the S's back without him or her seeing it. Use pictures of women for female Ss and pictures of men for male Ss.

■ Explain the task: Ss try to guess whose picture is on their back. Ss can use only Yes/No questions to find out who it is.

■ Model the task by asking a S to pin a picture on your back (e.g., the picture shows Mr. Gorbachev):

T: Am I an entertainer?
S: No, you aren't.
T: Am I a politician?
S: Yes, you are.
T: Do I live in North America?
S: No, you don't.
T: Do I speak Russian?
S: Yes, you do.
T: Am I Mr. Gorbachev?
S: Yes, you are!

■ Ss move around the class trying to identify their pictures. When a S correctly guesses the person's name, he or she sits down.

■ Stop the activity after about ten minutes. Find out how many Ss guessed the person's name correctly.

# 6 ENTERTAINMENT SURVEY

This is an open-ended follow-up activity to Exercises 3–5. The focus is on getting the Ss to express themselves using their own information, with emphasis on fluency, not on accuracy. The first part of this exercise is a free discussion on entertainment and entertainers.

## 1 Group work

■ If you teach a heterogeneous class with Ss from many different countries, tell the Ss to talk about entertainers and types of entertainment in your country (i.e., not in the Ss' own countries).

■ Ss work in groups of four or five. Set a time limit of about ten minutes. Ss take turns asking any of the questions on the list to others in the group. Encourage Ss to elaborate their responses:

S1: Do you like pop music?
S2: Umm, not really, but I love classical music.
S3: Oh, really? Who's your favorite composer?
S2: Brahms. I love his music! And how about you?
S3: . . .

## 2

■ One S in each group is a group secretary. Ss take turns and ask about each topic listed in the chart "Our Group Favorites," using these questions:

What is your favorite kind of music?
Who is your favorite actor?

■ Group secretaries write down each S's response.

## 3 Class activity

■ Present the "Useful expressions."

■ Group secretaries report their group's favorites to the class. Write the information on the board and then find the class favorites.

■ Optional: Books closed. Ss practice asking and answering questions on the theme of entertainment. Encourage Ss to ask questions and to give responses quickly, without pausing if possible. Start the activity by asking a question to a S:

T: Who's your favorite American actress, Carlos?
S1: Umm, Glenn Close.
T: Oh, really? I like her, too! OK, Carlos, ask someone else a question.
S1: Keiko, what kind of TV programs do you like?
S2: . . .

■ A more challenging way of doing thi activity is not to allow Ss to repeat a has already been asked.

# 7 LISTENING: TV game show

This exercise practices listening for likes and dislikes. The task is based on a popular American TV game show called *The Dating Game.*

■ Explain the situation: Linda will choose to have a date with Bill, Tony, or John, based on how many interests they have in common.

■ Books closed. Play the tape once. Ss listen only.

■ Books open. Point out that Ss need to write only one-word or two-word answers to complete the task.

■ Play the tape again while Ss complete the task. Use the pause button where necessary to give Ss time to complete the answers.

■ Play the tape straight through again for Ss to check answers.

Answers:

|  | *Music* | *Movies* | *TV programs* |
|---|---|---|---|
| Bill | classical | thrillers | news programs |
| John | jazz | westerns | talk shows |
| Tony | rock | horror films | game shows |
| Linda | pop | horror films | talk shows and game shows |

■ Class activity: Ask the class who the best date for Linda is.

Possible answer:

Tony is the best date for Linda because:

1. He and Linda both like horror films and game shows.
2. Linda never disagreed with something that Tony liked. However, she directly disagreed with both Bill and John on music (she said she didn't like classical or jazz).

■ If Ss think that Bill or John is a better date for Linda, have a short discussion and ask for their reasons.

# 8 CONVERSATION: Invitations

This exercise introduces making and accepting invitations, which is developed more fully in

Unit 15. It also introduces *there is,* and prepositions for describing days and times.

■ Optional: This is the first reference in the book to times of the day. If your Ss need practice telling the time in English, teach expressions like these:

1:00 = one o'clock
2:05 = five after two   *(or)*   two-oh-five
3:15 = [a] quarter after three   *(or)*   three-fifteen
4:20 = twenty after four   *(or)*   four-twenty
5:30 = half past five   *(or)*   five-thirty
6:45 = quarter to seven   *(or)*   six forty-five

■ Books open. Play the tape. Ss listen only.

■ Play the tape again or model each sentence. Ss repeat. Model the stress in "Would you **like** to **go**?" and "**That** sounds **good!**" Explain that the "Blue Note" is a jazz club.

■ Ss practice the conversation in pairs, using the "Look Up and Say" technique.

## 9 GRAMMAR FOCUS:
### *There is;* prepositions

This exercise presents the structure *there is* and the prepositions *on* and *at.* *There is* is introduced here in singular statement form only. A full presentation of *there is/are* is given in Unit 8. *There is,* which functions as an empty subject, will not be difficult for Ss who speak European languages since many of these languages have a similar structure. For Ss unfamiliar with this structure, it might be helpful to point out the equivalence between these sentences:

The jazz concert is at 10.
        = There's a jazz concert at 10.

■ Use the tape to present the sentences in the box.
■ Write these rules on the board for the prepositions *at* and *on,* or ask Ss to look at the Unit Summary in the Student's Book on page 126:

The jazz concert is <u>at</u> the Blue        *at* + place
   Note.
The jazz concert is <u>on</u> Friday.        *on* + day
The jazz concert is <u>at</u> 10 o'clock.        *at* + time

■ Elicit information about events in your city and write other examples on the board:

There's a soccer game <u>at</u> the university <u>on</u> Sunday.
   It's <u>at</u> 3:00.
There's a movie at the King Theater <u>on</u> Wednesday. It's <u>at</u> 7:00.

## 1

■ Ss write about the other events listed as in the example.

■ Ss read their sentences aloud. Check for article and preposition usage.

## 2 Pair work

This provides extra oral practice and reviews Wh-questions.

■ Remind Ss to use falling intonation with Wh-questions.

■ Ss practice the questions in pairs.

## 10 LISTENING

This exercise practices listening for information about times and days.

■ Explain the situation. Play the tape several times. Ss complete the task. Check Ss' answers.

Answers:

*Kramer vs. Kramer*
Times: 2, 4, 6, 8, 10 P.M.
Days: Mon., Thur.

*Dracula*
Times: 3, 5, 7, 9, 11 P.M.
Days: Fri., Sat., Sun.

*Gone with the Wind*
Times: 12, 4, 8 P.M.
Days: Wed., Thur.

## 11 WRITING

This exercise practices describing events in a city using real information, and making invitations.

*Preparation:* Ask Ss to bring English language newspapers to class for this task. If there are none available, Ss will have to translate information from other sources into English. Or you could bring newspapers or other local printed sources with information about events in your town or city and make copies for all Ss to use in class.

## 1

This activity can be done with Ss working individually, in pairs, or in groups. The main types of information Ss should include are:

the kind of event
place
day/date
time

Ss should add other information as appropriate (e.g., the kind of movie, the main actors and actresses).

■ Explain the task and go over the model. Ss write descriptions of three events. Move around the class and give help as needed.

■ Ss read their descriptions to the class.

**Alternative presentation**

■ Assign the writing task in part 1 for homework. In class, Ss read their descriptions to the class.

## 2 Pair work

■ Ss review Exercise 8 before starting the pair work task here.

■ Ss take turns inviting their partners to do something, using the information from their three descriptions of events.

## Optional activity: *Likes and dislikes*

This activity practices questions. Time: 15–20 minutes.

*Preparation:* In a previous class, ask Ss to write three statements about their likes and dislikes on the topics of music and entertainment (see examples in Figure 4.1). Collect the statements and use the information to make a class grid. In each box, write information about one student (without the student's name).

Make one photocopy of the grid for each S.

■ Give each S a copy of the grid. Explain the task: Ss move around the class trying to find out who each person is by asking questions. Tell Ss to look at the first box on the grid. Elicit example questions and write them on the board:

Do you like game shows?
Do you like Mozart?
What do you think of Grace Jones?

■ When Ss find the correct person, they write down the S's name in the box on the grid. Set a time limit of about 15 minutes.

■ When the time is up, find out which S has the most names.

---

## 12 READING: Is TV good or bad?

This exercise practices reading to identify people's opinions and to make inferences.

■ Books closed. Introduce the topic of television by asking questions around the class:

Do you like television?
Do you watch TV every day?
About how many hours a week do you watch TV?
What kind of programs do you watch?

■ Books open. Ss read the passage and try to guess the meanings of any new words. If Ss cannot guess the meaning of a word that they think is important, tell them to circle it.

■ Ask which words Ss circled and explain them. Also explain: *Sesame Street* = a popular children's program on educational TV.

### 1

■ Ss complete the task and then compare answers. Check Ss' answers.

Answers:

a) B   b) G   c) B   d) B   e) G   f) G   g) B
h) B   i) G   j) B

### 2

■ Ss complete the task.

■ Check Ss' opinions around the class and discuss their reasons for agreeing or disagreeing.

Figure 4.1

## Interchange 4: Can I help you?

This is a role play activity that requires Ss to talk about events in a city. Either use telephones or ask Ss to sit back to back during this activity.

■ This activity uses ordinal numbers. Present ordinal numbers (1–10) and write them on the board:

| | |
|---|---|
| 1st = first | 6th = sixth |
| 2nd = second | 7th = seventh |
| 3rd = third | 8th = eighth |
| 4th = fourth | 9th = ninth |
| 5th = fifth | 10th = tenth |

■ Explain the activity: Some Ss are going to be tourists visiting a city. They want information about things to do, so they call the Tourist Information Center. The other Ss are clerks at the Tourist Information Center. They have information about events in the city and will answer the tourists' questions. In part 2 of the activity, Ss change roles and partners. Encourage Ss to be imaginative and creative, and to use only English.

■ Divide the class into two groups (As and Bs) before beginning the activity. Ask all Student As (clerks) to look at page 106, and all Student Bs (tourists) at page 108.

■ Explain what Student As need to do. They should use the information on their page.

■ Now explain to the Student Bs that there are four events they want to get information about – two that are mentioned by name on their charts and two that only have the places mentioned.

They should use the information on the chart and the questions on the page.

■ Play the part of Student B and model the task with a Student A:

S: Hello?
T: Hi. I'm a tourist in your city. I'm calling from my hotel. What's on at the Film Center this week?
S: There's a . . .

■ Remind Ss how to ask for repetition and clarifications (e.g., "Please say that again," or "How do you spell/say that, please?").

## 1

■ Now Ss do the activity in A/B pairs. Set a time limit for parts 1 and 2 of 10–15 minutes. Remind Ss to sit back to back (if there are no phones). Tell Student Bs to fill in the information in the book. Go around and give help as needed.

■ If Ss are having any difficulty with the task, stop the activity and ask two Ss to do the role play in front of the class. Give helpful comments and elicit suggestions from Ss on how the role plays could be improved.

■ Stop the activity after about five minutes.

## 2

■ Ss switch partners and roles here, and continue with part 2.

■ After Ss have completed the activity, or after five more minutes are up, call on pairs to perform the activity in front of the class.

# 5 Tell me about your family

This unit has three cycles and introduces the themes of families and making small talk. It presents third-person questions and statements in the present tense.

## UNIT PLAN

### Cycle 1

**1** Word Power: *Introduces the vocabulary of family members*

**2** Relatives: *Further practice of the vocabulary of family members*

**3** Snapshot: *Information about typical North American families*

### Cycle 2

**4** Conversation: *Introduces third-person questions and statements in the present tense*

**5** Listening: *Practices listening for information about families of famous people*

**6** Pronunciation: *Practices third-person s*

**7** Grammar Focus: *Practices the grammar of third person in questions and statements in the present tense*

**8** Interesting People: *A fluency activity on the topic of families*

**9** Listening: *Listening for information about a famous person*

**10** Twenty Questions: *A game reviewing Yes/No questions*

**11** Writing: *Writing a short composition about one's family*

Interchange 5: *A communication activity that reviews asking questions*

### Cycle 3

**12** Conversation: *Common greetings and small talk*

**13** Small Talk: *Practices making small talk*

**14** Reading: *Practices reading for main ideas*

## 1  WORD POWER: The family

This exercise presents the vocabulary needed to talk about family members, which Ss will use throughout the unit.

### 1

■ Ss complete the task individually or in pairs without using their dictionaries. Then have Ss compare answers before you give them the correct answers.

Answers – Sam's family tree:

| Generation | Family members |
| --- | --- |
| 1st | grandfather & grandmother |
| 2nd | father & mother / uncle & aunt |
| 3rd | Sam/brother & sister-in-law/cousins |
| 4th | niece / nephew |

■ Model the pronunciation of each word. Model the voiced /z/ in "cousin," the dropped /d/ in "gran*d*mother" and "gran*d*father," and the correct pronunciation of "niece" /niys/ and "nephew" /'nefjuw/. Also model the correct position of the tongue for *th* /ð/ in "mo*th*er" and "fa*th*er" (i.e., the tip of the tongue lightly touches the back of the teeth).

### 2

*There are* is presented here for the first time. (*There is* was presented in Unit 4.)

■ Ss draw their family trees. Ss can either describe their immediate families (e.g., wife/husband/children or their mother/father/brothers/sisters).

■ Present the sentences to use for a single or a married person. Model the task by talking about your own family. Answer any questions.

■ Ask questions around the class like this:

T:  Tell us about your family, Ana.
S1: Well, there are six in my family. I have . . .
T:  And how about you, Keiko?
S2: . . .

## 2  RELATIVES

This is a "quiz" that provides a fun review.

### 1

■ Ask a S to read the first sentence and elicit the correct answer (i.e., "cousin").

■ Ss complete the task individually or in pairs. Then compare answers around the class.

Answers:

a) cousin    b) niece    c) sister-in-law    d) aunt
e) grandparents    f) father    g) grandmother

### 2  Pair work

■ Ss write three similar sentences individually and then read them aloud to a partner.

■ Optional: Call on Ss to read their sentences to the class. Other Ss complete them.

## 3  SNAPSHOT: Families

This exercise extends the topic of the unit by providing information for cross-cultural comparisons.

■ Explain "average," "percentage," and "alone."

■ Ss read the Snapshot and complete the task. Then Ss compare with a partner.

■ Ss give their answers around the class. Then compare Ss' answers with the information in the Snapshot.

## 4  CONVERSATION

This introduces the main grammar point of the unit – third-person questions and statements in the present simple.

■ Books closed. Set the scene: Two friends, Rita and Keiko, are talking about their families.

■ Write these questions on the board:

Is Keiko married?
What does she say about her family?
Does Rita have any brothers and sisters?

■ Play the tape. Ss compare answers.

■ Books open. Play the tape again. Present the conversation. Model the stressed and unstressed forms of *do* in **"What** do you **do?"** and the unstressed form of *does* in **"What** does your husband **do?"** The only vocabulary item Ss may not know here is *export business*. Explain that "No kidding" is used to express surprise; an equivalent expression is "Really?"

■ Ss practice the conversation in pairs.

## 5 LISTENING:
### Hollywood lives

This activity involves listening for key information.

■ Ask Ss questions about Jane Fonda and Madonna (e.g., "Is Jane Fonda British?" "Is she an opera singer?").

■ Play the tape. Ss listen only.

■ Play the tape again. Ss listen again. Ask them to write down information about each person's family. They should not write whole sentences, but key words or phrases only.

■ Ss compare the information they wrote down. Play the tape again if necessary.

Possible answers:

*Jane Fonda*
- daughter of famous actor, Henry Fonda
- sister of actor, Peter Fonda
- was married to Tom Hayden, a California state politician
- son named Troy; daughter, Vanessa (from first marriage)

*Madonna*
- big family
- the oldest daughter
- two sisters and three brothers
- first husband was American actor, Sean Penn

## 6 PRONUNCIATION:
### Third-person *s*

This exercise practices the pronunciation of the third-person *s*.

■ The phonological rule for final *s* for third-person present tense is the same as that for final *s* in plural nouns. (See explanation in teacher's notes in Unit 3, Exercise 6.)

### 1

■ Use the tape to present the set of verbs. Ss practice.

### 2

This can be done either as a class activity, in pairs, or individually.

■ To make it easier to refer to the three sounds, write the sounds on the board and number them:

| 1 | 2 | 3 |
|---|---|---|
| /z/ | /s/ | /ɪz/ |

■ Ask Ss to write the number of each sound beside each word. Play the tape to check Ss' answers.

Answers:

| 1 | 2 | 3 |
|---|---|---|
| /z/ | /s/ | /ɪz/ |
| buys | cooks | discusses |
| comes | helps | exercises |
| designs | takes | washes |
| studies | types | |
| | writes | |

■ Optional: Write additional verbs in third-person form on the board and ask Ss to pronounce them (e.g., agrees, answers, catches, helps, guesses, loves, passes, travels, thinks, watches, wants).

## 7 GRAMMAR FOCUS:
### Present tense – third person

This exercise practices questions and statements in the third-person singular and plural using the present tense.

■ Use the tape to present the questions and statements in the box. Ss repeat. Model the stress in the Wh-questions (e.g., **"What** does she **do?"**). Then model the stress in the Yes/No questions with *do* (e.g., "Does your **bro**ther go to **school?"** "Do your **chil**dren work in Chi**ca**go?").

■ Ss ask each other Wh- and Yes/No questions around the class:

S1: John, what does Tomiko do?
S2: She works in a bank. Um, Maria, does your husband work for the government?
S3: Yes, he does. Tom, . . . ?

■ Ss complete the conversations individually and then check answers with a partner.

Answers:

A: Tell me about your parents. What <u>do</u> they do?
B: Well, my father is retired, and my <u>mother</u> <u>manages</u> a boutique.
A: <u>Oh</u>. Do <u>they</u> live with you?
B: No, they <u>don't</u>. They <u>live</u> in Miami.

A: Do you have any brothers and sisters?
B: Yes, I have two sisters and one brother. My older sister <u>works</u> for United Airlines, and my younger sister <u>goes</u> to UCLA.
A: Oh, really? And <u>what</u> <u>does</u> your brother do? Does he <u>go</u> to school, <u>too</u>?

B: No, he <u>doesn't</u>. He is married and <u>teaches</u> in an elementary school.

■ Call on several Ss to read the conversations aloud, using the "Look Up and Say" technique. Check their pronunciation of third-person *s* and their use of stress.

■ Ss practice the conversations in pairs.

## Optional activity: *Game – Tic-Tac-Toe*

This activity practices making statements with third-person verb forms (e.g., work/works) in the present tense. (This game is known as Tic-Tac-Toe in Canada and the U.S. and as Noughts and Crosses in some other countries.) This game can be used in any unit by substituting different parts of speech. Time: 10–15 minutes.

■ Draw a grid with nine squares on the board. Ask Ss to call out verbs in the present tense and write them on the grid. (See Figure 5.1.)

| lives | go | studies |
| take | does | makes |
| sells | work | answer |

Figure 5.1

■ Now divide the class into two teams, Team X and Team O. Team X starts. They choose a verb from the grid and one S from the team makes a sentence with it:

S1: We want to make a sentence with "lives."
T: OK.
S1: Noriko lives in Osaka, Japan.
T: Team O, is that a good sentence?
S2: Yes, it is.

If the sentence is correct, mark X in the square over "lives"; if it is not correct, Team O gets a chance to make a sentence. If Team O's sentence is correct, mark an O over the verb they used. Then Team O gets a turn to choose a verb. The game continues until a team has three Xs or three Os in any direction. (See Figure 5.2.)

Figure 5.2

## 8 INTERESTING PEOPLE

This is an open-ended fluency activity. Ss should try to keep the conversation going without stumbling over pronunciation or grammar.

### 1 Group work

■ Model the task by having Ss ask you (or a S in the class) questions about your family. Ss need not limit themselves to the questions presented in this activity or unit. Encourage them to be creative.

■ Ss form groups. Explain that each person takes a turn answering questions about his or her family. The distinctions between single and married are only suggestions for describing one's immediate family. Married Ss can also discuss parents, brothers, sisters, etc. Ss can take notes if they wish (see part 2, Class activity).

■ Set a time limit of about 10 minutes. Move around and make sure all Ss get a chance to answer questions from their group.

### 2 Class activity

■ Ss choose one person in their group they want to talk about. They can make notes if they want to before beginning the class activity.

■ Groups take turns talking about Ss' families.

### Optional activity: *People in the news*

■ Group work: Each group chooses an interesting person who has been in the news recently. The group must "pool" their information on the person. One S in each group acts as secretary and takes notes. Ss start like this:

S1: Let's talk about . . .
S2: Or how about . . . ?

■ Group secretaries tell the class about the person their group talked about.

## Optional activity: *Occupations*

This activity practices forming compound nouns from verb + noun constructions (e.g., "She studies law" = "She's a law student"). Time: 10–15 minutes.

*Preparation:* Make a copy of Figure 5.3 on page 48 for each S.

■ Give each S a copy of the list (Figure 5.3). Give one or two examples, providing the name of the occupation using compound nouns. Elicit a few more examples from Ss around the class.

■ Ss work individually and then compare answers in pairs. Go around the class and give help as necessary.

■ Check Ss' answers.

---

## 9 LISTENING

This activity practices listening to information about a famous person and previews the activity in Exercise 10.

■ Explain the game "Twenty Questions": One player thinks of a famous person, place, or thing, and the other players try to guess who or what it is by asking a maximum of 20 Yes/No questions. If they cannot guess the answer, the first player wins.

■ Play the tape. Ss try to guess the famous person. Don't give them the correct answer yet.

■ If necessary, explain these key words: *famous, videos, hit album.*

■ Play the tape again. Check Ss' answers.

Answer:

Michael Jackson

---

## 10 TWENTY QUESTIONS

This activity is the same game Ss heard played in Exercise 9.

## Group work

■ Remind Ss of the rules of the game: They can only ask Yes/No questions with *be* or *do* (i.e., not Wh-questions). They have to think of a living person and use the present tense in the questions.

■ Ss form groups. Each S takes a turn thinking of a famous person and answering the group's questions. Set a time limit of about 10 minutes.

■ Optional: Find out if anyone in the group thought of someone the other group members could not identify. If so, let the rest of the class play the game with that S and try to guess the person's identity.

---

## 11 WRITING

This exercise practices writing a short description of a family.

### 1

■ Ss think about their families to get ideas and information they can use. Ask Ss to write down key words and phrases related to the topic. This is called "brainstorming." Brainstorm about your own family on the board:

seven in my family
brother, Carlos, lives in Sydney
married to an Australian
three younger sisters
Mary, 23, goes to school

■ Ss brainstorm about their families.

■ Show Ss how to use their notes to write a paragraph like the examples. Ss write first drafts of their compositions. They should concentrate on writing as much as they can in sentence form without worrying too much about spelling or grammar.

■ Ss check their drafts. Can they add any information? What do they need to revise or delete? What grammar and spelling need to be corrected?

■ Ss revise their drafts.

### 2

■ Ss exchange papers and answer their partners' questions.

■ Optional: Ss put their compositions on the class bulletin board for other Ss to read.

---

## INTERCHANGE 5:
Who's who?

This activity reviews asking questions and gives Ss an opportunity to find out more about one another.

## OCCUPATIONS

 1. He drives a truck.  _____

 2. She plays the guitar.  _____

 3. He collects rent.  _____

 4. She teaches history.  _____

 5. He designs jewelry.  _____

 6. She announces the news.  _____

 7. He manages a store.  _____

 8. She's a restaurant owner.  _____

 9. He teaches school.  _____

10. She drives a taxi.  _____

11. He drives a bus.  _____

12. She drives a truck.  _____

13. He manages an office.  _____

14. She sings opera.  _____

15. He works on a farm.  _____

16. She studies engineering.  _____

17. He studies music.  _____

18. She changes money.  _____

19. He collects garbage.  _____

20. She studies art.  _____

Figure 5.3

**1**

- Ask Ss to write some interesting information about any member of their family (e.g., parents, brother, sister, relatives). They should give information about at least two family members as in the examples given in the Student's Book. Explain that they should not put their names on their papers.

- Collect Ss' papers, edit them where necessary, and prepare a class chart as in Interchange 5 in the Student's Book (p. 107), with one box for each S's information.

- Make copies of the chart for all the Ss in your class. Now Ss are ready for the activity.

## 2 Class activity

- Give each S a copy of the chart. Model the kinds of questions Ss should ask from the information in the class chart you have prepared. (They should not ask questions like, "Did you write this?" and "Is this yours?")

- Set a time limit of about 10 minutes. Ss walk around asking each other questions.

- Ss compare answers.

- Find out who got the most names.

## Optional activity: *True or false?*

This activity practices making descriptions. Time: 10–15 minutes.

- Explain the task: Ss write six statements about themselves. Four statements should be true and two false:

| | |
|---|---|
| I have a pet snake named Bobby. | (F) |
| My younger brother is a detective. | (T) |
| My last name's Garcia. | (F) |
| I drive a red Ford. | (T) |
| (etc.) | |

- Form groups of four or five. Ss take turns reading their statements, and other Ss try to guess which statements are true or false.

- Ss report what they learned about each other to the class:

T:  Jill, what's the most interesting thing you learned about a classmate?
S1:  Well, John's younger brother is a detective.
T:  And how about you, Kathy?
S2:  . . .

## 12 CONVERSATION

This exercise practices opening a conversation, making small talk, and ending a conversation. These are basic skills in using a foreign language.

**1**

- Set the scene and explain the phrase "small talk."

- Play the tape once or twice. Ss listen.

- Explain that the expressions taught here can be used among friends or classmates. Present each expression for greeting someone. Model the correct stress in the reduced forms in **"How've** you **been?" "How**'re **things?" "How**'re you **doing?"** Point out that the last word receives the strongest stress.

- Ss practice the expressions.

- Present the expressions for making small talk and ending a conversation in the same way.

**2**

- Explain the task: Ss will hear greetings and questions and must choose the best response each time. Remind Ss to cover the expressions in part 1.

- Play the tape once or twice. Ss check their responses.

Answers:

| | |
|---|---|
| a) Yeah, see you later. | c) OK, thanks. |
| b) They are fine, thanks. | d) Great, thanks. |

### Alternative presentation (part 2)

- Books closed. Before Ss do the exercise, they listen to the expressions and try to think of suitable responses.

## 13 SMALL TALK

This is a fluency activity that follows up on Exercise 12.

## Class activity

- Books open. Explain the activity and go over the model conversation.

- Ss practice the conversation in pairs.

- Books closed. Ss move around the class and talk to three classmates, practicing opening conversations, making small talk, and ending conversations. If necessary, write what the Ss have to do on the board:

1. Greeting someone
2. Making small talk
3. Ending a conversation

---

## 14 READING: Touchy topics

This exercise practices reading for information and presents cultural information on the kinds of topics that are considered appropriate and inappropriate in social conversation in the U.S. and Canada.

■ Introduce the idea of "touchy topics" by saying:

T: Here are some questions I don't like people to ask me – "How old are you?" and "What's your salary?"

■ Ss read the passage silently and circle any words they cannot guess the meaning of. (Ss should not do tasks 1 or 2 yet.)

■ Explain any vocabulary the Ss ask about and go over these words if necessary: *polite, personal, private, politics,* and *religion.*

### 1 Pair work

■ Ss complete the task.

Answers:

a) Polite
b) Not polite
c) Not polite
d) Polite
e) Not polite
f) Polite
g) Not polite
h) Not polite
i) Not polite

### 2

■ Elicit Ss' answers around the class like this:

T:  Is the first question polite or not polite in your country, Jan?

S1: It's polite in my country.
T:  Is it the same in your country, Terry?
S2: It's . . .

■ Optional: Ask Ss to give examples of polite or impolite questions in their countries. If there is time, ask Ss what they say when someone asks them an impolite question. In a heterogeneous class, this is a good opportunity to do some cross-cultural comparisons.

### Optional activity: *Crossword puzzle*

This activity is good for reviewing vocabulary in the unit and for practicing spelling. It could be used with any unit. Time: 10 minutes.

■ Form pairs or small groups. Ss make a crossword puzzle grid of 12 by 12 lines.

■ Then Ss use words from the unit and try to fit in as many as possible on their grid (Figure 5.4).

| f | a | m | i | l | y |   |   |   | d | o |
|---|---|---|---|---|---|---|---|---|---|---|
| a |   | y |   |   | o | l | d | e | r |   |
| t |   |   |   |   | u |   |   |   | i |   |
| h | a | v | e |   | n |   |   |   | v |   |
| e |   |   |   |   | g |   |   | h | e | r |
| r |   |   |   |   | e |   |   |   |   |   |
|   |   | w | o | r | k | s |   |   |   |   |
|   |   |   | e |   |   |   |   |   |   |   |

Figure 5.4

■ After 10 minutes, stop the activity and find out who has the most words on the grid.

# 6 Do you play tennis?

This unit has two cycles and introduces the topics of sports, exercise, and leisure activities. It also presents adverbs of frequency and the present tense for describing habitual actions.

## UNIT PLAN

### Cycle 1

1. Snapshot: *Introduces the theme of daily routines and leisure activities*

2. Conversation: *Introduces adverbs of frequency and the simple present tense for habitual actions*

3. Listening: *Practices listening for information about how often people exercise*

4. Grammar Focus: *Practices adverbs of frequency (e.g.,* always, never)

5. My Busiest Day: *A fluency activity that reviews the simple present*

6. Writing: *Practices describing a day's activities*

### Cycle 2

7. Word Power: *Introduces the vocabulary of sports and exercise*

8. Conversation: *Introduces additional adverbs of frequency*

9. Pronunciation: *Practices reductions with* do *in questions*

10. Grammar Focus: *Practices additional adverbs of frequency (e.g.,* every day, once a week)

11. Listening: *Practices listening to questions*

    Interchange 6: *A fluency exercise involving a survey on leisure activities*

12. Reading: *A fitness survey*

# 1 SNAPSHOT: All in a day

This exercise introduces the theme of daily routines and leisure activities.

■ Books closed. Introduce the topic of daily activities and leisure time by asking Ss how much time they spend each day doing certain things (e.g., watching TV, talking on the phone, studying, commuting to work or school).

■ Books open. Ss skim through the list of activities for new vocabulary. If necessary, explain words like *prepare* and *laundry*.

■ Ss complete the task and then compare with a partner.

■ Optional: As a follow-up, ask Ss what other activities they spend time on in a typical day.

# 2 CONVERSATION: Routines

This conversation introduces adverbs of frequency.

■ Books closed. Introduce the topic of leisure activities by asking a few questions around the class:

T: What do you do on Sundays, Teresa?
S1: I go swimming.
T: How about you, Satoshi?
S2: Well, I play tennis on Sundays.

■ Set the scene. Explain the differences between these words:

| | | |
|---|---|---|
| day off | = | a day in the week when a person doesn't go to work (e.g., Saturday, Sunday) |
| holiday | = | national or official day when most people don't have to work or go to school (e.g., Christmas, Labor Day) |
| vacation | = | an extended time off from work (e.g., one or two weeks) when people usually go on a trip |

■ Write these questions on the board:

What does Chuck do on his day off?
What does Marie do on her day off?

■ Play the tape once or twice. Check Ss' answers.

■ Books open. Play the tape again. Present the conversation line by line. Explain these expressions:

| | | |
|---|---|---|
| lift weights | = | work out or exercise with weights |
| stay in shape | = | keep physically fit |
| couch potato | = | someone who stays home and watches TV all the time |

■ Ss practice the conversation in pairs.

■ Optional: Books closed. Ss practice the conversation using their own words (i.e., they don't need to memorize or use the exact language in the conversation).

# 3 LISTENING

This exercise practices listening for key words.

■ Set the scene. Play the tape once. Ss listen only.

■ Play the tape again. Ss complete the task and compare answers.

Answers:

Who likes to exercise?        Sue
Who doesn't?        Mark, Liz

■ Optional: Write this question on the board:

What do Mark, Sue, and Liz do on their day off?

Then play the tape again. Ss listen and take notes and then compare with a partner. Check Ss' answers.

Answers:

Mark:  never gets up before noon
        watches videos at home
        reads science fiction

 Sue:  goes to the gym in the afternoon
        lifts weights
        wants to lose five pounds by next month
        swims three times a week

 Liz:  takes long naps
        watches old movies on TV
        stays at home and reads magazines
        doesn't like to exercise

# 4 GRAMMAR FOCUS: Adverbs of frequency (1)

This exercise practices adverbs of frequency and the simple present for habitual actions.

■ Use the tape to present the sentences in the box. Model the correct pronunciation of *usually* and point out that it has three syllables. To explain the meanings of the adverbs, you can illustrate with a simple chart:

| | | |
|---|---|---|
| always | = | 100% |
| usually | = | 90% |
| often | = | 70% |
| sometimes | = | 30% |
| never | = | 0% |

Of course, these percentages are approximate.

■ Explain that the normal position for adverbs of frequency is before the main verb, though the adverb *sometimes* can also occur before the subject (e.g., "I sometimes read the paper," or "Sometimes I read the paper"). With the verb *be,* however, the adverb of frequency usually comes after the verb (e.g., "He is never late").

■ Ask Ss to give other sentences using the adverbs. Practice one adverb at a time:

T: *(Give cue)* Always.
S1: I always get up at five o'clock.
S2: I always have rice for breakfast.
S3: Susie always arrives late for class.

## 1

■ Ss cover the box and complete the task. Check Ss' answers.

Possible answers:

A: What do you usually do on your day off?
B: Nothing much. I always sleep until noon.

A: Do you usually go out on Saturday night?
B: Yes, I often do. I sometimes go roller-skating or I go to a movie.

A: Do you usually drive to school?
B: No, I never drive to school. I always take the bus.

A: What do you usually do after class?
B: I often meet friends for a drink or I sometimes go straight home.

A: Do you usually get much exercise?
B: Yes, I sometimes play tennis after work. And on Sundays, I often go to the gym.

■ Ss practice the conversations in pairs.

## 2 Pair work

■ Remind Ss to use falling intonation for Wh-questions and rising intonation for Yes/No questions. Model an example of each type of question with the correct intonation.

■ Ss practice the questions in pairs, giving their own answers.

## 3 Class activity

■ Ss write four questions of their own, based on the patterns just practiced. Some Ss might only mechanically substitute new words in the questions:

What do you usually do on Sunday afternoons?
What do you do in the evenings?
Do you usually play sports?

So encourage Ss to be more creative:

Do you often eat out?
What do you usually wear on weekends?
What do you always wear when you play tennis (or golf, etc.)?

■ Ss move around the class and ask their questions.

■ Optional: Ss work in pairs and take turns asking their original questions or new questions.

## 5 MY BUSIEST DAY

This is a fluency activity that reviews the simple present for habitual actions.

■ Books closed. Explain the expression "busiest day." Then ask Ss questions about their busiest day:

T: My busiest day is. . . . How about you, Toshi? What's your busiest day?
S1: Saturday.
T: And how about you, Maria?
S2: Umm, I guess my busiest day is Monday.

■ Books open. Read the model description aloud and explain any new vocabulary (e.g., "until 9 P.M.," "midnight," "a really long day").

■ Use the dialog and model the task with several Ss.

## Pair work

■ Ss take turns describing their busiest day in pairs. The questions provided here are just examples. Encourage Ss to ask additional questions of their own.

## Optional activity: *What's the question?*

This activity reviews adverbs of frequency and questions. Time: 10–15 minutes.

Each S will need five blank cards.

■ Divide the class into two teams – A and B – or into groups of four. Each S writes five statements, one on each card, using adverbs of frequency (e.g., "I usually stay home on my day off," "I work out twice a week").

■ Collect Ss' cards and put them in a pile face down.

■ Team A starts. One S takes a card and reads it to a S on Team B. That S tries to make a question (e.g., "Do you usually stay home on your day off?" "How often do you work out?"). Ss on both teams decide if the question is correct. If it is, Team B gets a point. If it isn't, Team A tries to make a question; if it is correct, they get the point instead. Keep a record of the team scores on the board. The team with the most points is the winner.

---

## 6 WRITING: Writing about a typical day

This exercise practices describing habitual actions, using adverbs of frequency and the present tense.

### 1

■ Explain the task: Ss choose a day to write about (e.g., busiest day, day off, favorite day). Give additional suggestions, if appropriate (e.g., the worst day of the week or month, payday).

■ Ss individually brainstorm by writing down words or phrases that come to mind as they think about their topic. Remind Ss to think about things they do in the morning, afternoon, and evening.

■ Now Ss write first drafts of their compositions, using their notes. (This could be given as a homework assignment.)

■ Ss read over their drafts and make any changes they want (e.g., reordering, adding, deleting information to improve content). Remind Ss to check grammar, spelling, and particularly their use of adverbs of frequency.

■ Optional: Ss work in pairs and exchange drafts. Encourage Ss to give suggestions on how to improve the drafts.

■ Ss write second drafts, incorporating changes and revisions. (This could also be a homework assignment.)

### 2 Group work

■ Ss take turns reading their compositions in groups. Encourage Ss to participate actively in group discussions by:

a) asking questions for more information: "What do you usually do after that?"
b) making comments: "You really enjoy your day off!"
c) giving positive feedback: "I like Mark's composition very much. There's a lot of information in it."

---

## 7 WORD POWER: Sports and exercise

This introduces the theme and vocabulary of sports and exercise.

### 1

■ Model the pronunciation of the words and the stress in "ae**ro**bics," "**bi**cycling," "**ka**rate," and "**ski**ing."

■ Ss complete the task. Check Ss' answers.

Answers:

| | |
|---|---|
| g | aerobics |
| d | baseball |
| f | bicycling |
| b | golf |
| e | hiking |
| c | karate |
| a | skiing |
| h | soccer |

### 2 Pair work

■ Explain the terms *team sports* and *individual sports*.

■ Pairs complete the task. Check Ss' answers.

Possible answers:

(Some of these words could be both individual sports and exercise.)

| *Team sports* | *Individual sports* | *Exercise* |
|---|---|---|
| baseball | bicycling | aerobics |
| soccer | golf | bicycling |
| | karate | golf |
| | skiing | hiking |

### 3

■ Ss do the task. Check Ss' answers and write them on the board.

Possible answers:

| *Team sports* | *Individual sports* | *Exercise* |
|---|---|---|
| basketball | fishing | jogging |
| football | swimming | push-ups |
| ice hockey | horseback riding | weight lifting |

## 8 CONVERSATION

This exercise introduces adverbs and adverbial phrases of time.

■ Books open. Use the picture to set the scene.

■ Books closed. Play the tape once or twice. Ss listen only.

■ Write some questions on the board and elicit Ss' answers.

Does Pedro work out?
Is Cathy in good shape?

■ If Ss have difficulty answering the questions, play the tape again.

■ Books open. Present the conversation line by line. Explain these words and expressions:

| | | |
|---|---|---|
| muscles | = | (point to your arm muscle) |
| work out | = | exercise |
| race (a verb here) | = | run very fast |
| Good for you! | = | That's great! *or* I'm happy for you. |
| chocolate milkshake | = | a chocolate drink usually made with milk and ice cream |

■ Ss practice the conversation.

## 9 PRONUNCIATION:
### Reduced form of *do*

This exercise focuses on the reduction and blending of sounds.

### 1

■ Play the first part of the tape. Model the reductions in "Do you" /dəjə/. Ss repeat.

### 2

■ Play the second part of the tape. Ss repeat the sentences with reduced forms.

■ Give additional sentences for practice:

Where do you go after class?
What time do you get up?
How often do you play sports?

## 10 GRAMMAR FOCUS:
### Adverbs of frequency (2)

This exercise introduces adverbial phrases of time, and questions with "How often . . . ?"

■ Use the tape to present the sentences in the box. Explain that people say "once" (not "one time"), "twice" or "two times," and "three times, four times," and so on. Point out that these adverbs normally occur at the ends of sentences (i.e., after the verb or object).

■ Elicit additional sentences from Ss using each adverb:

T: *(Gives cue)* Every day.
S1: I walk to school every day.
S2: I read the paper every day.
T: *(Gives cue)* Once a week.
S3: I go to the movies once a week.
S4: I do my homework about once a week.
T: *(Gives cue)* Three times a year.
S5: I go to the dentist about three times a year.

### 1

■ Before Ss write their answers, present the questions and call on Ss to answer. Since this is a grammar exercise, correct any errors.

■ Ss do the written task.

### 2 Pair work

■ Ss use their answers from part 1 and do the second task in pairs. Go around the class and listen for grammatical accuracy and correct intonation. Make notes on whatever difficulties Ss may have.

■ Use your notes and go over any difficulties with the class. Write examples on the board.

## 11 LISTENING

This exercise practices listening for questions and choosing appropriate responses.

■ Books open. Set the scene and play the tape. Ss check the correct responses and then compare with a partner.

■ Play the tape again. Check Ss' answers.

Answers:

a) I don't usually do much.
b) Well, I sometimes do.
c) About twice a week.
d) Yes, once or twice a year.
e) I play tennis and I swim.
f) Golf.

### Alternative presentation

■ Books closed. Ss listen to the tape and think of appropriate responses. Then books open. Ss listen again and check the correct responses.

## INTERCHANGE 6:
## Leisure survey

This is an information-sharing activity that reviews present tense questions and statements, and adverbs of time.

### 1

■ Ss look over the survey quickly (p. 107). Explain any new vocabulary (e.g., *library, museum, handball, martial arts, backpacking, calisthenics*).

■ For question 1, "How often do you . . . ?", Ss ask questions using the cues on the form (e.g., "How often do you go to a movie?"). Ss should check the appropriate column on the form for each answer they get. Explain that if a S answers "never," it is not necessary to check the form.

■ For question 2, "What kinds of sports do you play?", Ss ask only this one question (i.e., Ss do not ask a question about each of the sports in turn). If a S replies with a sport not on the list, tell Ss to write the sport under "Other."

■ For question 3, "What kinds of exercise do you do?", Ss again ask only this one question.

■ Show Ss on the board how to mark down responses on their survey forms when they interview their classmates:

1. How often do you . . .
1. How often do you . . .

| | About once a week | About once a month | About once a year |
|---|---|---|---|
| go to a movie? | 卌 | ||| | |
| eat out? | || | 卌 || | | |

■ Explain how the activity works: Each S moves around the class and talks to five people. When Ss have finished interviewing five people, they sit down. Set a time limit of about 10 minutes.

■ Ss do the activity.

## 2 Class activity

■ Ss form groups of five or six with a secretary in each group to tabulate their information.

■ Group secretaries report their information to the class and write it on the board. (This is not a scientific survey since some Ss will have been interviewed more often than others.)

■ Discuss any new vocabulary Ss themselves have supplied.

## 12 READING: Fitness

This exercise practices reading a survey for specific information. It could be assigned as homework.

■ As preparation, Ss read the questionnaire quickly and circle any words they do not know. Explain words that Ss circled and any other vocabulary if necessary (e.g., *vacuum, on my feet, farming, delivery, involves, heart,* 1 mile = 1.6 kilometers).

■ Ss work individually and complete the questionnaire. Move around the class and give help as needed.

■ Point out the "Fitness Index" at the bottom of the questionnaire. Ask Ss to calculate their total points and then read their fitness profiles.

■ Optional: Either Ss compare answers around the class, or find out which Ss are in really good shape according to the fitness index.

### Optional activity: *Free time*

This activity practices the present tense with adverbs of frequency. Ss try to identify classmates by finding out what they do in their free time. Time: 10 minutes.

*Preparation:* In a class that precedes this activity, write these cues on the board:

*Free time*

I like . . . (sports, music, TV, videos).
I . . . every day.
I usually/often/sometimes . . . in the evening.
I . . . on Saturday/Sunday.
For my summer vacation, I usually. . . .

Ask Ss to use the cues to write sentences about themselves (for a total of five sentences). Tell Ss not to write their names on the paper. Collect all the sentences and then use them to make a grid. Include three sentences from each S and provide a blank for "Name" (see Figure 6.1).

Make a photocopy of the grid for each S.

■ Give each S a copy of the grid. Explain the task: Ss ask questions based on the information in the grid and fill in the correct name for each box. Elicit the kinds of questions Ss could ask based on the information in the first box on the grid. Write the questions on the board.

■ Set a time limit of about 10 minutes. Ss move around the class asking each other questions and filling in the names on their grids.

■ When the time is up, find out who has the most names.

I lift weights every day.
I always go to my aerobics class on Saturday morning.
For my summer vacation I usually go hiking in the mountains.
Name: _____

I like rock music a lot.
I sometimes watch TV in the evening.
I take piano lessons on Saturday afternoon.
Name: _____

Figure 6.1

# Review of Units 4–6

This unit reviews talking about habits and leisure activities, asking Wh- and Yes/No questions with *do/does,* and using adverbs of frequency.

## UNIT PLAN

**1** What's On at the Movies?: *Reviews Wh- and Yes/No questions with* be

**2** TV and Radio: *Reviews Wh- and Yes/No questions with* be *and* do

**3** An Interesting Person: *Reviews third-person* s *with the present tense*

**4** A Day in the Life of . . . : *Reviews adverbs of frequency and practices talking about routines*

**5** Listening: *Practices listening to questions*

## 1 WHAT'S ON AT THE MOVIES?

This exercise reviews Wh- and Yes/No questions with *be* and practices talking about movies and time.

*Preparation:* Make photocopies of the movie section in a local English language newspaper for Ss to use. You may use several different newspapers if you want Ss to have information from various sources. If an English language newspaper is not available, make your own "Local Movie Guide" in English and make photocopies of it.

### Pair work

■ Explain the task and model it. Encourage Ss to use expressions they have learned ("I'm not sure," "I don't know," "I think it's . . ."):

T: Are there any good movies playing?
S: Yes, there's an interesting movie at the Center Theater.
T: Oh? What's the name of the movie?
S: It's *Nightmare on Elm Street.*
T: What kind of movie is it?
S: Well, I think it's a horror film.
T: Oh, a horror movie. Who's in it?
S: Gee, I don't know, but it's an American movie.

T: What times is it showing?
S: It's on at seven and nine tonight. Would you like to see it?
T: Yeah. Let's go to the seven o'clock show. OK?

■ Ss do the task. Go around the class and give help as needed.

■ Books closed. Ss perform the conversation in front of the class. Elicit positive comments about the conversations, and then suggest how they could be improved.

■ Optional: Ss look at other events listed in the entertainment section of the newspaper (e.g., concerts, plays, TV) and have similar conversations.

## 2 TV AND RADIO

This exercise reviews Wh- and Yes/No questions with *be* and *do.*

### 1 Pair work

■ Explain the task. Then model the task and show Ss how to elaborate:

S: Do you watch TV a lot?
T: No, not very much. I don't have the time!
S: How often do you watch TV?

T: Well, about three times a week, I guess. Usually on weekends.

■ Ss do the task in pairs. Go around the class and give help as needed.

## 2

■ Ss change partners and do the task.
■ Optional: Take a class poll on the Ss' TV and radio interests and habits.

### Alternative presentation

■ Ss work in groups of four and use the questions in both parts to have a discussion about TV and radio. Set a time limit of about 10 minutes.
■ Class activity: Groups report to the class about their TV and radio interests and habits.

## 3 | AN INTERESTING PERSON

This exercise reviews third-person *s* with the present tense.

### 1 Pair work

■ Explain the task. Go over the model and point out different types of information Ss could include (e.g., age, habits, interests, hobbies). Elicit questions like these from Ss and write them on the board:

How old is he?
What language does he speak?
What kind of music does he play?

■ Ss do the task. Go around the class and give help as needed.

### Alternative presentation

■ Ss write a short description of a person as in the model.
■ Ss work in pairs and take turns reading their descriptions to each other and answering questions.
■ Ss revise their descriptions and use them for the task in part 2.

### 2 Group work

■ Ss form groups of four and do the task. Encourage Ss to ask questions.
■ Optional: Groups choose one of the people they heard about and tell the class about that person.

## 4 | A DAY IN THE LIFE OF . . .

This exercise reviews talking about habits and routines with adverbs of frequency.

## 1

■ Explain the task. Go over new vocabulary: *commute* and *take care of children*.
■ Use the board to demonstrate how to fill out times for the activities:

| 8 hours | sleep |
| 1½ hours | eat |
| 40 minutes | commute |

Ss could use symbols (e.g., 1′30″ = 1 hour and 30 minutes) or abbreviations (e.g., hour = hr., hrs.; minute = min., mins.).

■ Elicit other habits and routines Ss could add to the list (e.g., jog, drive) and write them on the board.
■ Ss work individually and do the task.

### 2 Group work

■ Explain the task. Go over the model dialog.
■ Ss form groups of four and do the task. One S is the group secretary and writes down the information.
■ Explain now to calculate group averages: Ss add up the total amount of time the group spends on each activity and then divides it by the number of Ss in the group.

### 3 Class activity

■ Group secretaries report their averages to the class.
■ Optional: Write the group averages on the board. Ask Ss to help you find the class average for each activity.

## 5 | LISTENING

This exercise practices listening to questions and reviews the topic of "small talk" (Unit 5, Exercise 14).

■ Books closed. Set the scene.
■ Play the tape once. Ss listen only.
■ Books open. Explain the task. Play the tape once or twice, pausing after each question. Ss do the task.

■ Ss compare answers. Check Ss' answers.

Answers:

a) Polite
b) Not polite
c) Polite
d) Not polite

e) Polite
f) Not polite
g) Polite
h) Polite

■ Optional: If you did not already have a class discussion on the topic of small talk after the Reading in Unit 5, elicit cross-cultural differences from Ss here. This may be particularly interesting in a heterogeneous class.

## Test 2

See page 151 for general instructions on using the tests. Test 2 covers Units 4–6. Photocopy the test (pp. 155–157) and distribute it in class. Allow 45–60 minutes for the test. Listening material for tests is on Side 4 of the Class Cassette, and the test answer key and tape transcripts are at the back of the Teacher's Manual.

# 7 It was terrific!

This unit has two cycles and practices describing weekend activities and vacations. It introduces the past tense with Wh-questions, Yes/No questions, and statements.

## 1 SNAPSHOT: The weekend

This exercise introduces the theme of weekend activities and also presents useful verbs for talking about activities.

■ Books closed. Introduce the theme of weekend activities by asking Ss what they usually do on the weekend. Write some of the things they do on the board:

meet friends for coffee
go shopping

■ Books open. Explain new vocabulary: *events, hobbies, garden.*

■ Ss read the information and complete the task.

■ Optional: Take a class poll and list on the board the ways the class typically spends a weekend. Start with one S's list of four activities and build up from there. Compare Ss' information with that in the Snapshot.

## 2 CONVERSATION: Monday morning

This exercise introduces the past tense by talking about the weekend. Exercises 2–7 should be scheduled as closely as possible to the beginning of the week. (Ss are not ready to talk about their own weekends until after the past tense has been presented and practiced in Exercise 3.)

■ Books closed. Set the scene. Ask Ss to listen for how some of the people responded to the question "How was your weekend?" Ss shouldn't write anything down.

■ Play the tape. Ask Ss what responses they heard.

■ Books open. Present the conversations. Explain that "work around the house" = do housework and/or house repairs.

■ Ss practice the conversations in pairs using the "Look Up and Say" technique.

■ Ss change partners and practice again, this time covering the conversations and looking only at the pictures for cues.

## 3 GRAMMAR FOCUS: Past tense (1)

This exercise presents the past tense in Wh-questions and statements with both regular and irregular verbs.

■ Use the tape to present the questions and statements in the box. Explain the auxiliary verb *did* for the past tense (e.g., "What *did* you do?"). Give other examples:

Where did you go on Saturday?
What time did you get up this morning?
What did you eat for breakfast?

■ Before starting part 1, go over some of the past tense forms of the irregular verbs in the list on page 133 of the Student's Book. Tell Ss to refer to this chart whenever they need to.

### 1

■ Optional: Go through the task orally with the class by calling on Ss to complete the conversations.

■ Ss complete the conversations individually and then compare answers with a partner.

Answers:

A: What <u>did</u> you do on the weekend?
B: I <u>went</u> to a movie. I <u>saw</u> *Casablanca.** It <u>was</u> terrific!

A: How <u>was</u> your weekend?
B: It <u>was</u> great! I <u>met</u> some friends on Saturday, and we <u>went</u> to an outdoor concert.

A: What <u>did</u> you do on Saturday night?
B: I <u>had</u> friends over and <u>cooked</u> dinner for them. Then we <u>watched</u> a video. And what <u>did</u> you do on the weekend?
A: Oh, I <u>stayed</u> home and <u>studied.</u>

A: What <u>did</u> you do on Sunday?
B: I <u>went</u> to Boston with my friend. We <u>took</u> a tour of the city. Then we <u>went</u> shopping.

**Casablanca* is a classic American movie with Humphrey Bogart and Ingrid Bergman.

■ Ss practice the conversations in pairs.

### 2 Pair work

■ Books closed. To prepare Ss for this activity, model the task by asking questions about the weekend around the class. Help Ss with their responses and write a few of them on the board. Ss practice.

■ Ss do the task in pairs (or in groups).

## 4 PRONUNCIATION: Past tense

This exercise presents the three different ways of pronouncing the regular past tense ending -*ed:* /d/, /t/, and /ɪd/. The rules are:

1. Use /d/ if the verb ends in a vowel or voiced consonant (except /d/).
2. Use /t/ if the verb ends in a voiceless consonant (except /t/).
3. Use /ɪd/ if the verb ends in /d/ or /t/.

This information is mainly for the teacher. The most important thing for Ss to know is when to add the extra syllable /ɪd/.

## 1

■ Play the tape. Ss practice.

## 2

This can be done either as a class activity, in pairs, or individually.

■ To make it easier to refer to the three sounds, write the sounds on the board and number them:

*1*      *2*      *3*
/d/    /t/    /ɪd/

■ Explain the task: Ask Ss to write the number of each sound beside each word.

■ Ss do the task and then compare answers.

■ Play the tape. Ss check their answers.

Answers:

| *1* | *2* | *3* |
| /d/ | /t/ | /ɪd/ |
| called | cooked | waited |
| listened | talked | started |
| phoned | looked | invited |
| tried | | rented |
| lived | | |

■ Optional: Write additional verbs in regular past tense form and ask Ss to pronounce them.

---

## 5 WORD POWER: Verbs

This exercise presents useful verbs to describe past events.

■ Check that Ss understand the verbs by using them in simple sentences (e.g., "I typed three letters on Sunday," or use hand gestures to show typing).

■ Model the pronunciation of each verb, paying attention to the tricky ones (e.g., *read, bought, took, brought, cooked*).

### 1 Pair work

■ Explain the task. Ss complete it.

■ Check Ss' answers.

Answers:

a) typed (the others describe outdoor physical activities)
b) bought (the others have to do with school or study)
c) danced (the others have to do with seeing or hearing something and are not physical actions)
d) spoke (the others are physical actions that involve taking something from one place to another)
e) rode (the others have to do with food or drink)

## 2

■ Ss complete the task without a dictionary and then compare with a partner. (Ss can check their answers by looking at the verb list on page 133 of the Student's Book or in their dictionaries.)

Answers:

a) walk   type   run   climb
b) study   write   read   buy
c) dance   listen   watch   see
d) speak   take   bring   carry
e) cook   drink   ride   eat

---

## 6 LISTENING

This exercise practices listening for key words in order to get the gist of a conversation.

### 1

■ Set the scene: People are talking about their weekends; each person did something that is connected with one of the headlines. (One headline is a distractor and is not used.) Explain the word *headline*.

■ Go over each headline. Ask Ss to guess what the headlines mean. For example, "Singer's Concert A Sell-Out" = "A singer gave a concert. All the tickets were sold." Talk about the other headlines in the same way.

■ Play the tape. Ss listen only.

■ Explain the task: Ss match each person's name to the correct headline.

■ Play the tape again. Ss do the task. Check Ss' answers.

Answers:

A. Angela – Fog Closes Airport
B. John – Singer's Concert A Sell-Out
C. Gary – Storm Causes Power Blackout

## 2

This task can be done either individually or in pairs. Ss try to say what happened in their own words.

■ Play the tape again. Ss listen and write down key words or phrases. (Ss do not have to write sentences.)

■ Check Ss' answers.

Possible answers:

Angela – stayed home all weekend / couldn't take her trip
John – paid $60 for his concert ticket
Gary – was stuck in elevator / met his new neighbor

■ Ss use their notes and take turns describing what happened in their own words.

## 7  ANY QUESTIONS?

This is a fluency activity that provides further practice with the past tense as well as practice in an essential conversational skill – asking follow-up questions to continue a conversation. The important thing here is for Ss to ask follow-up questions quickly without pausing.

### Group work

■ Model the task by asking a S to make a statement about something he or she did on the weekend and show how to ask follow-up questions. These can be both Yes/No questions and Wh-questions.

S:  I went for a drive.
T:  Did you go with a friend?
    *(or)*   Where did you go?

Ss repeat the follow-up questions. Then point to a S to ask another follow-up question. Continue in this way until at least four questions have been asked.

■ Ask Ss to look at the example questions in the exercise and suggest other follow-up questions (e.g., "What was the movie?" "Did you enjoy it?").

■ Ask Ss to form groups and try the activity. Go around the class. Since this is essentially a fluency activity, give assistance only if it is really needed.

This kind of activity should be practiced regularly to promote conversational fluency. You can use other kinds of statements; they do not all have to be in the past tense. They could be related to what Ss have studied in a unit like this:

S1:  I really hate horror movies.
S2:  Why do you hate horror movies?
S1:  . . .
S3:  What kinds of movies do you like?

## 8  CONVERSATION:
## On vacation

This conversation introduces the past tense with Yes/No questions, and "How long . . . ?" with *was/were*.

## 1

■ Books closed. Set the scene. Write these questions on the board:

Where did Celia go?
How long was she there?
What cities did she visit?
Did she like the food?

■ Play part 1 of the tape. Check Ss' answers.

■ Books open. Play the tape again. Explain these words:

wonderful    =  really great
fantastic    =  very very good
sumo match   =  Japanese-style wrestling
sushi        =  pickled rice with raw fish

Model the stress on: "**won**derful," "**beau**tiful," and "fan**tas**tic."

## 2

■ Ask Ss to suggest what each photograph is about and accept any ideas they may have. The photos show:

1. a Japanese bride and groom wearing traditional wedding kimonos
2. someone wearing a yukata (i.e., a cotton kimono worn in the summer in Japan) and sitting in a Japanese inn
3. a scene from a kabuki play (i.e., traditional Japanese theater)
4. sumo wrestlers

■ Play part 2 of the tape. On the first listening, Ss identify the two photos being talked about.

Answers:

The wedding photo and the Japanese inn photo.

■ Play the tape again. Ask Ss if they can remember anything else that Celia said about the two pictures. Elicit answers around the class.

Possible answers:

*Wedding photo:* Celia's school friend, Aki, and his bride, Sashiko; there were lots of guests; the food was very good

*Japanese inn photo:* Celia stayed in a Japanese inn for three days, slept on the floor, wore a Japanese robe called a *yukata*

---

## 9 GRAMMAR FOCUS:  Past tense (2)

This exercise practices Yes/No questions with *do* in the past tense, and "How much . . . ?" with *was/were.*

■ Use the tape to present the questions and statements in the box. Model these stress patterns:

Did you **go** to **Kyo**to? (*kyo-to*)
How **long** were you **there?**
I was **there** for **three weeks.**
We were **there** for a **month.**

■ Either present the conversations orally or ask Ss to complete the conversations individually.

■ Ss compare answers in pairs. Check Ss' answers. Explain the terms *month, year, Winter Carnival,* and *cold.* Model the stress in the word "va**ca**tion."

Answers:

A: Did you go away for the weekend?
B: Yes, I did. My family and I went to Disneyland. We had a great time!

A: Did you enjoy your trip to England?
B: Yes, we did.
A: How long were you there?
B: We were there for a month.

A: Did you take a winter vacation last year?
B: Yes, I did. I went to Quebec City for the Winter Carnival. I had a wonderful time, but it was really cold.

■ Ss practice the conversations in pairs.

■ Optional: Books closed. Ss change partners and practice the conversations again.

---

## 10 VACATIONS

This open-ended fluency task is a follow-up to Exercise 9. The focus here is on getting the Ss to give as much information as they can about a real trip or vacation they have taken.

## Group work

■ Go over the questions. The whole class repeats each question. Explain the word *sightseeing.*

■ Model the task by talking about a recent trip or vacation you have taken. Get Ss to ask appropriate questions from the list in the book and encourage them to ask additional questions of their own.

■ Ss work in groups and take turns talking about their trips or vacations. Go around the class and give help wherever necessary.

■ Call on one S from each group to tell the class about his or her vacation. Encourage the class to ask questions for more information.

### Optional activity: *Chain story – A terrible vacation*

This activity practices narratives in the past tense. Time: 10 minutes.

■ Ss work in groups of four or five. Explain the task: Ss make up an interesting story about a terrible vacation where everything went wrong. One S starts the story, and then the other Ss take turns adding more sentences to it.

■ Model the task:

T:  I just got back from a terrible vacation!
S1: We went to the beach and rented a cabin, but it rained every day!
S2: The cabin was full of bugs and the roof leaked.
S3: . . .

■ Ss do the task. Set a time limit of about five minutes. Go around the class and give help where needed.

■ Groups take turns telling one of their stories to the class. Which group had the worst vacation?

---

## 11 WRITING: Writing a postcard

This exercise practices writing a short narrative in the past tense.

### 1

■ Go over the model with the class. Explain these words:

| | |
|---|---|
| Harrods | = famous department store in London |
| *The Mousetrap* | = long-running mystery play by Agatha Christie |

"Guess what!" = expression used to announce something surprising

Buckingham Palace = official residence of the British monarch (currently Queen Elizabeth II)

"Love," = a common way of ending postcards and letters to relatives and close friends (for others, "See you soon!" and "Take care!" are appropriate)

### 2

■ Explain the task: Ss choose a trip or vacation to write about and use the questions in Exercise 10 to make notes.

■ Point out the different ways to close a postcard (e.g., "Bye!" "See you!" "Take care!" "Wish you were here!").

■ Ss use their notes to write first drafts. (This could be a homework assignment.) Move around the class and check that Ss have included sufficient information.

■ Now Ss revise their drafts. Remind them to check grammar and spelling, especially past tense forms.

■ Ss exchange postcards and read about each other's vacation.

## INTERCHANGE 7:
### Photo album

This is a fluency activity that practices making up a vacation story based on the pictures provided. This is a good activity to train Ss to think in English and can also be fun if Ss are imaginative.

■ Ss work in pairs. Student A looks at page 109 and Student B looks at page 110.

■ Tell Ss to look at the photos on their pages. Ask Ss to think of where each photo was taken and what each photo is about. Encourage them to make up interesting information about each photo using the five questions to help them.

■ Ss do the activity. Student A starts ("I had a really interesting vacation. I went to . . .") and Student B asks questions. Set a time limit of about five minutes.

■ Then it is Student B's turn. Set a time limit again of about five minutes.

■ Optional: Ss change roles and partners and try the activity again.

■ Optional: Ask one Student A to describe the photos, and other Ss in the class ask questions. Repeat with a Student B.

### Optional activity

In a previous class, ask Ss to bring real vacation photos to talk about.

■ Ss work in groups and talk about their vacations and their photos.

## 12 READING: Vacation postcards

This activity practices reading for main ideas.

■ Ask Ss to read the three postcards. Tell them to try to guess the meanings of any words they do not know and to circle any other words.

■ Ss compare their circled words in pairs to see if they can help each other. Explain that Corfu is an island off the Greek coast, and the Smithsonian and the National Gallery are two famous museums in Washington, D.C.

### 1

■ Ss complete the task.

Answers:

a) T   b) F   c) T   d) T   e) F   f) T

**Alternative presentation**

■ Ss read the True/False statements first and then skim the postcards for the answers.

■ Check any vocabulary Ss do not know (as explained above).

### 2

This task encourages Ss to look for the relationships between ideas in texts, and it can be done either individually or in pairs.

■ Ss do the task.

Answers:

*Postcard A:* After the sentence beginning "I toured the island . . ." as this introduces the topic of shopping (i.e., prices)

*Postcard B:* After "Great food!" as this provides the link with the subject of restaurants

*Postcard C:* After the sentence beginning "And there's a new musical . . ." as this introduces the topic of musicals.

## Optional activity: *Picture story*

This activity practices the past tense by making up a story about a vacation. Time: 15–20 minutes.

*Preparation:* Collect pictures from magazines or newspapers showing people, actions, scenes, and events. Each group needs 8 to 10 pictures.

■ Ss work in groups of four or five. Give each group a set of pictures. Explain the task: Ss describe an imaginary vacation they took together using the pictures to make up a story about the trip.

■ Model how the vacation story might begin and encourage Ss to be imaginative and to describe an interesting and unusual vacation:

Last summer, our group went on a trip to . . .
We flew to . . .
Here's a picture of the plane we flew on.

■ Set a time limit of about 15 minutes. Move around the class and give help where needed.

■ Groups take turns describing their vacations and showing their pictures to the class. The class asks questions. Which group had the most interesting vacation?

# 8 You can't miss it!

This unit has three cycles and introduces language about housing and neighborhoods. It presents prepositions for describing locations within a city and *there is / there are*.

## UNIT PLAN

### Cycle 1

**1** Word Power: *Presents names of places in cities*

**2** Locations: *Introduces prepositions for describing locations*

**3** Listening: *Practices listening for locations*

**4** Where Is It?: *A fluency activity on describing locations*

**5** Pronunciation: *Practices vowel contrast /eɪ/ and /ɛ/*

### Cycle 2

**6** Conversation: *Introduces* there is / there are *and* one, any, some, *and practices talking about neighborhoods*

**7** Grammar Focus: *Practices* there is / there are *and* one, any, some

**8** In the City: *A more extended fluency activity on describing locations*

### Cycle 3

**9** Snapshot: *Introduces the topic of housing*

**10** Conversation: *Introduces expressions for describing housing and neighborhoods*

**11** Houses and Apartments: *A fluency activity on describing housing and neighborhoods*

Interchange 8: *A communication activity that practices asking about cities, neighborhoods, and shopping*

**12** Reading: *Skimming and scanning housing ads for key words*

**13** Writing: *Practices writing ads for apartments or houses*

# 1 WORD POWER: Places

This exercise presents the vocabulary used throughout the unit and the structure "It's a place where you. . . ."

## 1

■ It is not necessary to pre-teach the vocabulary in the Word Power since the task enables Ss to learn the words by themselves.

■ Ss complete the task and then compare with a partner.

■ In checking Ss' answers, model the correct pronunciation of each word. Model the stress in "It's a **place** where you **wash** and **dry clothes**."

Answers:

a) buy medicine
b) wash and dry clothes
c) borrow books and read newspapers
d) get stamps and mail letters
e) have a meal
f) buy groceries
g) see a movie or play

■ Books closed. Pairs take turns. One S asks a question (e.g., "What's a drugstore?") and the partner gives the definition (e.g., "It's a place where you buy medicine.").

## 2 Pair work

■ Go over the six place names, but don't give definitions if possible.

■ Model the task by writing on the board:

A bank is a place where you . . .

Elicit answers from Ss and write the better ones on the board.

■ Ss work in pairs and write definitions for the six places. Go around the class and give help as needed.

■ Check Ss' answers. Write the best definitions on the board.

Possible answers:

*A . . . is a place where you . . .*

| | |
|---|---|
| bank | get/keep money. |
| bookstore | buy books and magazines. |
| bus station | get on/off a bus *(or)* get/catch/<br>    take buses to another city. |
| coffee shop | have coffee, drinks, and snacks. |
| gas station | get gas for your car. |
| gym | work out/exercise. |

# 2 LOCATIONS

This exercise introduces the prepositions *across . . . from, on, next to, near, on the corner of,* and *opposite.* It is not necessary to pre-teach these prepositions as the task is designed to help Ss learn them.

## 1 Pair work

■ Explain the task: Ss do the task orally by saying each question and statement aloud as they try to find each place on the map. Prepare Ss for this by having the class repeat the questions and the statements.

■ Model the correct stress on "**su**per**mar**ket," "**laun**dromat," and "**li**brary." Point out that in the statements the word *the* is unstressed.

■ Ss work in pairs and complete the task. Check answers.

Answers:

*It's . . .*

a) on the corner of Elm and Third.
b) across the street from the bank.
c) next to the gas station.
d) near the movie theater on Second.
e) opposite the post office.
f) on First Street.

## 2

■ Ss cover the list of prepositional phrases and take turns asking about six more places on the map. Check answers around the class.

Possible answers:

| *Where's . . . ?* | *It's . . .* |
|---|---|
| the bus station | on Third Street next to the Sheraton Hotel. |
| Japan Air Lines | on the corner of Elm and Second opposite the library. |
| Long's Drugstore | on Maple opposite the laundromat and gas station. |
| the school | on First across the street from the pool. |
| Denny's Coffee Shop | on the corner of Second and Elm. |
| the bookstore | next to the bus stop and across the street from the city park. |

## Optional activity: *What am I thinking of?*

This activity practices Yes/No questions. Time: 5–10 minutes.

■ Form groups of four or five, or divide the class into two teams.

■ Explain the activity: One S thinks of something in the classroom. The other Ss try to guess what it is by asking Yes/No questions.

■ Model the task:

T: I'm thinking of something in the classroom.
S1: Is it near the window?
T: No.
S2: Is it on the teacher's desk?
T: Yes.
S3: Is it big?
T: No.
S4: Does it cost a lot?
T: No.
S5: Is it red?
T: Yes.
S6: Is it something you eat?
T: Yes.
S7: Are you thinking of an apple?
T: Yes!

The S who guesses the object has the next turn.

■ Now Ss play the game in groups.

## 3 LISTENING

This exercise practices listening for locations on a map.

### 1

■ Set the scene. The map of Vancouver is authentic. Ask Ss if anyone has been to Vancouver.

■ Explain the task and ask Ss to mark the places (a–f) with a pencil.

■ Play the tape several times. Ss do the task and then compare answers. Check Ss' answers.

Possible answers:

a) The library is on the corner of Robson and Burrard.
b) Eaton's is on Granville St. Mall, across the street from the Castle Hotel.
c) The Four Seasons Hotel is on Howe Street, opposite the Mandarin Hotel.
d) The Orpheum Theatre is on the corner of Smithe and Granville St. Mall.
e) The YMCA is opposite the B.C. Hydro Building, near the corner of Nelson and Burrard.
f) The Art Gallery is on Robson Street, opposite Robson Square.

### 2

This task could be done for homework.

■ Ss write sentences about six places on the map and then compare with a partner. Go around the class and give help as needed.

■ Check Ss' sentences around the class by asking Ss to read some of their sentences to the class or by writing them on the board.

## Optional activity

*Preparation:* Bring copies or photocopies of a map of your city or town for Ss to use. Choose 10 less well-known places on the map for them to locate.

■ Class activity: Ss will have a class "competition" or game. Explain that you will ask the question "Where is . . . ?" about 10 different places on the map. Tell Ss to raise their hands as soon as they know the answer. Call on the first S who raises his or her hand after each question to give the answer to the class.

■ Alternatively, Ss work in groups and make their own lists of 10 less well-known places on the map. Then groups take turns asking "Where is . . . ?" to other groups or to the whole class.

## 4 WHERE IS IT?

This exercise reviews what Ss have learned thus far in the unit.

### Pair work

■ While you draw a simple map of one or two familiar local streets on the board, model the task by asking questions to the class:

Where's . . . ?
What's this street?
What's on the corner?
What's next to . . . ?

■ Ss work in pairs and draw a similar map of one or two familiar streets of their choice. They should include cross streets, some buildings, and landmarks, if any. Walk around the class and encourage pairs to take turns asking questions about the places on their maps while they are drawing them:

A: Where's . . . ?
B: It's . . .

■ Optional: Ss exchange maps or put them on the wall and ask each other about local places and locations.

## Optional activity

This activity is a "test your memory task" and is fun to do. Time: 10–15 minutes.

■ Explain the task: Ss will draw maps of their school or campus.

■ Model the task by drawing a simple diagram that shows the location of your school building and its immediate vicinity (e.g., the street it's on, a nearby cross street, the campus area).

■ Ask Ss to think about the building their classroom is in and what other things are nearby (e.g., pay phone, trees, grass, bus stop, mailbox, street lights, parking lot, coffee shop, other buildings or stores).

■ Ss work in pairs and try to draw a map of the school building with as much information as possible about things on the street and in the surrounding area. Set a time limit of about five minutes.

■ When the time is up, find out how many things Ss were able to put on their maps.

■ Optional: If you want, Ss could go outside the school building to check their maps for accuracy and for things they might have missed. Set a time limit of 10–15 minutes.

---

## 5 PRONUNCIATION: Vowel contrast /ey/ and /ɛ/

This exercise introduces a contrast that is difficult for many Ss – /ey/ (as in "name") and /ɛ/ (as in "get"). /ey/ is a diphthong (i.e., a combination of two vowel sounds).

### 1

■ Model the difference in vowel quality between /ey/ and /ɛ/.

■ Play the first part of the tape several times. Ss practice.

### 2

■ Prepare Ss for the task by writing these headings on the board:

*1.* /ey/    *2.* /ɛ/

Tell Ss to copy down the headings on a piece of paper for the task.

■ Ss work individually and do the task. Then Ss compare answers.

■ Play the second part of the tape and check Ss' answers.

Answers:

| *1.* /ey/ | *2.* /ɛ/ |
|-----------|----------|
| name      | spend    |
| cake      | went     |
| game      | met      |
| came      |          |
| take      |          |

■ Optional: Elicit additional words with these vowel sounds and write them on the board.

## Optional activity

This exercise uses the vowel contrast /ey/ and /ɛ/ to build vocabulary and helps Ss discover spelling patterns for each sound. This kind of activity can be used with other sound contrasts as well. Time: 10 minutes.

■ Write the sound /ey/ on the board. Ask Ss for words with that sound and write them on the board. Elicit as many examples as possible:

/ey/
came
eight
station
name
neighbor
mail
tail
sale

■ Go over the list with the Ss and then ask them how many different spelling patterns they can see for the sound /ey/. Write the patterns on the board:

c*a*me, st*a*tion, n*a*me, s*a*le  = *a*
*ei*ght, n*ei*ghbor  = *ei*
m*ai*l, t*ai*l  = *ai*

■ Now write the sound /ɛ/ on the board and repeat the activity.

---

## 6 CONVERSATION: The neighborhood

This exercise presents *there is / there are* and *one, any, some.*

- Books open. Set the scene.
- Play the tape once. Ss listen.
- Explain these words:

ma'am = used to address a woman (who is usually older and who the speaker does not know personally; the equivalent term for a man is "sir")

move in = start to live in a new house or apartment

- Ask Ss why they think the woman in the conversation tells Jack about the barbershop. (*Answer:* She thinks he needs a haircut.)
- Present the conversation line by line. Model the pronunciation for "just moved in" (the *t* in *just* is dropped, and the *d* in *moved* is linked to *in*), "are there any," and "there are."
- Ss practice the conversation.

---

## 7 GRAMMAR FOCUS:
*There is, there are; one, any, some*

This is the first full presentation of *there is / there are* in questions and statements. For an explanation of *there is / there are,* see teacher's notes in Unit 4, Exercise 9.

- Use the tape to present the language in the box. Point out that *one* replaces the singular noun "a laundromat," and that *some* replaces the plural noun "grocery stores." Explain that *any* is used with questions and negatives (indefinite) and that *some* is used with affirmative statements (definite). Point out that *but* is used to signal contrasting information.
- Practice the sentences in the box as a drill. Substitute other places in your neighborhood or city and elicit answers with "There is a . . ." or "There are some . . ." by asking questions:

Is there a bus stop around here?
Is there a pay phone near here?
Are there any restaurants around here?
Are there any coffee shops near here?

- Ss do the task and then compare with a partner.

### Alternative presentation

Class activity: Ss complete the conversations orally before they do the task individually and then compare with a partner.

- Check Ss' answers and explain these expressions:

OK, I'll try it.  = I will try it.
You can't miss it!  = It's easy to find.

Answers:

A: Excuse me. Is there a pay phone around here?
B: Yes, there is. There's one on the corner of Jade and King.
A: Thanks a lot.

A: I'm new in town. Are there any good restaurants near here?
B: No, there aren't, but there are some opposite the shopping center on Young Street.
A: Oh, great!

A: Are there any hotels near the airport?
B: Yes, there are two, the Plaza and the Royal. I like the Plaza.
A: OK, I'll try it. Thanks.

A: Is there a gas station near the school?
B: No, there isn't, but there's one downtown on Fourth Street next to the bank. You can't miss it!
A: OK, thanks.

- Ss practice the conversations in pairs.

---

## 8 IN THE CITY

This is a fluency activity and a follow-up to Exercise 7. Here the focus is on getting Ss to respond quickly and to provide the information asked for.

### Group work

- Explain the activity by showing Ss how to use the model dialog and cues. Encourage Ss to give additional information in their answers:

T: Is there a good bookstore near the school?
S1: Yes, there's a good one on Ford Street. It's next to the department store. They have really good books there.
S2: What's it called?
S1: I'm not sure, but I think it's called Waldenbooks.

- Present the "Useful expressions" and add other expressions of your own (e.g., "I can't remember," "Sorry, I have no idea").
- Ss practice the activity in groups of four or five.
- Optional: As a follow-up, ask about other local places and elicit Ss' answers.

## 9 SNAPSHOT: Housing in the United States

This exercise introduces the theme of housing.

■ Books closed. Explain these words before Ss read the Snapshot:

| | | |
|---|---|---|
| housing (noun) | = | a place to live |
| mobile home | = | a movable trailer home used as a permanent residence |
| condominium (*also* condo) | = | a building with apartments that people own rather than rent; it's also known as a coop (pronounced **co-**op) |
| typical | = | usual |
| square feet | = | unit of measurement (plural of *square foot*) |

■ Books open. Ss read the Snapshot, do the task, and then compare with a partner.

■ Check Ss' responses around the class.

■ Write typical information about housing in your country or in the Ss' countries on the board and then compare this information with the Snapshot.

## 10 CONVERSATION [cassette]

This exercise presents expressions used in talking about houses or apartments. The key language presented is "What's it like?" and "How big is it?" These questions are presented functionally here rather than grammatically.

### 1

■ Books closed. Set the scene: Kim is telling her friend Dan about her new apartment. Write these questions on the board:

Where does Kim live?
Does she like it?
What's it like?

■ Play the first part of the tape several times. Check Ss' answers.

■ Books open. Present the conversation line by line. Explain these words: ·

| | | |
|---|---|---|
| *just* in "I just moved . . ." | = | something that happened recently |
| *fairly* in "fairly big" | = | not too small; big enough; or bigger than average |

| | | |
|---|---|---|
| a Jacuzzi | = | a spa or a hot tub with whirling water |

■ Model the pronunciation and stress in "Ja**cuz**zi" and "**neigh**borhood."

■ Ss practice the conversation in pairs.

■ Books closed. Ss role play the conversation.

### 2

■ Explain that Ss will now listen to Dan talk about his apartment. Tell Ss to listen for key words or phrases and to try to write down one or two things Dan says. This task could also be done as a group activity in which Ss pool their information.

■ Play the second part of the tape several times. Check answers.

Possible answers:

*Positive things Dan says about his apartment:*

- on Seventh Street
- near the shopping center on Eighth Street
- rent only $100 a month
- pretty big apartment (large living room, good kitchen)

*Negative things Dan says about his apartment:*

- bedroom window next to a parking lot
- airport two blocks away (planes landing every two minutes)
- Dan can't sleep at night
- there are bugs (roaches)

## Optional activity: *Housing survey*

This activity practices asking for information about housing. Time: 10–15 minutes.

*Preparation:* Make a photocopy of the "Housing Survey" form (Figure 8.1, p. 74) for each S.

■ Give each S a copy of the survey. Explain that Ss use their forms to interview three other Ss. Tell them to mark down the information they get on the form.

■ Ss move around the class and interview other classmates. Encourage Ss to use the "Look Up and Say" technique when asking the survey questions to each other.

■ Optional: Ss report their findings to the class. Write the information on the board and find the class averages.

## Housing Survey

1. Where do you live?    _____ house    _____ apt.    _____ dorm    _____ other

2. How do you like it there?    _____ excellent    _____ good    _____ bad

3. How many rooms does it have?    _____ 1–2    _____ 3–4    _____ 5 or more

4. Do you share it with anyone?    _____ yes    _____ no

5. Do you have a private kitchen?    _____ yes    _____ no

6. Do you have a private bathroom?    _____ yes    _____ no

7. Is there a room for studying?    _____ yes    _____ no

8. Do you have a room for entertaining friends?    _____ yes    _____ no

9. Is there a yard?    _____ yes    _____ no

10. Is there parking available?    _____ yes    _____ no

11. Is it near . . . ?    _____ shops    _____ public transportation

    _____ schools    _____ recreation facilities

12. Do you like the neighborhood?    _____ yes    _____ no

13. Is it quiet?    _____ yes    _____ no

14. Is it safe?    _____ yes    _____ no

15. Do you want to move?    _____ yes    _____ no

    Why or why not?    _____

    _____

    _____

Figure 8.1

## 11 HOUSES AND APARTMENTS

This is an open-ended fluency activity in which Ss must try to answer questions as quickly as possible without communication breakdowns.

### Group work

■ Model the questions for pronunciation and stress. Ss repeat. Do not include any answers here.

■ Model the task by eliciting questions about where you live and elaborate your responses:

S1:  Do you live in a house or an apartment?
T:   Well, I live in a condominium. It's called West Tower.
S2:  Where is it?
T:   It's near Central Park on First Street. It's opposite the Cambridge Theater.
S3:  How big is your condo?
T:   . . .

■ Now Ss try the activity in groups. Go around the class and give help as needed.

■ Optional: As a follow-up class activity, Ss take turns asking about where other Ss live.

## INTERCHANGE 8:
### Just moved!

This is a class activity that reviews much of the language Ss have learned up to now. Four Ss sit at the front of the class, and the rest move about getting information they need. This activity can take 15–30 minutes.

*Preparation:* Make four large signs (one for each of the three clerks and one for the manager) to identify their roles (Figure 8.2). The signs should be placed on the four Ss' desks at the front of the classroom (or behind them on the wall or board).

GREYHOUND BUS STATION

ROBINSON'S DEPARTMENT STORE

7-ELEVEN MARKET

APARTMENT MANAGER

Figure 8.2

Move four desks to the front of the room for the three clerks and manager. Move the rest of the desks out of the way.

■ Explain the task.

■ Ask for four volunteers to sit at the front of the class. Each one gets a sign. They use the information on page 111. This is the only information they will need. The rest of the class should not look at page 111. Now identify each S who has a sign and explain his or her role to the class:

1. Clerk at the Greyhound Bus Station: Answers questions about departure and arrival times, and the price of bus tickets.
2. Clerk at the 7-Eleven market (a small grocery store): Answers questions about the cost of items in the store and helps customers at the check-out counter.
3. Clerk at Robinson's Department Store: Answers questions about things for sale in the store and helps customers pay for purchases.
4. Apartment manager: Answers tenants' questions and gives information about the location of places and things in the apartment building and in the town.

■ Explain that the rest of the Ss are new tenants. There are four different tenant cue sheets on pages 112–113. At this point, assign Ss' roles as Tenant 1, 2, 3, and 4. Their task is to follow the six different instructions on their cue sheets. Point out that each instruction is a "mini role play."

■ Model the first task for each tenant. Start with the first set of instructions for Tenant 1. Tell all tenants to look at page 112 at Tenant 1's card. Tell the clerks and manager to look at page 111 at the information for the clerk at the Greyhound Bus Station. This will show all Ss (tenants, clerks, and manager) how to use their cue sheets and information. Encourage Ss to use their own language, to be creative, and to have fun! Model examples to show Ss how the conversation can be role played:

Tenant 1:  *(Walks over to the clerk at the Greyhound Bus Station.)*
           Excuse me . . .
Clerk:     Can I help you?
Tenant 1:  Yes, please. I want to go to Denver.
Clerk:     Denver? Oh, sure. There are two buses today.
Tenant 1:  Oh, good! What time?
Clerk:     There is one at ten A.M. and one at three-thirty this afternoon.

Tenant 1 writes down the times in the blank in the book.

- Optional: Go quickly through the tenants' cues (there are about six different types of instructions that require certain question forms from the Ss), modeling possible language to use.

- Ss quickly read through their cue sheets. Check if any S needs further clarification for what to do or ask during the role play.

- Point out that when the instruction says "Ask someone . . . ," the Ss who are tenants should only ask another tenant who is walking around; they should not ask the clerks or the manager sitting in the front of the classroom.

- Either tell tenants to sit down when they have completed the task, or stop the activity after about 10 minutes.

- Ss compare answers. Check Ss' answers around the class.

## 12 READING: For rent

This exercise practices scanning for key words and information.

### 1

- Explain these key words: *needed, available, furnished, unfurnished, bachelor, location, single person, partly.*

- Explain the task: Tell Ss to scan the ads quickly for key information; they do not need to read word for word. Set a time limit of about three minutes.

- Check Ss' answers.

Answers:

Unfurnished studio apt. – N
Large room – A
New large 3-bedroom house – A
Family with 3 children – N
4-Bedroom house – A
Writer – N
Small apt. – A
For rent: 2-bedroom house – A

- Ask Ss which key words they used for the task.

### 2 Pair work

- Ask Ss to reread the ads and to try to find suitable housing for the ones they marked *N*. Check Ss' answers.

Answers:

Unfurnished studio apt. + Large room
Family with 3 children + 4-Bedroom house
Writer + For rent: 2-bedroom house

The other two "Housing Available" ads are distractors.

## 13 WRITING

This exercise practices writing housing ads.

- List these topics on the board and tell Ss to include some of them in their ads:

kind of housing
size
furniture
neighborhood
shops
schools
restaurants
public transportation

- On the board, show Ss how to write ads in normal language (i.e., not in "newspaper style" as the ads are written in the Student's Book):

*Housing needed*
We are looking for a large house. We have three children, a dog, and a cat. We want a house near a high school for about $550 a month. Call us at 987-2651.

*Housing available*
I have a three-bedroom apartment for rent. It's on Black Street in a quiet building near a park. It has two large bedrooms and it's nicely furnished. The rent is $350 a month. Contact Mrs. Bentley at 239-6438.

### 1 Class activity

- Divide the class into two groups: Group A = those with housing available, and Group B = those needing housing. This is not a group activity as each S writes his or her own ad.

- Ss write drafts of their ads. Move around the class and give help as needed.

- Ss exchange ads and give each other comments and suggestions.

- Ss revise their drafts.

### 2

- Ss put their ads on a bulletin board and try to match them.

- Find out how many ads the class was able to match.

## Optional activity: *Planning a student center*

This activity practices planning and describing a student center. Time: 15–20 minutes.

■ Explain the task: Ss work in groups and plan a student center for the school (i.e., a room where Ss can meet, socialize, and plan student activities).

■ Write these questions on the board:

What room do you want to use?
What equipment and furniture do you need for it?

What's the floor plan like? (Draw a plan for it.)
What days and hours is the center open?
Do students pay to use it?
What do students do there?

■ Form groups of four. Now groups use the questions to help them plan a student center. Go around the class and give help as needed.

■ Class activity: Groups report their plans to the class (drawing their "floor plans" on the board if necessary). Ask which group has the most interesting plan.

# 9 Which one is Judy?

This unit has two cycles and practices describing people and what they are doing. It introduces the present continuous and the language of physical description.

## UNIT PLAN

### Cycle 1

**1** Snapshot: *Introduces the theme of fashion and clothing*

**2** Conversation: *Presents the present continuous*

**3** Grammar Focus: *Practices questions and statements in the present continuous*

**4** What's Going On?: *Uses nonverbal listening cues to practice the present continuous*

**5** Find the Differences: *A fluency activity based on picture descriptions*

### Cycle 2

**6** Pronunciation: *Practices sentence stress*

**7** Word Power: *Introduces adjectives and phrases used in describing people's physical appearance*

**8** Listening: *Practices listening for a description of a person*

**9** Who Is It?: *A fluency activity that practices asking questions about someone*

**10** Writing: *Practices writing a description of someone*

Interchange 9: *Practices identifying people in a photo*

**11** Reading: *Practices reading for main ideas*

# ☐1 SNAPSHOT: Fashion firsts

This exercise serves to introduce the topic of what people wear and includes some interesting information about fashions.

■ Ss read the information, using their dictionaries as necessary.

■ Ss complete the task and then compare with a partner.

■ Optional: Elicit from Ss information about the kind of clothes worn in their countries that are not worn in other countries.

# ☐2 CONVERSATION

This conversation introduces the present continuous.

## 1

■ Books open. Set the scene. Play the tape. Ss listen.

■ Present the conversation. Explain that "good to see you" is used between friends who have not seen each other for a while; "She couldn't make it" = She couldn't come.

## 2

■ Talk about some of the people in the picture:

T: What's this man wearing?
S: Slacks and a shirt.

■ Play the tape. Ss complete the task.

Answers:

*Kevin:* standing near the window and wearing white slacks and a yellow polo shirt
*Michiko:* talking to Kevin and wearing black pants and a green pullover sweater
*Rosa:* dancing with John and wearing a purple dress

# ☐3 GRAMMAR FOCUS:
Present continuous

This exercise practices the present continuous.

The present continuous is used to describe incomplete actions or events (e.g., "She's opening the door.") and events that are true at the moment of speaking, or "momentary" actions (e.g., "He's

wearing blue jeans." = "He doesn't always wear blue jeans."). Events that are permanent or unchanging (i.e., states or habits) are described with the present simple (e.g., "Paul lives in Australia." "Mary goes to school.").

■ Use the tape to present the questions and statements in the box. Point out that *be* in the present continuous is normally reduced in conversation (i.e., "You're wearing blue jeans," "She's wearing a miniskirt").

■ Ask follow-up questions about Ss in the class:

What's Nobu wearing?
Who's sitting next to Lou?
What's Rita doing?
Is Judy sitting next to Kate?

## 1

■ Ss complete the conversations individually.
■ Check Ss' answers.
Answers:

A: Which one is Yoko? What is she wearing?
B: She is sitting on the sofa. She is wearing a green blouse.

A: Are Bill and Helen coming to the party?
B: No, Bill is studying for an exam, and Helen is working late.

A: Where is Nick going?
B: He is getting some beer from his car.

A: Is Antonio dating Diane?
B: No, he is going out with Cindy these days.

A: How are you going home?
B: Steve is giving me a ride, I hope!

■ Ss practice in pairs.

## 2 Pair work

This is a memory test and practices colors, the present continuous, and the vocabulary of clothing and accessories.

■ Review the vocabulary of colors, using the color chart.

■ Ask questions around the class about the color of things people are wearing (e.g., "What color is Ann's dress?" "What color is Kenji's jacket?").

■ Model the task by having a S come to the front of the class. Look at the S for five seconds and then look away from her or him. Try to describe as much of what she or he is wearing as you can.

■ Ss sit back to back and describe each other.

**3**

■ Go through the questions, and then Ss write five similar questions of their own.

■ Ss take turns asking their questions to the class.

## Optional activity: *Tic-Tac-Toe*

This activity practices making questions or statements with the present continuous. (See teacher's notes in Unit 5 on page 46 for more details on this activity.) Time: 5–10 minutes.

■ Draw a grid with nine squares on the board. Ask Ss to call out verbs in the *-ing* form (e.g., walking, running, eating) and then write them on the grid.

■ Divide the class into two teams, Team X and Team O. Team X starts by choosing a verb and making either a question or a statement with it. If it is correct, write an X over the verb on the grid. If it is not correct, Team O gets a chance to use the same word in a question or statement. If Team O makes a correct sentence, write an O on the grid. The game continues until one team gets tic-tac-toe (i.e., a row of three Xs or Os on the grid).

■ Optional: This activity could be played in pairs or small groups and would give Ss more chances to make sentences or questions.

## 4 WHAT'S GOING ON?

This exercise involves listening to sound effects. Its purpose is to elicit the present continuous.

**1**

■ Explain the task: Ss will hear only the sounds of people doing things (i.e., they will not hear a conversation). Ask Ss to guess what each person is doing and to come up with interesting suggestions. They should make notes (key words only) about the sounds.

■ Play the tape several times.

## 2 Pair work

■ Ss compare and talk about their answers as in the model dialog.

■ Check Ss' suggestions around the class.

Answers:

1. Someone mixing a drink in a blender
2. Man taking a shower (and singing)
3. Man using a vacuum cleaner

4. Man walking a dog
5. Someone sleeping (snoring)

## 5 FIND THE DIFFERENCES

This is an information-sharing activity that reviews the present continuous for describing people and what they are doing.

## 1 Pair work

■ Explain the task and go over the questions.

■ Ss form pairs, cover each other's pictures, and write down any differences they find. Set a time limit of about five minutes.

## 2 Class activity

■ Ss call out the differences they found in the pictures. Help them with the present continuous if necessary. Which pair of Ss found the greatest number of differences?

Answers:

*In Student A's picture:*
Dave is wearing a white shirt.
Ann is sitting.
Nick is sitting between Ann and Kevin.
Nick has a drink in his hand.
Fay is wearing a pink blouse.
Kate is standing.

*In Student B's picture:*
Dave is wearing a black shirt.
Ann is standing.
Nick is sitting between Fay and Kevin.
Nick does not have a drink in his hand.
Fay is wearing a green blouse.
Kate is sitting.

## Optional activity: *Sentence-making contest*

This activity practices describing pictures using the present continuous. Time: 10–15 minutes.

*Preparation:* Collect magazine pictures showing people doing different activities – one picture for each group. Each picture should have several people in it.

■ Form groups of five or six and give each group a picture. One person in each group is the secretary. Explain the task: Groups try to make as many different sentences as they can about their picture using the present continuous:

This woman is wearing a red dress.
A man is getting into a car.
A dog is walking on the sidewalk.

- Groups start the task. Remind the group secretaries to write the sentences down. Go around the class and give help where needed. Set a time limit of about three minutes.

- Now groups exchange pictures and do the task again. Continue the activity (with a time limit of about three minutes for each picture) until every group has made sentences for all the pictures.

- Find out which group has written the most sentences for each picture. Group secretaries read their sentences aloud.

## 6 PRONUNCIATION: Sentence stress

This exercise introduces the use of sentence stress, which gives a natural rhythm to spoken English.

The rhythm of spoken English is determined by the occurrence of stressed syllables. Stressed syllables occur at more or less equal intervals in English. The other syllables in a sentence are reduced or blended to accommodate the regular beat of the stressed syllables. This contrasts with many other languages where syllables receive more or less the same stress. Ss should aim for a stress-timed rhythm as in English, rather than a syllable-timed rhythm as in languages like French, Spanish, and Japanese.

### 1

- Use the tape to present the sentences. Point out the stressed syllables (i.e., those that appear in bold type). Ss repeat.

### 2 Pair work

- Play the second part of the tape or read the sentences with the correct stress. Ss do the task. Check Ss' answers.

Answers:

<u>Which</u> one is <u>Sarah</u>?
<u>She's</u> <u>standing</u> near the <u>door</u>.
She's <u>wearing</u> a <u>red</u> <u>dress</u>.

(The stressed words are underlined here, though in words of more than one syllable, for example, *standing,* only one syllable may in fact be stressed.)

## 7 WORD POWER: People

This exercise presents the words and phrases needed to describe people's physical appearance.

### 1

- Ss look at the pictures and study the vocabulary.

- Present the vocabulary by having Ss repeat each phrase in a sentence. Use these patterns:

*Age:* She's about 20. She's in her thirties. He's in his fifties.
*Height:* He's short. She's medium height.
*Hair:* She has straight black hair. He's bald. He has a beard / a moustache.

- Now ask each S to give a sentence using a word or phrase from the exercise. Check that Ss use the correct pattern. Refer Ss to the Unit Summary on page 129 for *be* + adjective and *have* + noun patterns.

### 2 Pair work

- Ss work in pairs and practice describing each person in the picture. (This task can be done for written homework.)

- Compare Ss' descriptions around the class.

Possible answers:

*Person #1:* He's about 55. He's medium height. He's bald and has a beard.
*Person #2:* She's in her twenties. She's fairly short. She has straight black hair.
*Person #3:* She's about 35. She's medium height. She has curly brown hair.
*Person #4:* He's in his thirties. He's pretty tall. He has curly black hair, a beard, and a moustache.
*Person #5:* She's in her seventies. She's short. She has gray hair.
*Person #6:* She's about eighteen. She's medium height. She has long red hair.
*Person #7:* He's in his fifties. He's tall. He's bald and has a moustache.
*Person #8:* He's about twelve. He's short. He has curly blond hair.

- Optional: Ss take turns describing their classmates.

### Optional activity: *True or false?*

This activity practices describing people. Time: 10 minutes.

- Ss write six statements about themselves – four are true and two are false:

I'm pretty tall.   (T)
I have straight black hair.   (F)
I'm in my twenties.   (F)
I'm wearing blue jeans.   (T)
I'm wearing a green sweater with pink
   stripes.   (T)
I'm wearing a watch.   (T)

■ Now Ss work in groups of four or five and take turns reading their statements. If a S hears a false statement, he or she says "False!" and then gives the correct information:

S1: I'm pretty tall. I have straight black hair.
S2: False! You don't have straight black hair. You have curly black hair.
S1: I'm in my twenties.
S3: False! You're not in your twenties. You're in your fifties!

## 8 LISTENING: Missing person

This exercise practices listening to a description of a person and identifying key words.

### 1

■ Set the scene: A young woman is calling the police to report a missing person.

■ Play the first part of the tape. Ss listen.

■ Play the tape again. Ss take notes. Ss write down only key words (words that describe height, age, dress, hair).

### 2 Pair work

■ Ss compare their notes and answer the three questions in part 1.

Answers:

Who is missing? (Mrs. Rose Baker = her grandmother or "Grandma")
What does the person look like? (78 years old, 5 feet tall, curly gray hair, wears glasses)
What is the person wearing? (a red dress, a white jacket, and a hat with flowers on it)

■ Play the second part of the tape. Ss listen.

■ Check Ss' understanding of what happened.

Answer:

Grandma went out on a date with a new boyfriend, Mr. Franklin, age 83.

## 9 WHO IS IT?

This is a fluency activity that practices identifying people.

### Pair work

■ To prepare Ss for the task, review the questions that Ss will ask each other. Then model the task and have Ss ask you questions.

■ Ss practice the task in pairs. Set a time limit of about two minutes for each S's turn.

### Optional activity: *Family photos*

This activity practices identifying people from descriptions. Time: 10–15 minutes.

*Preparation:* Ss need to bring four or five photos of family members and relatives (or friends). These should be pictures of individuals (i.e., not group photos).

■ Form groups of four or five. Explain the task: Ss shuffle all the photos together and put them face up on a table. Then Ss take turns describing someone in one of their photographs and the other Ss try to find the correct picture from the description. Model the task:

T:  My older sister is twenty-four. She's a student. I guess she's pretty tall, and she has curly black hair.
S1: Is this your sister?
T:  No, it isn't.
S2: Please describe her again.
T:  OK. She's twenty-four and she has curly black hair.
S3: Oh, is *this* your sister here?
T:  Yes, that's her!

When a S finds the correct photo, she or he turns it over and then gets a point. The S with the most points is the winner.

■ Now groups start the task. Go around the class and give help where needed. After about 10 minutes, find out who the winners are.

## 10 WRITING

This activity practices writing descriptions of people.

*Preparation:* Either bring interesting color pictures of people from magazines, or ask Ss to bring their own magazine pictures. Each picture should show just one person with a distinctive appearance and clothes. They do not all have to be pictures of models; pictures with people performing actions are also suitable. Each pair of Ss needs one picture.

## 1

■ Give each pair of Ss a picture. Ask Ss to look at the picture and to think about how to describe the person in it.

■ Ask Ss to look at the example in the Student's Book on page 58. Write these words and phrases on the board (i.e., for topics that Ss can use when making notes before writing):

Age
Height
Hair
Clothing
Where is she/he?
What is she/he doing?

■ Explain that even though Ss work in pairs using the same picture, they should work independently when making notes and writing their descriptions.

■ Ss make notes using the key words on the board and then write their compositions. Move around and give help as needed.

■ Ss compare their descriptions with their partner.

■ Optional: Ask several pairs of Ss to show their pictures to the class and then take turns reading their compositions.

## Optional activity: *Game – Fashion Match*

This activity practices writing descriptions of people and involves matching photos of people with descriptions of them. Time: 10–15 minutes.

*Preparation:* Bring color photos of people from magazines or fashion catalogs – four photos for each S.

■ Give each S in the class a set of four photos. Ss write a description of each person, each on a separate piece of paper:

She's about 20. She has long blond hair.
She's wearing jeans and a yellow sweater.
She's riding a bicycle.

■ Arrange the class into groups. Groups shuffle the descriptions they wrote and put them in a pile face down. Then they shuffle their photos and put them in another pile face down.

■ Show Ss how to play the game. Ask a S in one group to turn over a photo and show it to the class.

Then ask the same S to turn over a description and read it aloud. Does it match the photo? If it matches, the S keeps both the card and the photo; if it doesn't match, the S puts the photo turned up on the table and the description at the bottom of the pile of descriptions.

■ Ss play the game and continue until all the photos have been matched. The S with the most photos is the winner.

---

## INTERCHANGE 9:
## We are the world

This activity provides practice of the present continuous and the language of physical descriptions. (*We Are the World* is a recording by a group of popular entertainers; profits from sales went to African famine relief organizations.)

■ Before starting the task, divide the class into A/B pairs. Tell Student A to look at page 114, and Student B at page 116. Remind Ss not to look at each other's pictures.

## 1 Pair work

■ Explain the task. Then present the model conversation. Ss practice it in pairs.

## 2

■ Pairs take turns asking about people on their lists. Student A starts the task.

■ When pairs finish asking questions, they check their answers by looking at each other's picture.

■ Optional: Ask Ss to identify other people in the picture:

T: Who else do you know in this picture?
S: . . .
T: Which one is she/he?
S: . . .

---

## 11 READING: The dating game

This practices reading for main ideas.

■ Present the pre-reading questions and elicit answers from Ss.

■ Ss read the passage and try to guess any unknown words. Tell Ss to circle any words they cannot guess. Explain any words Ss do not know.

■ Ss read the passage again.

■ Check Ss' comprehension by asking questions:

Do parents choose dates for young people in North America?
What is a "blind date"?
What does "go Dutch" mean?

## 1 Group work

■ Ss work individually and complete the task.

■ Ss work in groups and compare their answers.

## 2 Class activity

■ Ss think of other differences between dating in North America and in their country. Elicit answers, such as:

Boys and girls don't date.
Boys and girls always go out in groups.

# Review of Units 7–9

This unit reviews *there is / there are,* the past tense, and the present continuous in questions and statements.

## UNIT PLAN

**1** What Can You Remember?: *A fluency activity that reviews the past tense*

**2** Listening: *Practices listening for information and inferencing*

**3** Helping a Stranger: *Reviews* there is / there are *and prepositions, and practices giving locations*

**4** Charades: *A game that reviews questions in the present continuous*

**5** Role Play: *Reviews describing a person's appearance*

## 1 WHAT CAN YOU REMEMBER?

This exercise reviews the past tense.

### 1 Pair work

■ Model the task and show how to give extended answers:

S1: What time did you get up yesterday?
T: Well, my alarm rang at six o'clock, and I turned it off. Then I listened to the morning news on the radio for thirty minutes. Finally, I got up at six-thirty.
S2: What did you have for breakfast?
T: Umm, let me see. Yesterday, I had my usual breakfast – coffee, toast, and cereal.
S3: Did you drink your coffee black?
T: No, I had milk and sugar in it.
S4: Did you have anything else?
T: Oh, I almost forgot! I had peanut butter on my toast.
S4: Ugh! You had peanut butter on toast for breakfast?
T: Yes, I really like it. You should try it!
S2: Well, here's the next question. What did you wear yesterday?
T: Let me think. Oh, yes, I wore . . .

■ Pairs do the task. Encourage Ss to ask follow-up questions and to give lots of details in their responses. Go around the class and give help as needed. Note any incorrectly used past tense forms. When Ss have finished the task, write their questions and answers on the board, and underline the past tense forms:

| *Questions* | *Answers* |
|---|---|
| What time <u>did</u> you <u>get</u> up? | I <u>got</u> up at . . . |
| <u>Did</u> you <u>meet</u> anyone interesting? | Yes, I met . . . No, I <u>didn't</u> (<u>meet</u> anyone). |
| How many calls <u>did</u> you <u>make</u>? | I made . . . calls. I <u>didn't</u> <u>make</u> any (calls). |
| What <u>was</u> the best thing . . . ? | I <u>saw</u> my friend. I <u>got</u> my paycheck. |

■ If Ss had trouble with past tense, use the verb forms on the board for a quick drill.

### 2

■ Books closed. Ss change partners. Explain the task.

■ Ss do the task. Tell Ss to keep score of how many questions they ask. Stop the activity after about 10 minutes.

■ Find out which Ss asked the most questions.

## 2 LISTENING

This exercise reviews listening for key information and inferencing.

### 1

■ Books closed. Set the scene: Inspector Dobbs is interrogating Frankie, a suspect in a robbery, about what he did last Saturday.

■ Play the tape. Ss listen.

■ Books open. Explain the task: Ss look at the pictures and listen for Frankie's answers to Inspector Dobbs's questions about what he was doing at different times on Saturday. Tell the Ss that if the picture and Frankie's answers are the same, they write **T** for true in the box; if they are different, they write **F** for false.

■ Play the tape again. Ss do the task.

■ Optional: Play the tape one more time, using the pause button to stop the tape after each question-answer exchange for each picture.

■ Ss compare answers. Check Ss' answers.

Answers:

|  |  |
|---|---|
| 1 P.M. | T |
| 3 P.M. | T |
| 5 P.M. | T |
| 6 P.M. | T |
| 8 P.M. | F |
| 10:30 P.M. | F |

### 2 Pair work

■ Explain the task: Ss use the pictures and the T/F information to answer the questions. (You may want to play the end of the tape one more time.) Check Ss' answers around the class.

Answers:

What did Frankie do after he cleaned the house? He went out at 8 P.M.
Where did he go? He (probably) went to the hotel.
What did he do? He (probably) robbed the hotel.
When did he come home? He (probably) came home at 10:30 P.M.

■ Find out how many Ss think Frankie robbed the hotel.

## 3 HELPING A STRANGER

This exercise reviews *there is / there are* in questions and statements, prepositions, and giving locations.

### Pair work

■ Explain the task: One S is a visitor to your city, and the other S lives there. Model the task and give as much real information as possible:

S: Excuse me. Can you help me? I'm on vacation here. Is there a department store nearby?
T: Yes, there is. There's one downtown on Main Street. It's called Robinson's.
S: What's it near?
T: Well, it's near the Bank of Japan. And it's opposite the Holiday Inn. You can't miss it!
S: Thanks. And . . .

■ Ss do the task in pairs. Remind Ss to switch roles and do the task again.

■ Optional: Ss perform the role play in front of the class.

## 4 CHARADES

This game is a fun activity and reviews making questions with the present continuous.

### Class activity

■ Explain how to play the game of Charades: One S mimes an action and others try to guess what she or he is doing.

■ Model the activity and elicit Ss' guesses:

T: *(Mimes putting stamps on envelopes.)*
S1: Are you eating crackers?
T: *(Moves head to indicate "No.")*
S2: Are you gluing paper?
T: *(Moves head to indicate "Maybe.")*
S3: I know! Are you putting stamps on letters?
T: Yes, I am! OK, now it's your turn . . .

■ Continue playing the game until everyone gets a chance to mime an action, or stop the activity after about 15 minutes.

■ Review any action verbs that Ss had difficulty using.

## 5 ROLE PLAY: Lost at Disney World

This exercise reviews describing a person's appearance.

■ Ss form A/B pairs. Explain the situation: On a trip to Disney World, one of the Ss in the class gets lost there. Student A gives a description of the missing classmate to Student B, the security officer at Disney World.

- Go over the instructions for both roles.

- Model the task:

A: Excuse me, officer. My classmate got lost. Can you help me?
B: Sure. Um, is your classmate a man or a woman?
A: A woman.
B: OK. And how old is she?
A: Gee, I guess she's about nineteen.
B: All right. And how tall is she?
A: ...

- Student As look around the room and choose one of their classmates to be the "lost person" they will describe. Remind them not to give the person's name to their partner.

- Tell Student Bs to fill out the "Lost Person Report" form completely and then look around the class to find the lost student.

- Ss do the role play. Go around the class and give help as needed. Stop the activity after 5–10 minutes.

- Find out how many security officers were able to find the lost students.

- Optional: If time is available, tell Ss to switch partners and roles and then try the role play again.

## Test 3

See page 151 for general instructions on using the tests. Test 3 covers Units 7–9. Photocopy the test (pp. 158–161) and distribute it in class. Allow 45–60 minutes for the test. Listening material for tests is on Side 4 of the Class Cassette, and the test answer key and tape transcripts are at the back of the Teacher's Manual.

# 10 Guess what happened!

This unit has two cycles and teaches Ss how to talk about past events and experiences. It introduces the present perfect and reviews the past tense for narration.

## UNIT PLAN

### Cycle 1

**1** Snapshot: *Introduces the topic of cars and transportation*

**2** Conversation: *Introduces the present perfect*

**3** Grammar Focus: *Practices the present perfect for describing indefinite events and the past tense for definite events*

**4** Pronunciation: *Practices linking sounds*

**5** Have You Ever . . . ?: *A fluency activity using the present perfect and the past tense to talk about personal experiences*

**6** Word Power: *Introduces verbs for describing actions and activities*

### Cycle 2

**7** Conversation: *Practices narratives*

**8** Grammar Focus: *Introduces connecting words*

**9** Listening: *Practices listening for a sequence of events*

**10** A Strange Thing Happened to Me: *A fluency activity that practices narratives*

**11** Writing: *Practices writing a narrative*

Interchange 10: *Practices telling a story based on pictures*

**12** Reading: *Practices reading for main ideas*

## 1 SNAPSHOT: Car facts

This exercise presents some interesting facts about cars and driving, which are topics continued in Exercises 2 and 3.

- Ss read the information without using a dictionary.

- Check if there is any vocabulary Ss cannot guess. Explain that *detailing* in "Steve's Detailing" = a special kind of car cleaning business for luxury cars.

- Ss complete the task and compare with a partner. (The present perfect is used here, but save explanation of it until Exercise 3.)

- Optional: Take a class poll by eliciting information from the Ss' task and writing it on the board.

## 2 CONVERSATION

This exercise introduces the present perfect for referring to an indefinite event in the past.

### 1

- Books closed. Set the scene: Two friends are traveling in a car. Write these questions on the board:

Who's driving?
What kind of car is it?
How fast are they going?
Where are they going?

- Play the first part of the tape. Ss listen for answers.

- Check Ss' answers.

- Books open. Present the conversation. Explain these expressions:

You're doing nearly 80! = You are traveling at a speed of nearly 80 miles an hour (130 kilometers an hour).
speeding ticket = a fine for driving over the speed limit
How long till we get there? = How long is it until we get there?

- Point out that the *t* in "don't worry" /down 'wɜriy/ is blended (i.e., it is not pronounced).

- Ss practice the conversation in pairs.

### 2

- Play the second part of the tape. Ss listen. It is not necessary for Ss to write anything here; they only need to follow the situation.

- Check Ss' understanding of what happened by eliciting suggestions:

T:  What happened?
S1: A police car stopped them.
T:  Why?
S2: For speeding.
T:  What did the police officer ask for?
S3: The officer asked Jill for her driver's license.

Answer:

A police officer stopped Jill for speeding and asked to see her driver's license.

## 3 GRAMMAR FOCUS: Present perfect

This exercise practices the present perfect for indefinite past events and the past tense for definite past events.

- The present perfect is used here to refer to events that occurred within a time period beginning in the past and continuing up to the present; that is, the present perfect is used for the "indefinite past." For example, "*Have you ever driven a sports car?*" means "at any time in your lifetime." By comparison, the simple past describes a completed event in the past.

- Put the two diagrams in Figure 10.1 on the board to show Ss the difference between the past and the present perfect.

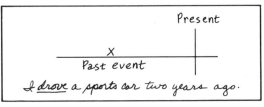

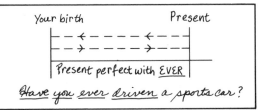

Figure 10.1

■ Use the tape to present the questions and responses in the box. Ss practice. Model the correct stress (e.g., "Have you **ever driven** a **sports car?**"). (The past participle form *gotten* is found only in American and Canadian English; it is not used in British English.)

■ Ask follow-up questions with "Have you ever . . .?" around the class:

Have you ever been to . . . ?
Have you ever seen a James Bond movie?
Have you ever eaten Spanish food?
Have you ever gotten a speeding ticket?

■ Either Ss complete the task individually, or the whole class could complete the conversations orally.

■ Either tell Ss to check their answers with the irregular verb list showing participle forms given on page 133 in the Student's Book, or check Ss' answers around the class.

Answers:

A: Have you ever gotten a traffic ticket?

B: Yes, I have. Once I got a ticket that cost me $50!

A: Have you ever been late for an important appointment?

B: Yes, I have. I was 30 minutes late for my wedding. Would you believe it!

A: Have you ever lost your keys?

B: Yes, I have. I lost them twice last month!

A: Have you ever seen a house on fire?

B: No, I haven't. But I saw a car on fire the other day.

A: Have you ever forgotten where you parked your car?

B: No, I haven't, but my brother always does. It drives him crazy!

■ Explain these expressions:

| | |
|---|---|
| Would you believe it! | = shows surprise or disbelief |
| on fire | = burning |
| It drives him crazy! | = something makes him angry or frustrated |

■ Point out that the present perfect can introduce a topic (e.g., "*Have you ever gotten* a traffic ticket?"). However, if we continue to talk about

the topic (i.e., ticket), we use the past tense (e.g., "Once I *got* . . ."), because the topic is now a definite event in the past. (Ss should not practice the conversations in pairs yet, as they will be asked to do this in Exercise 4.)

## Optional activity

■ Write a list of 10–15 phrases on the board like these:

won a prize
seen a ghost
gone on a diet
ridden a donkey
seen a Tom Cruise movie
met someone from the Soviet Union
missed the last train home
gone to a party on the wrong day

Elicit as many phrases as possible from Ss.

■ Class activity: Ss take turns asking classmates questions with the present perfect around the class:

S1: Carlos, have you ever won a prize?
S2: Yes, I have. I won a speech contest once. Sharon, have you ever seen a ghost?
S3: . . .

## Optional activity

■ Give Ss sample sentences:

I've never been to Mexico, but I've eaten Mexican food.
I've never been to the opera, but I've seen a lot of musicals.

■ Ss compose their own sentences and share them with classmates.

---

## 4 PRONUNCIATION: Linking sounds

This exercise practices linking a final consonant sound with a following vowel sound (e.g., Look out = "Loo kout").

### 1

■ Explain the notion of "linking sounds" – the final consonant of a word is linked to the sound of a following vowel.

■ Write the first sentence on the board and mark the linking sounds as you say them. Ss repeat.

■ Play the first part of the tape. Ss practice the questions again using linking sounds.

## 2

■ Tell Ss to look at the conversations in Exercise 3 again. Ask them to mark the linking sounds. This can be done individually or in pairs.

■ Play the second part of the tape. Ss check answers.

Possible answers:

The linking sounds are marked in the Answer section for Exercise 3.

■ Call on Ss to read the sentences aloud to the class. Check that Ss are linking the sounds correctly. Write sentences on the board that Ss have trouble with and mark where the linking sounds are.

■ Now Ss practice the conversations.

## 5 HAVE YOU EVER . . . ?

This is a fluency activity that allows Ss to use the present perfect and to describe past events in the past tense.

## 1

■ Ask Ss to write five questions about interesting or unusual events using the present perfect. Remind them to use the list on page 133 for present perfect forms.

■ Move around the class and give Ss help as needed. For this activity to work, at least half of the questions should be about things that can be answered "Yes." Ss should write these kinds of statements:

Have you ever seen a Rambo movie?
Have you ever ridden a horse?
Have you ever had a pet?

## 2 Class activity

■ Model the task by calling on one S to ask a question and another S to answer. Go around the class until a S answers the question with "Yes." Help the S to elaborate by asking follow-up questions in the past tense.

T: Have you ever had a pet?
S: Yes, I had a rabbit once.
T: What was its name?
S: Peter.
T: Was he a good pet?
S: No, he made a mess all over the house.

■ Ss go around the class and ask their questions. Remind Ss to ask follow-up questions and get as much information as possible. Set a time limit of 5–10 minutes.

## 3

■ Call on Ss around the class to report something they found out:

S: Ann had a pet rabbit once. Its name was Peter. He wasn't a very good pet. He always made a mess.

## 6 WORD POWER: Verbs

This activity extends and reviews Ss' knowledge of verbs.

## 1 Pair work

■ Explain the task. The only word Ss may not know is *chores* (= work around the house).

■ Ss complete the word map in pairs.

■ Check Ss' answers.

Answers:

| *Doing household chores* | *Going places on foot* | *Using money* |
|---|---|---|
| clean | hike | buy |
| cook | run | pay |
| wash | walk | sell |

| *Talking to people* | *Using transportation* |
|---|---|
| explain | fly |
| ask | drive |
| tell | ride |

■ Optional: Ask Ss to add two more words for each category. Check answers around the class and write them on the board.

Possible answers:

| *Doing household chores* | *Going places on foot* | *Using money* |
|---|---|---|
| iron | climb | bargain |
| sweep | jog | deposit |
| vacuum | skip | save |
| dust | tiptoe | spend |

| *Talking to people* | *Using transportation* |
|---|---|
| answer | pedal |
| complain | row |
| describe | sail |
| question | steer |
| reply | |

**2**

■ Model the task by writing these headings on the board and filling in the first verb from the list of words in the word map:

*Verb*   *Past tense*   *Participle*
ask     asked        asked

■ Ss do the task and then compare with a partner. Ask Ss not to look at the irregular verb list on page 133 until they have compared answers and want to make a final check.

■ Optional: If there is time in class (or for homework), Ss can make up sentences with the past or present perfect forms of the verbs.

## Optional activity: *Chain story – Shopping spree*

This activity practices narrating a story in the past tense. Time: 10 minutes.

■ Explain the task: Ss tell a story about an unusual shopping expedition. One S gives the first sentence of the story. The next S repeats that sentence and adds another sentence. Model the task with some Ss:

T:  I went downtown on Saturday afternoon.
S1: I went downtown on Saturday afternoon, and I bought some boots.
S2: I went downtown on Saturday afternoon, I bought some boots, and then I met my friend, Bob.
S3: . . .

■ Form groups of five. Ss take turns adding sentences around the group until the story comes to an interesting end.

---

## 7 CONVERSATION:
### An embarrassing situation

This exercise reviews the past tense and introduces connecting words in narratives.

**1**

■ Books closed. Set the scene: Ss will hear someone describe an embarrassing situation. Explain that "embarrassing situation" = when you feel awkward or uncomfortable because of a situation you are in. Write on the board:

Where was Bill on Sunday?
What embarrassing thing happened to him?
What did he do first?

What did he do after that?
Who helped him?

■ Play the tape once or twice. Ss compare answers. Do not correct answers at this point.

■ Books open. Ss read the conversation and check their answers.

■ Play the tape again. Present the conversation line by line. Point out that people often open a conversation with "Guess what happened?" "Do you know what happened?" or "You know what?" without meaning it literally because it is only used as an attention getter. Model the stress in "How em**bar**rassing!"

■ Ss practice in pairs. Remind them to use the "Look Up and Say" technique.

## 2 Pair work

■ Books closed. Ask Ss to tell Bill's story in their own words.

## Optional activity

This activity offers an opportunity for Ss to personalize.

■ Ask Ss to think about something embarrassing that has happened to them. Then model the activity by telling the class about something that happened to you:

T: I was in an embarrassing situation once. I forgot my mother's fiftieth birthday. So the next day, I bought her fifty red roses.

■ Ss practice talking about embarrassing situations in pairs. Write useful questions and expressions on the board:

What happened?
What did you do?
How did you feel?
How embarrassing!
How awful!
Really? That's too bad!

---

## 8 GRAMMAR FOCUS:
### Connecting words

This presents connecting words (also called "sequence markers") for use in narratives.

■ Use the tape to present the sentences in the box. Explain that these connecting words show the order of events in a story. The connecting words *after that, next,* and *then* are interchangeable.

■ Ask if Ss know other connecting words or phrases (e.g., *afterwards, later, a few minutes later, the next day, the day after that*) and write them on the board.

## 1  Pair work

■ Go over the task by reading the dialog aloud and then telling Ss to number the events in Lisa's story from 1 through 6.

■ Ss do the task in pairs. Check Ss' answers.

Answers:

| | |
|---|---|
| 2 | I went to the airline counter, and they gave me a form to fill in. |
| 6 | My luggage arrived at midnight, and the airline brought it to the hotel. |
| 4 *or* 5 | I went out and bought some new clothes. |
| 5 *or* 4 | I went to my hotel and checked in. |
| 3 | They gave me $50 to buy a few things. |
| 1 | I waited for my luggage, but it didn't arrive. |

## 2

■ Ss work individually or in pairs. Tell Ss to add connecting words to Lisa's sentences in part 1. Check Ss' answers.

Possible answers:

(1) First I waited for my luggage, but it didn't arrive. (2) Then I went to the airline counter, and they gave me a form to fill in. (3) Next they gave me $50 to buy a few things. (4) After that, I went out and bought some new clothes. (5) Then I went to my hotel and checked in. (6) Finally my luggage arrived at midnight, and the airline brought it to the hotel.

■ Students take turns and practice the conversation in pairs.

## Optional activity: *Strip story*

A good activity to try here is a strip story. For this activity you need a story that consists of a fixed sequence of events.

*Preparation:* Figure 10.2 is an example of a strip story. Make copies and then cut the story along the lines and give one sentence to each S or pair.

■ Either form groups of 10, or have a whole class activity with Ss working in pairs. Each S gets one or more sentences from the story.

■ Explain the activity: The S with the sentence marked #1 starts by reading the sentence aloud to the group or class. The other Ss see if they have the second sentence in the story, and then that S

reads a sentence. Continue in this way until the story is finished.

---

## 9  LISTENING: And *then* what happened?

This exercise practices listening for key information and connecting words, and for the sequencing of events.

### 1

■ Books closed. Explain the situation.

■ Play the tape. Ss listen only.

■ Books open. Play the tape again. Ss listen and do the task.

■ Ss compare answers. Ss listen again if necessary.

Answers:

| | |
|---|---|
| 3 | called his parents |
| 2 | went to the police station |
| 4 | sold his camera |
| 6 | called the airline company |
| 5 | moved to a hostel |
| 1 | went to the embassy |

### 2  Pair work

■ Ss take turns and use their answers to help them tell Ken's story.

■ Write the beginning of this conversation on the board to help model how Ss should do the task:

Friend:  How was your vacation?
Ken:     Well, it was OK, but someone stole my bag one day.
Friend:  Gee! What did you lose?
Ken:     I lost my . . .
Friend:  That's terrible! What did you do?
Ken:     . . .
Friend:  And then what did you do?
Ken:     . . .
Friend:  After that what happened?

■ Optional: Pairs take turns telling Ken's story to the class.

---

## 10  A STRANGE THING HAPPENED TO ME

This exercise gives Ss a chance to be creative and to have fun making up an interesting story together.

The *Titanic*

----------------------------------------------------------------------

#1    One of the world's worst ship disasters was the sinking of the *Titanic*.

----------------------------------------------------------------------

The *Titanic* sailed on its first voyage in April 1912.

----------------------------------------------------------------------

It sailed from Southampton in England on its way to New York.

----------------------------------------------------------------------

There were over 2,000 people sailing on the ship to New York.

----------------------------------------------------------------------

But on the night of April 14, 1912, it hit an iceberg and sank.

----------------------------------------------------------------------

There were not enough lifeboats on board for all the passengers.

----------------------------------------------------------------------

Because of this, more than 1,500 passengers drowned.

----------------------------------------------------------------------

For many years after that, people tried to find the wreck of the *Titanic*.

----------------------------------------------------------------------

Finally, in 1985, a French ocean explorer found the wreck at the bottom of the Atlantic.

----------------------------------------------------------------------

He used a submarine to take photographs of the ship.

----------------------------------------------------------------------

Figure 10.2

## 1 Group work

Model the task by showing how the example dialog can be continued to tell a story. Ask Ss to help you and encourage them to come up with interesting and fun ideas:

T:  Last week, a strange thing happened to me.
S1: The phone rang at four o'clock in the morning.
S2: First, I jumped out of bed.
S3: Then I answered it and heard a horrible voice say, "I have your dog! How much do you want to pay for it?"
S4: I answered, "I don't have a dog!"
S5: I hung up the phone and went back to bed.

■ Set a time limit of about five minutes. Ss work in groups until their stories come to an interesting end or until the time is up. Go around the class and give help as needed.

## 2 Class activity

■ Groups take turns telling their stories. The class decides which group had the best story.

## Optional activity: *The good and the bad*

This activity practices describing events with the past tense. Time: 15 minutes.

■ Write these sentences on the board:

The best thing that happened to me last week was . . .
The nicest thing that happened to me yesterday was . . .
The worst thing that happened to me this week was . . .
An unusual thing that happened to me recently was . . .
A funny thing that happened to me recently was . . .

■ Model how you can describe an experience beginning with one of the sentences on the board:

T:  The best thing that happened to me last week was a surprise birthday party. It was my birthday on Sunday. At seven o'clock in the evening, the doorbell rang. I opened the door and saw twenty friends standing there. Then they all shouted "Surprise! Happy Birthday!" It was a wonderful surprise.

■ Ss work in groups and take turns describing an event beginning with any one of the phrases. Other Ss ask questions. Set a time limit of about 10 minutes.

■ Ask each group to choose one person who had an interesting experience to tell the class about it.

## 11 WRITING

This exercise practices writing a narrative using the past tense and connecting words. This writing task could be done for homework.

### 1

■ Explain the task and go over the model composition.

■ Ss can either write the same story their group told the class in Exercise 10.2, or they can write a new story of their own.

■ Ss make notes about the main events in their story. Encourage them to be creative and to add a lot of details.

■ Ss use their notes to write their compositions.

■ When Ss finish writing, ask them to check their past tense forms and connecting words.

### 2

■ If Ss wrote the same story that their group told, those Ss should get back together as a group and exchange papers. Ask them to see how similar or how different their written stories are. But if Ss wrote new stories of their own, they should exchange papers with other Ss who wrote new stories.

■ Optional: Ss put their stories on the board or wall for everyone to read.

## INTERCHANGE 10:
We saw a UFO!

This activity practices narratives.

■ Explain that UFO = an abbreviation for an "Unidentified Flying Object." Ask the class questions about UFOs:

Have you ever seen a UFO?
Do you think there really are UFOs?

## 1 Group work

■ Books open. Ss look at the pictures on page 115. Ask questions about each picture and elicit Ss' suggestions about what happened in each one:

What did Jim and Debbie do last summer?
Where did they go?
What did they see?
What happened after that?

■ Ss form groups of four. Ss take turns and use the pictures to tell an interesting and creative story together as a group. Move around the class and give help as needed. Set a time limit of about 10 minutes for this part of the activity.

## 2

■ Now tell the groups to finish their stories. Encourage them to think of a creative, unusual, or surprising ending. Give them a few minutes to complete this part.

## 3 Class activity

■ Groups take turns telling their stories to the class. The class decides which group had the best UFO story.

---

## 12 READING: To catch a thief

This exercise practices reading for key ideas. In order to do the tasks, Ss do not need to understand every word in the passage.

■ Before Ss read the passage, ask them to look at each picture in part 1 and figure out what is going on. Elicit suggestions from the Ss and introduce these key words: *burglar, karate, kick, arrest* (verb), *award, jail.*

■ Ss read the passage and try to get the main ideas. They can read it in pairs if necessary.

## 1

■ Ss do the task. Move around the class and give help as needed. Check Ss' answers.

Answers:

1. Ann is cycling in a bike race.
2. Ann is having dinner in a restaurant with her boyfriend.
3. She and her boyfriend are entering the house, and the burglar is hiding behind the door. A stereo, TV, and computer are in boxes just outside the door.
4. Ann is chasing the burglar down the street.
5. The burglar is trying to hit Ann, but she is using a karate move to block his blows.
6. Ann is using a karate kick to knock the burglar to the sidewalk.
7. Ann is receiving an award from the governor of Iowa.
8. The burglar is in prison.

## 2 Pair work

■ Ss cover the passage and use the pictures to tell the story in their own words:

S1: She was in a competition.
    That night, she and her boyfriend . . .

## Optional activity: *Picture story*

This activity practices the past tense. It is a variation on the optional activity also called "Picture Story" in Unit 7 in the Teacher's Manual. Time: 15–20 minutes.

*Preparation:* Ask each S to bring two or three pictures from magazines or newspapers showing interesting people, actions, scenes, and events. The pictures do not need to be related.

■ Group work: Ss pool their pictures and lay them out on a desk. They have to link the pictures to tell an interesting story. Encourage Ss to make up interesting or unusual stories. If necessary, model how a story could begin by showing how some of the pictures might be linked together.

■ Set a time limit of about 10 minutes. Move around the class and give help as needed.

■ Class activity: Groups take turns telling their stories and the class asks questions. Which group had the most interesting story?

# 11 It's an interesting place

This unit has two cycles and practices describing cities and countries. It presents adjectives and adverbs, and the modal verb *should*. There is no pronunciation exercise in this unit.

## UNIT PLAN

### Cycle 1

**1** Snapshot: *Introduces the topic of cities*

**2** Word Power: *A vocabulary-building exercise on adjectives*

**3** Conversation: *Introduces adjectives and adverbs*

**4** Grammar Focus: *Practices adjectives and adverbs*

**5** Home Sweet Home: *A fluency activity on describing cities*

**6** Listening: *Practices listening for information about cities*

**7** My Favorite City: *A fluency activity on describing a favorite city*

### Cycle 2

**8** Conversation: *Introduces* should *and* shouldn't

**9** Grammar Focus: *Practices questions and statements with* should

**10** Listening: *Practices listening to information about countries*

**11** On Vacation: *Practices describing vacation places*

**12** Writing: *Practices describing a country*

Interchange 11: *A communication activity involving planning an itinerary*

**13** Reading: *Practices reading for key ideas*

## 1 SNAPSHOT: City living

This exercise introduces the theme of the unit – cities and countries.

■ Books closed. As a warm-up activity, ask Ss questions about their favorite town or city:

What's your favorite town in . . . ?
What do you think is the most interesting city in . . . (Europe, Canada, the United States)?

■ Books open. Ss read the Snapshot and do the task. Then Ss compare information with a partner.

■ Compare Ss' information around the class.

## 2 WORD POWER: Adjectives

This exercise presents adjectives used to describe cities and countries.

### 1 Pair work

■ Model the pronunciation of the words. Explain that "interesting" /ˈɪntrɪstɪŋ/ has only three syllables, and "expensive" is stressed on the second syllable.

■ Ss match the adjectives in pairs without using their dictionaries. Ask Ss to use these patterns:

S1: What's the opposite of . . . ?
S2: I think it's . . . (or) It's . . .

■ Check Ss' answers.

Answers:

a) ugly
b) small
c) expensive
d) dirty
e) cold
f) boring
g) new
h) noisy
i) dangerous
j) dry

### 2

■ Ss do the second task individually and then compare with a partner.

■ After Ss complete the second part of the activity, ask them to discuss their city. Do not prolong the discussion too much as this theme is developed more fully in Exercises 4 and 5.

## 3 CONVERSATION

This exercise presents adjectives and adverbs.

### 1

■ Books closed. Set the scene. Write these questions on the board:

Where's the man from?
What's it like there?
Is it expensive?

■ Play the first part of the tape. Ss listen for answers. Check Ss' answers.

■ Books open. Present the conversation line by line. Model the stress on adjectives and adverbs (e.g., "It's a **great ci**ty!" and " . . . but **apart**ments are **fair**ly ex**pen**sive").

■ Ss practice the conversation in pairs.

### 2

■ Play the second part of the tape. Ss write down key words about transportation and shopping.

■ Ss compare notes. Play the tape again if necessary. Check Ss' information.

Answers:

*Transportation:* good subways and buses.
*Shopping:* great shopping centers and department stores; Eaton's is one of the biggest shopping centers in the world.

■ Optional: Books closed. Ss practice both parts of the conversation using their own words.

## 4 GRAMMAR FOCUS:
Adjectives and adverbs

This introduces adjectives and adverbs in two different patterns:

1. article + (adverb) + adjective + noun
2. *be* + (adverb) + adjective (without noun)

■ Ss need to avoid using "it's an interesting" and "it's interesting city." Put this information on the board to clarify the patterns:

```
        art +   adj   + noun
It's an   exciting    city.

        art + adv +   adj   + noun
It's a    very    exciting    city.
```

*be* +  adj

It's  exciting.

*be* + adv +  adj

It's  very  exciting.

- Use the tape to present the sentences in the box.

- Point out the linked consonants and vowels in "It's an exciting city."

- Ask Ss questions around the class about cities they know. Use the patterns in the box and other adjectives:

T:  What's Kyoto like?
S1:  It's an old city.
S2:  It's not very big.
S3:  It's a pretty interesting place.
S4:  It's very beautiful.

## 1

- Ss complete the matching task either individually or in pairs. Check Ss' answers.

Answers:

_c_ Oh, really? It's beautiful. It has a great harbor and beautiful beaches.

_d_ No, it's very old. It has lots of fascinating streets, canals, and buildings.

_a_ Oh, yes, it is. It's very exciting, but it's pretty crowded.

_b_ No, I hate it! It's very boring. That's why I moved away.

- Explain that the *sc* in "fa**sc**inating" is pronounced /s/, "ca**nal**" is stressed on the second syllable, and "moved away" = left a city and went to live in another one.

- Ss practice the conversations in pairs.

## 2

- Ss complete the task individually. Tell Ss to write sentences about the city your class is in and remind them to use adjectives from the box and from Exercise 2.

- Call on Ss to read some of their sentences to the class. Ask whether other Ss agree or disagree with the descriptions.

---

## 5 HOME SWEET HOME

This is a fluency activity in which Ss use adjectives and adverbs in describing their cities or hometowns.

## Pair work

- Model the task by having Ss ask about your hometown. Ss use the questions listed on the page. Give full answers using adjectives and adverbs.

- Elicit other questions from the Ss and write them on the board.

- Ss work in pairs and take turns talking about their cities. Move around the class and give help as needed. Set a time limit of about 10 minutes.

- Optional: As a follow-up, either ask pairs around the class to give short descriptions of the places they talked about, or have the class ask several Ss about their cities or hometowns.

## Optional activity

- For a change of focus, ask Ss to think about towns, cities, or places they don't like to visit. Model the task by describing a place you really don't like. Encourage Ss to ask "Why?":

T:  I really don't like . . .
S1:  Why? (*or* Why not?)
T:  Well, it's cold and wet in the winter there. And it's not very clean. In fact, it's really dirty downtown and in the parks.
S2:  Is it expensive there?
T:  Yes, it's a very expensive place. The prices are really high in the stores, hotels, and restaurants.

- Ss work in pairs and describe places they don't like.

- Optional: As a follow-up, pairs tell the class about the places they talked about.

## Optional activity: *Cheap fun*

This activity practices describing events and activities in a city. Time: 10–15 minutes.

- Explain the task: This is a brainstorming activity. Ss have to think of interesting and fun things they can do in their city for a fixed amount of money (e.g., for less than $5 each, or the equivalent amount in your currency). The group that comes up with the longest list is the winner. One S in each group is the secretary and takes notes.

- Model the kinds of suggestions needed and the language to use:

T:  Take the train to . . . Temple. Look at the carvings on the temple walls. They are over five hundred years old. Have lunch at the cafe outside the temple. It costs two dollars for the train fare, one dollar for the temple, and two dollars for lunch. The total is five dollars.

■ Ss form groups of four and do the task. Set a time limit of about 10 minutes. Go around the class and give help as needed.

■ Class activity: Group secretaries read their suggestions to the class.

# 6 LISTENING

This exercise practices listening for key words and for information about hometowns.

■ Books closed. Set the scene.

■ Play the tape. Ss listen.

■ Books open. Explain the task. Point out that if the speaker doesn't say anything about a particular category, Ss should leave it blank.

■ Play the tape again once or twice. Ss complete the chart.

■ Ss compare answers. Check answers around the class.

Answers:

|  | Interesting | Big | Expensive | Beautiful |
|---|---|---|---|---|
| 1. Joyce | N | N |  | Y |
| 2. Lou | Y | Y | Y |  |
| 3. Nick | N | Y |  | N* |

*Nick did not actually say this, but it was implied.

# 7 MY FAVORITE CITY

This is an additional oral fluency activity on describing cities.

## Group work

■ Go over the model and elicit questions Ss could ask to get more information.

■ To encourage Ss to ask questions, model the task by first giving only one piece of information about your favorite city:

T:  My favorite city in Europe is Lisbon.
S1:  Where is it?
T:  It's in Portugal.

Proceed in this way so Ss get the idea that they should keep asking questions to get more information. They can extend their questions:

S2:  How long were you there?
S3:  What did you do?

■ Call on Ss to take turns talking about their favorite city and answering other Ss' questions.

## Optional activity

■ Ss write short compositions about their favorite city, using the model in Exercise 7 as an example. Write the following list of topics on the board:

location
size
climate
shopping
transportation
restaurants

■ Ss make notes about the topics. Then Ss use their notes to write compositions. This part could be done for homework.

■ Ss exchange compositions or put them on the board for everyone to read.

# 8 CONVERSATION

This exercise introduces the modal verb *should* for giving advice, and the theme of traveling and vacations.

■ Books closed. Review the names of the seasons if necessary. Set the scene and write these questions on the board:

What's the best time of year to visit?
What's the weather like then?
What are the beaches like?
What places should you see?

■ Play the tape once or twice. Ss compare answers.

■ Books open. Play the tape again. Ss listen.

■ Present the conversation line by line. Explain these expressions: "Can you tell me a little about Mexico?", "What would you like to know?", and "I can't wait to go there!" Present the vocabulary: *should* (for advice or suggestions), *winter, spring, ruins, miss* ("You shouldn't miss . . ." = You should see/go to . . . ). Explain that the Mayan ruins are near Mérida, which is the capital of the state of Yucatán, Mexico. The Mayas were a race of Indians in southern Mexico and Central America whose civilization reached its height around A.D. 1000.

■ Model the stress in "**What** would you **like** to **know?**"

■ Ss practice the conversation in pairs.

■ Optional: Books closed. Either Ss practice the conversation using their own words, or Ss take turns and talk about a country they have visited.

---

## 9 GRAMMAR FOCUS:
### Modal verb *should*

This exercise practices the modal verb *should* in questions and statements.

■ Use the tape to present the sentences in the box. Explain that modal verbs usually occur with a main verb. Point out that in positive statements and questions the main verb, rather than the modal verb, is usually stressed more strongly:

What should I **do** there?
You should **go** to Mexico City.

■ In negative statements, both the modal verb and the main verb are stressed:

You **should**n't **miss** the Mayan ruins.

■ Show how Yes/No questions, other Wh-questions, and statements can be made with *should:*

Should I take warm clothes?
How much money should I take?
You should take your camera.

### 1

■ Explain the task. Ss complete the task individually and then compare with a partner.

■ Check Ss' answers and then present the conversation line by line. Ss repeat.

Answers:

A: When's a good time to visit San Diego?
B: You should go in the spring or summer.
A: Where do you think I should stay?
B: You should stay in a motel.
A: What places do you think I should see?
B: You should see the San Diego Zoo.
A: Anything else?
B: Yes, you shouldn't miss Sea World.
A: And does San Diego have any good museums?
B: Yes, you should go to the San Diego Museum of Art.
A: And how about shopping? Is San Diego good for shopping?
B: Yes, you should go to Old Town for shopping.
A: Gee, thanks. I'm sure I'll have a great vacation.

### 2

■ Ss practice the conversation in pairs.

---

## 10 LISTENING

This exercise practices listening for information about countries and identifying false information.

### 1

■ Tell Ss that they will hear information about three different countries. One statement about each place is incorrect, and the Ss have to try to identify it.

■ Play the tape. Ss listen only. Play the tape again. Ss take notes.

### 2

■ Play the tape again if necessary. Ss compare answers. Check answers around the class.

Answers:

*Japan:* Mount Fuji is the highest mountain, not Mount Everest.
*Argentina:* People speak Spanish, not Chinese.
*Italy:* The capital city is Rome, not Madrid.

---

## 11 ON VACATION

This fluency activity gives Ss additional practice with *should.*

### Group work

■ Before Ss form groups, have them read the example dialog and questions to help them prepare for the task.

■ Ss form small groups of three or four. Ss take turns talking about a place they have visited.

■ Optional: As a follow-up, Ss take turns talking about interesting places and the class asks questions.

### Optional activity

■ Ss work in groups of four and choose a country or city that none of them have ever visited, but one they would like to go to someday. Ss prepare a short class presentation on it, using information from guide books, encyclopedias, libraries, or travel brochures about the following topics:

place
location
weather
best time of the year
people
food

shopping
what to see and do
What makes the place so interesting or special?

■ Groups prepare a short talk about the place.

■ Class activity: Groups give their presentations to the class: Algeria is a beautiful country in North Africa . . .

## 12 WRITING

This exercise practices writing a short description of a country.

**1**

■ Ss think of a country to write about. They should include three or four different pieces of information in their descriptions, but should not include the name of the country. Ss must include one "clue" that will help their partner identify the country. This task will not work if Ss write vague descriptions that could be about any country in the world.

■ Ss write their compositions. Go around the class and give help wherever needed. (You might want to give this as a homework assignment.)

**2**

■ Ss exchange papers and try to guess the name of the country their partner wrote about.

■ Optional: As a follow-up, Ss take turns reading their descriptions to the class. Other Ss call out the name of the country as soon as they think they know what it is.

## INTERCHANGE 11: On tour

This activity offers a lighthearted change of pace and practices using the language of the unit in order to plan a vacation for a fairly "odd" family. The activity is in three parts.

Part 1: Ss work individually and plan an itinerary for the Winkley family. This could be done for homework.
Part 2: Ss work in pairs and compare their information.
Part 3: Pairs revise their itineraries and then compare with other Ss in the class.

**1**

■ Explain the situation: Ss are travel agents and will plan an interesting vacation for the Winkley family. Explain *itinerary* (= a detailed plan of places to visit). Tell the Ss that even though the family is traveling together, the individual members do not have to do the same things at the same time each day – for example, one member might go on a tour while two others do something else.

■ Have the whole class read through the information about the family on page 117. Ask for suggestions about the different kinds of activities each family member might like to do, based on the information given:

T:  What should Mrs. Winkley do?
S1: She should go to the museum.
S2: And she should paint a picture of the river from the bridge.
S3: I think she should go to the opera house.
S4: Yes, and she should see a play, too.

■ Ss individually make notes about what the Winkley family should do on vacation. Extra paper may be needed for this task if Ss plan separate activities for each member in the family. Set a time limit of about 15 minutes.

## 2 Pair work

■ Ss compare information in pairs as in the example dialog.

**3**

■ Pairs work together to make a revised itinerary from their notes.

■ Pairs compare their new itineraries with other pairs and decide which one is the most interesting.

■ Optional: Ss report their itineraries to the class.

## 13 READING: Famous cities

This practices reading for key information and inferencing.

**1**

■ This could be done either as an individual, pair, or group activity. Remind Ss that they do not need to know every word in the passage and that they should try to guess (e.g., they should be able to guess *gondola* since the text says the city has canals but no roads).

■ Ss read each passage and try to identify each city. Then they compare with a partner or partners. Check Ss' answers.

Answers:

#1: Venice
#2: Chicago
#3: Rio de Janeiro

■ Tell Ss to look at each paragraph and ask how they chose the correct city. This is to encourage development of Ss' inferencing strategies. If a S cannot understand a vocabulary item (e.g., *Renaissance*), ask other Ss to try to make a guess. Show them how to guess from context (e.g., *Renaissance* refers to buildings here, so it probably describes a kind of architecture). Although it's not necessary for Ss to get the precise meaning of words like *Renaissance,* they can use their dictionaries if they wish to.

## 2

■ Ss do the task orally in pairs or groups. Compare answers around the class.

Answers:

*Paragraph #1:*
– Because the city has no roads; it has canals.
– They take gondolas; they visit St. Mark's Square to see its Renaissance buildings and go to its cafes.

*Paragraph #2:*
– In the Midwest (of the U.S.).
– For its music, opera, theater, museums, and architecture.

*Paragraph #3:*
– They go to its beaches and mountains.
– They dance the samba in the streets.

## Optional activity: *Dream vacation*

This activity practices planning an imaginary vacation. Time: 10–15 minutes.

■ Explain the situation: A group of Ss won first prize in a lottery. They can plan a three-week vacation anywhere they like in the world. They have to decide what countries to visit and the things they want to see and do there.

■ Model how Ss can describe the vacation using the present tense:

T: Our vacation starts in Hawaii. We go to Hawaii for four days. We stay in a luxury hotel in Waikiki. We go swimming and windsurfing, and we rent a limousine and driver for sightseeing. Then we fly to . . .

■ Ss do the activity in groups. One S in each group is the secretary and takes notes. Set a time limit of about 10 minutes. Go around the class and give help as needed.

■ Group secretaries read their plans to the class.

# 12 It really works!

This unit has two cycles and practices talking about health problems and buying things in a drugstore. It presents giving advice with imperatives and modals, and making requests with modals.

## UNIT PLAN

### Cycle 1

**1** Snapshot: *Presents facts about the common cold*

**2** Word Power: *Introduces the parts of the body*

**3** Conversation: *Introduces imperatives for giving advice*

**4** Grammar Focus: *Practices positive and negative imperatives*

**5** Listening: *Practices listening for health problems and advice*

**6** Pronunciation: *Practices consonant contrast /θ/ and /t/*

**7** Problems and Advice: *A fluency activity involving giving advice with imperatives and* should

Interchange 12: *Practices imperatives with giving instructions*

### Cycle 2

**8** Conversation: *Introduces modal verbs with requests*

**9** Grammar Focus: *Practices modal verbs* can, could, may, *and* would *for requests*

**10** Containers: *Introduces partitive phrases (e.g., "a bottle of")*

**11** Listening: *Practices listening for correct responses*

**12** Role Play: *A fluency activity that practices making requests*

**13** Reading: *Practices reading for main ideas and inferencing*

**14** Writing: *Practices writing descriptions of home remedies*

## 1 SNAPSHOT: The cold facts

This exercise presents interesting facts about the common cold.

■ Books closed. Introduce the topic of the Snapshot by asking questions about colds:

T:   Does anyone have a cold today?
S1:  I have a cold.
T:   Oh, that's too bad. Do you often get colds, Carla?
S1:  Yes.
T:   And about how many colds do you get each year, Jean-Claude?
S2:  Oh, I guess I get about two or three colds a year.
T:   What cold medicine do you take?
S2:  . . .

■ Books open. Ss complete the task. Tell Ss not to use their dictionaries but to try to guess any new vocabulary they don't know.

■ Explain any vocabulary Ss didn't understand.

■ Ss compare information with a partner.

■ Compare Ss' information around the class.

## 2 WORD POWER: Parts of the body

This exercise teaches parts of the body.

**1**

■ Model the correct pronunciation of each word in the list. Ss repeat.

■ Ss work individually or in pairs and match the 12 words given with the numbers on the pictures.

■ Ss compare answers.

Answers:

| | | |
|---|---|---|
| 1. head | 5. neck | 9. back |
| 2. eye | 6. ear | 10. hand |
| 3. nose | 7. arm | 11. leg |
| 4. mouth | 8. chest | 12. foot |

■ Explain that Ss must now write down the word for numbers 13–20. Ss can use their dictionaries. Check Ss' answers.

Answers:

| | |
|---|---|
| 13. knee | 17. tooth/teeth |
| 14. finger | 18. chin |
| 15. toe | 19. stomach |
| 16. ankle | 20. elbow |

**2**

This part could be done as a class activity.

■ Elicit suggestions around the class:

T:   Which parts of the body does a cold affect?
S1:  Well, my nose always gets red.
S2:  And sometimes my head aches.
S3:  I cough a lot and then my chest hurts.

### Optional activity: *Game – Simon Says*

Your Ss might enjoy this game, which reviews parts of the body and practices basic action verbs.

■ Explain the rules of the game to the class: Ss stand up. You give a series of commands, some of which start with the phrase "Simon says . . .":

T: Simon says touch your toes.

The class must obey these commands. Sometimes, however, you give a command without "Simon says":

T: Touch your toes.

When Ss hear a command without "Simon says," they shouldn't do anything. Tell Ss that if they do an action without hearing "Simon says . . ." or if they do the wrong action, they will be out of the game. The last S standing is the winner and leads the next game.

## 3 CONVERSATION

This exercise introduces the topic of health problems and presents imperatives for giving advice.

■ Books closed. Set the scene and write these questions on the board:

What's the matter with the man?
What advice does his friend give?

■ Play the tape. Check Ss' answers.

■ Books open. Play the tape again. Ss listen.

■ Present the conversation line by line. Explain these expressions:

What's the matter? = What's wrong?
Do you know what you should do? = Here's my advice.
chicken stock = a soup or broth made by boiling chicken in water
It really works! = It has very good results.

■ Ss practice the conversation in pairs.

■ Optional: Books closed. Ss practice the conversation again using their own words.

---

## 4 GRAMMAR FOCUS: Imperatives

This exercise introduces positive and negative imperatives.

■ Use the tape to present the sentences in the box. Point out that "Don't" is stressed here. Give further practice of positive and negative imperatives by having one S in the class call out a positive imperative and another S turn it into a negative:

S1: See me after class.
S2: Don't see me after class.

### 1

■ Before Ss complete the matching task, present the list of problems and advice. Model the correct pronunciation and explain any new words. *Ache* in "headache" and "backache" is pronounced /eyk/, not /æʃ/ or /ɑ ʃ/.

■ Ss do the task individually. Ss can choose more than one piece of advice for each problem if appropriate.

### 2 Pair work

■ Model the dialog in the book for Ss to use in comparing answers.

■ Check Ss' answers around the class.

Suggested answers:

| | |
|---|---|
| a bad headache | b, f, g, h |
| a sore throat | a, b, c, d, k |
| a backache | b, c, e, j |
| a cough | c, f |
| a toothache | b, i |
| a fever | b, c, f, g, k |
| a burn | c, l |
| the flu | b, c, d, f, g, j, k |

■ Optional: Books closed. Ss ask about one of the health problems given and other Ss give suggestions.

### 3

■ Explain the new vocabulary:

stress    = when you have trouble relaxing because you have too many problems or worries
insomnia = when you have trouble sleeping

■ Ss do the task individually and then compare with a partner.

■ Call on Ss around the class to read their sentences.

### Optional activity: *Charades*

Ss might enjoy a game of Charades while reviewing the vocabulary for illnesses and health problems. Time: 20 minutes.

■ Form groups of four. Each group thinks of the names of several illnesses or health problems – one for each member of the group to mime. Ss may use their dictionaries to help them go beyond the vocabulary presented in the unit (e.g., a broken leg, a sprained ankle).

■ Class activity: Groups take turns miming or acting out their illnesses or health problems in front of the class. Other groups call out their guesses (e.g., "You have a hangover," "You have a toothache"). Keep score. Which group gets the most correct guesses?

### Optional activity: *Dear doctor*

This activity practices writing descriptions of health problems and giving suggestions. Time: 20 minutes.

■ Explain the first part of the task: Ss work in pairs and write a letter to a doctor in a newspaper health column. They should describe a problem (e.g., underweight, overweight, shyness, fear of cats, sleeplessness). Write an example on the board:

Dear Doctor,
I have trouble sleeping. I go to bed at 9 every night. But I don't fall asleep until 2 A.M. It makes me bad tempered and sleepy all day. Help! What should I do?

Sleepyhead

■ Pairs think of a problem and write a letter, signing it with an interesting name.

■ Collect the letters, mix them up, and hand them out randomly to pairs. Make sure no pair gets the same letter they wrote.

■ Explain the second part of the task. Pairs read a letter and write a short letter of advice:

Dear Sleepyhead,
Here are some things you should try:
1) Don't go to bed so early. Wait until you are really tired.
2) Don't drink coffee or tea in the evening.
3) Drink a glass of warm milk before you go to bed.

4) Listen to some relaxing music or a radio talk show.

Good luck!
Doctor Rock

■ Now pairs read their letters and write replies. Go around the class and give help as needed.

■ Pairs take turns reading their letters to the doctor and their letters of advice to the class; or put all the letters on the wall or bulletin board for everyone to read.

# 5 LISTENING

This exercise practices listening for health problems and advice.

■ Set the scene and then play the tape once. Ss listen only for the people's problems and write down key words and phrases. Ss compare answers.

Answers:

*Problems*
Speaker #1 has a hangover.
Speaker #2 has a black eye.
Speaker #3 has hay fever.

Explain that "hay fever" = an allergy due to plant pollen in the air.

■ Play the tape again. Ss listen for the advice and write down key words. Check Ss' answers.

Answers:

*Advice*
For Speaker #1: Eat four raw eggs and drink a bottle of warm beer.
For Speaker #2: Put some raw steak over the eye for at least an hour.
For Speaker #3: Take Contac 500 (a decongestant).

# 6 PRONUNCIATION:
## Consonant contrast /θ/ and /t/

This exercise practices the contrast between the voiceless fricative /θ/ and the aspirated plosive /t/. The sound /θ/ is made with the tip of the flattened tongue touching the tips of the upper teeth and forcing out a voiceless stream of air. The sound /t/ is made with the tip of the tongue touching (or almost touching) the tooth ridge. The /t/ is aspirated – released with a puff of air – in initial position and in medial position before a

stressed vowel. A common pronunciation error is to substitute /t/ for /θ/ or not to aspirate /t/.

## 1

■ Model the sounds with /θ/. Point out the position of the tongue.

■ Play the first part of the tape. Ss practice. Ss with a hand mirror can observe the position of the tongue.

## 2

■ Model the contrast /θ/ and /t/.

■ Play the second part of the tape. Ss practice. Tell Ss to check for aspiration by holding a piece of paper close to the mouth as they pronounce the sound /t/. The aspiration should cause the paper to move.

## 3

■ Before playing the third part of the tape, ask Ss to make two columns on a piece of paper with /θ/ and /t/ as the headings. Ss use this list to check off the sounds they hear.

■ Play the tape. Check Ss' answers.

Answers:

| /θ/ | /t/ |
|---|---|
| think | take |
| thousand | time |
| anything | seventy |
| healthy | pretty |

# 7 PROBLEMS AND ADVICE

This is an open-ended communication activity that practices giving advice with the imperative and *should*. This exercise reviews *should*, which was presented in Unit 11.

## 1 Group work

■ Explain the activity and any new vocabulary. Encourage Ss to suggest interesting or unusual home remedies rather than standard drugstore medications.

■ Model the dialog by asking Ss for advice for a fever:

T:  What should you do for a fever?
S1: Put an ice bag on your head.
S2: You should drink strong cold tea.
S3: I think you should take a cold shower.

Explain that *you* here means people in general.

■ Ss practice the task in groups. One S in each group acts as group secretary and writes down the most interesting advice for each problem.

## 2 Class activity

■ Group secretaries report their advice for each problem. Which group gave the most interesting or unusual advice?

## INTERCHANGE 12:
### Keeping in shape

This activity provides useful practice with the imperative and reviews parts of the body. It is also a fun physical exercise.

### 1 Class activity

This part demonstrates a complete set of actions required for one exercise.

■ Books open to page 118. Demonstrate each action as Ss read the directions. Ss should practice saying the actions, but not perform them at this stage.

■ Books closed. Ss stand and perform each action as you read the directions.

### 2

This part presents the language needed to do other kinds of physical actions.

■ Books open. Demonstrate each action as Ss read the directions. Ss should practice saying the action without performing it.

■ Books closed. Ss stand and perform each action as you read the directions.

■ For this part of the activity, you should call out any of the directions Ss have practiced. This is a check to see if Ss can make the correct responses. You might want to think of an exercise and prepare a set of actions in advance by writing down the instructions.

### 3 Group work

This part is an optional follow-up that could be done on a different day.

■ Ss think of an exercise to tell their classmates.

■ Ss form groups of four and take turns giving directions. Move around the class and give help as needed.

■ Ask several Ss who had interesting or fun exercises to give their directions to the whole class to perform.

■ Optional: If you have access to a TV monitor and videocassette player and an exercise video in English, play it for the class and exercise together in English!

## 8 CONVERSATION

This exercise introduces requests with modal verbs.

■ Books closed. Set the scene and write these questions on the board:

What does the customer want?
Why does she want it?
What does she buy?

■ Play the tape. Ss listen for answers.

■ Books open. Play the tape again. Ss check their answers.

■ Present the conversation line by line. Explain that "He doesn't have any energy" = He feels tired all the time. Point out that in conjoined phrases (e.g., "a large or small bottle") the indefinite article is optional in the second phrase. The pronoun "one" takes a plural "ones." "Some" is unstressed in the expression "Can I have some multi-vitamins?"

■ Ss practice the conversation.

■ Optional: Books closed. Ss practice the conversation using their own words.

## 9 GRAMMAR FOCUS: Modal
### verbs *can, could, may, would*

This exercise introduces modal verbs for polite requests. Partitive phrases are also practiced here and developed in Exercise 10.

■ Use the tape to present the questions and statements in the box. Ss practice. Point out that these modal expressions are considered more polite ways of stating a request than direct requests such as "Give me . . ." or "I want . . ." Indirectness is a politeness strategy in English, as it is in many other languages. It distances the speaker from the request, thus making it less face-threatening.

■ Point out the different kinds of nouns (e.g., eggs, milk, toothpaste) that require different partitive phrases (e.g., a carton, a bottle, a tube). Point out that the preposition *of* in partitive phrases and *for* in "something for a cold" are unstressed.

■ Give additional practice with modal verbs by reading aloud phrases and have Ss form requests with *can, could, may,* or *would*:

T:  a bottle of milk
S1:  Could I have a bottle of milk, please?
T:  *(Continue with these phrases)*

something for a burn
some flu tablets
something for a sore throat
something for an insect bite
some ointment
a bottle of aspirin

■ Point out that the expression "I'd like something for . . ." must be followed by an illness or health problem. Then Ss complete the conversations in pairs using the phrases in the box.

■ Check Ss' answers around the class.

Possible answers:

A:  Can I have a box of cold tablets?
B:  Oh, sure. These are pretty good. Anything else?
A:  No, that's all, thanks.
B:  OK. That's $5.75.

A:  I'd like something for a sunburn.
B:  Of course. Try this cream. It's very good.
A:  Can I have something for a stomachache?
B:  Here you are. That'll be $8.95 altogether.

A:  May I have something for a sore throat? And could I have a package of cough drops?
B:  OK. Do you want a large or small package?
A:  A small one, please.
B:  All right. Let me get that for you.

■ Explain some of the expressions and their pronunciation in the conversations (e.g., "Anything **else?**", "**That**'ll be **eight nine**ty-**five**," "**Let** me **get that** for you"). Then Ss practice the conversations in pairs.

✓

Optional activity: *Wonder drug*

This activity practices preparing an ad for a new "miracle" drug. Time: 15–20 minutes.

■ Explain the task: Ss work in groups of four and think up a new wonder drug that can be used for a specific problem (e.g., to improve your memory, to make you younger or taller, to save you from having to do any exercise).

■ Write these questions on the board to help Ss plan their ads:

What is the drug for?
What does it look like?
How often do you take it?
How much does it cost?

Where do you buy it?
What's it called?

■ Groups use the questions to prepare an ad for a magazine or a newspaper. One S is the group secretary. Go around the class and give help as needed. Stop the activity after 15 minutes.

■ Groups read their ads to the class. The class decides which group has the most interesting ad.

---

## 10  CONTAINERS

This exercise presents partitive phrases.

### 1

■ Ss cover the list of partitive phrases. Present the words *box, can, tube, bottle, package,* and *jar*.

■ Ask how many things Ss can think of for each container. Write their suggestions on the board (e.g., "a box of chocolates").

■ Ss complete the task in pairs. Point out that some words have several answers. Check answers around the class.

Possible answers:

a tube of toothpaste
a box of matches
a can of shaving cream
   tube
a jar of cold cream
a jar of ointment
   tube
a can of hair spray
a package of gum
a bottle of shampoo
   tube
a box of tissues
   package

### 2  Pair work

■ Ss talk about the price of each item. Encourage them to use these patterns:

S1:  How much is a tube of toothpaste in . . . ?
S2:  A large one is about . . .
S3:  A small one costs about . . .

---

## 11  LISTENING

This exercise practices developing Ss' ability to retain information in English while processing a sentence.

- Books closed. Set the scene and play the tape. Ss listen only.

- Books open. Explain the task: Ss choose the response that best matches each question or request.

- Play the tape once or twice. Ss do the task. Check Ss' answers.

Answers:

a) Yes, it really works!
b) I drink warm lemon juice with honey.
c) Yes, here's some extra-strength aspirin.
d) Sure. Do you want a large or small box?
e) All right. Anything else?
f) Yes, they're excellent.

### Optional activity: *Brand name products*

- Explain that the term "brand name product" = a product that is well known through advertising. Elicit examples from the Ss (e.g., Contac cold medicine, Bayer aspirin, Vick's cough drops).

- Ss work in groups and take turns talking about the brand name medicines they use for common illnesses (e.g., headaches, coughs, colds, muscle aches).

- Ss talk about and compare prices of other brand name items they usually buy in a drugstore (e.g., shampoo, soap, toothpaste, hair styling gel or mousse, cologne, perfume, nail polish).

---

## 12 ROLE PLAY: In a drugstore

This is a fluency activity that gives Ss a chance to use everything they have learned thus far in the unit.

- Ss form pairs and choose roles. Explain the situation and the task.

- Point out that Student As, the customers, have three things on a shopping list and should ask for each item, one at a time (i.e., not all items at once). Explain to Student Bs, the clerks, that vitamin C is available in bottles of 100 or 500 tablets and that the toothpaste comes in small and large tubes. Encourage Ss to be creative (e.g., to ask about other things as well).

- Model how the role play should begin with you as the clerk greeting a customer:

T: Good morning, Bob. How are you? What can I do for you today?
S: Hi, Betty. Well, I'm OK. But I went to the pool yesterday and got too much sun. Could I have something for a sunburn?
T: Sure . . .

- Before Ss do the role play, ask them to cover their partner's information. Set a time limit of about five minutes. Now Ss do the task. Move around the class and give help as needed.

- Several pairs act out their role plays in front of the class. Follow up by giving or eliciting suggestions on how the role plays could be improved.

- Ss change both roles and partners. This time they use their own information.

### Optional activity: *Absent again!*

This activity practices making telephone calls and giving medical excuses for being absent from class. Time: 10–15 minutes.

- Explain the task: One S is calling the teacher or the school office to give a medical excuse for not coming to school. Encourage Ss to think of interesting excuses for being absent. Model the task:

T: Hello?
S: Hello. This is Chen. I'm sorry I can't come to class today.
T: Oh? I'm sorry to hear that. What's wrong?
S: Well, I went hiking with some friends on Saturday and I hurt my ankle.
T: Oh, that's too bad. Well, I hope you feel better soon. Take care.
S: Thanks. Goodbye.
T: Bye.

- Pair work: Ss sit back to back and practice making telephone calls. Go around the class and give help as needed.

- Ss switch roles and try the activity again.

- Optional: Pairs perform the activity in front of the class.

---

## 13 READING

This exercise practices reading for main ideas and inferencing.

- Explain the term *home remedy*. Then either present the pre-reading questions to the class or tell Ss to discuss them in groups.

- Present key vocabulary: *bee sting, meat tenderizer, handkerchief.* Encourage Ss to guess meanings of other words while reading.

- Ss read the passage quickly, silently, for main ideas. Tell Ss to skip any words they don't know.

## 1

- Ss read the passage again and then cover the passage and do the task. Ss compare answers.
- Check Ss' answers. Ask them to find the key words in the passage that helped them choose the correct answer.

Answers:

a) T   b) T   c) F   d) T   e) F   f) T

## 2

- Ask Ss around the class to describe some home remedies they use.

---

## 14 WRITING

This exercise practices writing descriptions of home remedies. The first part of this exercise could be given as homework.

### 1

- Ss think of an interesting home remedy for a simple illness (e.g., a cold, the flu, a headache). Go over the model composition.
- Ss work individually and quickly write down their ideas in note form.
- Ss use their notes and write short compositions. Go around the class and give help as needed.
- Remind Ss to check their grammar, especially use of imperatives, and spelling.

## 2 Group work

- Ss take turns reading their compositions aloud to their group.
- Each group chooses one composition to read to the class (i.e., one that described the most interesting, funny, or unusual home remedy).
- Optional: Collect the compositions and correct errors. Ss rewrite them neatly. Make a class "book" by photocopying the compositions and stapling them together. An artistic S could provide the cover artwork.

## Optional activity: *Home remedies*

This activity practices describing habits in the present tense. Time: 15–20 minutes.

*Preparation:* Photocopy the "Home Remedy Survey" form (p. 112) – one copy for each S.

- Explain the task: This is a class survey activity in which Ss interview five classmates to find out what home remedies they use for common health problems.
- Give each S a copy of the form. Ss interview classmates and write the information on the survey in note form. Set a time limit of about 15 minutes.
- Ss take turns telling the class about any unusual or interesting home remedies they heard about.

## Home Remedy Survey

What do you do for . . .?

a headache _____

_____

a stomachache _____

_____

a burn _____

_____

a backache _____

_____

a sore throat _____

_____

Classmates interviewed: _____

Figure 12.1

_____

_____

_____

_____

# Review of Units 10–12

This unit gives further practice describing past experiences, describing places, giving advice, and giving instructions. It reviews present perfect, past tense, the modal verb *should,* and imperatives.

## 1 WHAT WAS IT LIKE?

This exercise reviews present perfect, past tense, and describing past experiences.

### Group work

■ Present any new vocabulary. Use the model to explain the task. Remind Ss to use the present perfect when asking about an indefinite event and the past tense when describing a particular event. Encourage Ss to elaborate in their answers.

■ Ss do the task. Go around the class and give help as needed.

■ Optional: Each group repeats one of their discussions for the class.

## 2 LISTENING

This exercise reviews listening to descriptions of events.

### 1

■ Books closed. Set the scene. Play the tape. Ss listen.

■ Books open. Go over the questions and tell the Ss to take notes. Play the tape again once or twice.

■ Ss use their notes to answer the questions. Check Ss' answers.

Answers:

*Where were they?* Max was having a dinner party on Saturday. Doris was doing a little shopping downtown on Saturday.

*What happened? What did they do?*

*Max*
Went out around 5 P.M.
Came back home but couldn't get in: forgot his keys.
Broke a window and climbed in.
Started to cook dinner.
A few people came around 7 o'clock.
His new stove caught on fire.
Finally decided to go out for pizza.

*Doris*
Walked around downtown.
Did a little shopping.
Someone ran into her and he grabbed her handbag.
She shouted "Thief!" but nobody helped her.
Went to the nearest police station.
Described the robber.
Police haven't caught him yet.

### 2 Pair work

■ Ss take turns and use their notes to describe what happened. Go around the class and give help as needed.

■ Optional: Pairs take turns and describe what happened to Max and Doris, but they add one false piece of information. Other Ss try to identify the false information.

## 3 MOTHER NATURE

This exercise reviews the modal verb *should*, asking for and giving advice, and describing places.

### Group work

■ Explain the task and model it by eliciting Ss' questions. If you want, bring a picture of the place you describe:

S1: What's your favorite place?
T: I think my favorite place is Yosemite National Park.
S2: Where is it?
T: It's in California.
S3: What's it like there?
T: It's beautiful. There are lots of mountains and rivers . . .

■ Ss do the task in groups. Go around the class and give help as needed.

■ Optional: Each group decides which place was the most interesting and tells the class about it. Other Ss ask questions.

## 4 CITY TOUR

This exercise reviews the modal verb *should* and connecting words.

### 1 Group work

■ Go over the task and model the dialog.

■ Ss form groups of four. One S is the group secretary and writes down the one-day itinerary. Go around the class and give help as needed.

### 2 Class activity

■ Group secretaries take turns reading their itineraries to the class.

■ The class decides which tour is the best. Find out why they liked it the most.

## 5 HERE'S HOW TO DO IT

This exercise reviews the imperative and practices writing instructions on how to use something.

### 1 Group work

■ Explain the task and go over the model instructions.

■ Ss work in groups of four and do the task. Go around the class and give help as needed.

### 2

■ Groups take turns reading their instructions to the class. Make suggestions and elicit additions and possible corrections from Ss.

### Optional activity

■ Groups think of something else to write instructions for. This time they do not tell the name of the object.

■ Groups write their instructions and then take turns reading them to the class. Other Ss try to guess what the object is and what process is being described.

### Test 4

See page 151 for general instructions on using the tests. Test 4 covers Units 10–12. Photocopy the test (pp. 162–165) and distribute it in class. Allow 45–60 minutes for the test. Listening material for tests is on Side 4 of the Class Cassette, and the test answer key and tape transcripts are at the back of the Teacher's Manual.

# 13 May I take your order, please?

This unit has three cycles and practices the language of food, making a restaurant reservation, and ordering a meal. It presents countable and uncountable nouns, and the modal verbs *would* and *will*.

## UNIT PLAN

### Cycle 1

**1** Snapshot: *Introduces the topic of food*

**2** Conversation: *Practices making restaurant reservations*

**3** Role Play: *A fluency exercise on making reservations*

**4** Word Power: *Presents countable and uncountable nouns*

### Cycle 2

**5** Conversation: *Introduces* would *and* will

**6** Pronunciation: *Practices reductions of* would *and* will

**7** Listening: *Practices listening for key words*

**8** Grammar Focus: *Practices* would *and* will *for requests and intentions*

**9** Role Play: *A fluency activity on ordering a meal in a restaurant*

### Cycle 3

**10** Conversation: *Practices thanking someone for a meal and saying goodbye*

**11** Writing: *Practices writing a restaurant review*

**12** Reading: *Practices reading for information*

Interchange 13: *A role play set in a restaurant*

# 1 SNAPSHOT: Food facts

This exercise introduces the theme of the unit – food and restaurant orders – and presents some of the vocabulary used in the unit.

■ Books closed. As a warm-up activity, ask Ss questions:

What do you usually have for breakfast, Keiko?
What's your favorite restaurant, Nicola?
What do you like to order there?

■ Books open. Ss read the Snapshot, using their dictionaries if necessary.

■ Before Ss complete the task, model the pronunciation of the food items in the Snapshot and ask questions:

Have you ever eaten roast beef?
Do you like beef stew?

■ Ss complete the task and compare with a partner.

■ Compare Ss' information around the class.

### Alternative presentation

Ask students what they think the favorite meat in the U.S. is, and the most popular restaurant orders and ice cream flavors. Then Ss read the Snapshot and do the task.

# 2 CONVERSATION:
Reservations

This exercise practices making restaurant reservations and reviews making requests with *may, can, could.*

**1**

■ Books open. Set the scene. Play the tape. Ss listen.

■ Present the conversation. Model the stress in "reser**va**tion" and "**cer**tainly." Explain that "certainly" is a more formal way of saying "Yes" or "All right."

■ Ss practice the conversation.

**2**

■ Explain "Special Request" on the reservation form.

■ Play the tape. Ss listen.

■ Play the tape again. Ss complete the task.

■ Ss compare answers. Then check answers around the class.

Answers:

*Date*: Saturday,          *Name*: Ms. Parker
    the 16th              *Phone*: 549-2237
*Time*: 6:45             *Special request*: Quick
*Number in party*: 4         service

# 3 ROLE PLAY: Calling a restaurant

This is a fluency activity that follows up on Exercise 2.

■ Explain the task. Encourage Ss to be creative and to use their own words and information (e.g., Ss could have special requests, such as sitting in the nonsmoking section, having a highchair for a baby).

■ Ask Ss to review Exercise 2 for the language they will need (but Ss should not look at Exercise 2 while doing the task). Student B needs to think of the name of a restaurant before answering the phone.

■ Call on two Ss to model the task and help them elaborate and improvise as necessary.

■ Ss work in pairs, sit back to back, and practice the role play.

■ Call on Ss to act out the role play again with the same partner in front of the class.

# 4 WORD POWER: Countable and uncountable nouns

This exercise presents countable and uncountable nouns. The distinction between countable and uncountable nouns is likely to be difficult for many Ss since (a) not all languages make this distinction; (b) for languages that do, words countable in English may be uncountable in another language or vice versa; and (c) many nouns can be used both as countable and uncountable in English (e.g., wine/wines).

**1**

■ Introduce the distinction between countable and uncountable nouns. Explain that nouns that take a plural *s* are thought of as discrete and countable units (e.g., an apple / apples, a knife / knives). In fact, you can count them: one apple, two apples, etc.

■ Model the pronunciation of the nouns. Explain that the words "potatoes" and "bananas" are stressed on the second syllable, and "tableware" = utensils, dishes, etc., that we use when we eat.

■ Ss complete the task individually or in pairs. Check Ss' answers.

Answers:

| *Fruit* | *Vegetables* | *Tableware* |
|---|---|---|
| an apple | beans | bowls |
| bananas | carrots | a knife |
| oranges | potatoes | plates |

Possible additional answers:

| *Fruit* | *Vegetables* | *Tableware* |
|---|---|---|
| apricots | mushrooms | cups |
| melons | an onion | a fork |
| a pear | peas | a glass |
| strawberries | a tomato | spoons |

## 2

■ Explain that uncountable nouns do not normally take a plural *s* and are not thought of as discrete and countable units (e.g., rice, beef). To describe differing amounts of these things, we use partitive phrases like those taught in Unit 12 (e.g., a pound of beef, a bag of flour, a glass of juice). We don't say "two beefs." However, sometimes an uncountable noun takes a plural *s* to show different varieties (e.g., wines of France, cheeses of Norway).

■ Ss complete the task individually or in pairs. Check Ss' answers.

Answers:

| *Drinks* | *Meat* | *Grain and grain products* | *Milk products* |
|---|---|---|---|
| orange juice | beef | flour | yogurt |
| water | pork | rice | cream |

Possible additional answers:

| *Drinks* | *Meat* | *Grain and grain products* | *Milk products* |
|---|---|---|---|
| beer | chicken | bread | cheese |
| coffee | duck | cornstarch | cottage cheese |
| lemonade | fish | dough | ice cream |
| tea | lamb | pasta | milk |

■ Optional: As a follow-up, ask Ss to try to find as many countable and uncountable nouns as they can to describe things in the classroom (e.g., bags, briefcases, furniture). Show Ss how to do the task:

T:  Is paper countable or uncountable?
S1: I think it's uncountable.
T:  Good. What about bags?
S2: . . .

■ Ss work in groups. One S is the group secretary and makes two lists, one for countable nouns and one for uncountable nouns. Ss can use their dictionaries to check and to talk about the nouns they choose. Set a time limit of about five minutes.

Possible answers:

| *Countable nouns* | *Uncountable nouns* | |
|---|---|---|
| blackboard | chalk | make-up |
| book | furniture | money |
| bulletin board | hair | paper |
| desk | ink | string |
| pencil | lipstick | water |

---

## 5  CONVERSATION: Ordering a meal

This exercise presents the modal verbs *would* and *will* for requests in the context of ordering in a restaurant.

■ Books closed. Set the scene. Write these questions on the board:

What does the customer order to eat?
What does he order to drink?

■ Play the tape once or twice. Ss compare answers.

■ Books open. Play the tape again. Ss listen.

■ Use the tape to present the conversation. Ss practice. Model the stress in these questions:

**Would** you **like** a salad?
**What** kind of **dres**sing would you **like**?

■ Explain that "Thousand Island," "Italian," and "French" are common dressings used on salads and that "french fries" are potatoes, deep fried in oil – they are not really French.

■ Ss practice the conversation in pairs.

■ Books closed. Ss try the conversation again using their own words, substituting other foods if they like.

---

## 6  PRONUNCIATION: Reduced forms of *would* and *will*

This exercise practices reduced forms of the modal verbs *would* and *will*. Natural conversational English contains many reductions that Ss should be aware of. The need for reductions is caused by the location of the stressed words. The words in between are reduced to allow the stressed words to occur at more or less regular intervals. Ss should avoid giving each word the same amount of stress.

## 1

■ Play the tape. Model the stressed words and the reduced forms of *would* ('d) and *will* ('ll). Ss practice.

**What'll** you **have?**
**I'd** like a **small sal**ad.
**I'll** have a **Se**ven-**Up.**

## 2

■ Play the tape and Ss practice. Give additional sentences to practice if necessary:

I'd like to see the menu again.
I'd like the check, please.
I'd like some more coffee.
I'll have the roast beef.
I'll have Thousand Island, please.
I'll have dessert, please.

---

## 7 LISTENING

This exercise practices listening for restaurant orders as well as recognizing correct and incorrect orders.

## 1

■ Books open. Set the scene.

■ Ss listen to the first part of the tape once or twice and complete the order.

■ Ss compare answers with a partner. Check Ss' answers.

Answers:

| *Tom's order* | *Tina's order* |
|---|---|
| a cup of coffee with cream and sugar | a chicken sandwich french fries |
| a piece of apple pie | iced tea |

## 2

■ Play the second part of the tape. Ss listen only; they do not need to take notes. Elicit Ss' answers about what happened and write them on the board.

Answers:

Tina ordered french fries, but the waiter brought her mashed potatoes with gravy.
Tom ordered apple pie, but the waiter forgot to bring it. (It's the waiter's first day.)

---

## Optional activity: *Unexpected guests*

This activity practices planning a menu. Time: 15 minutes.

*Preparation:* Bring supermarket food ads from newspapers – two or three ads for each group. These should be different kinds of food items that could be used in planning a dinner menu.

■ Ss work in groups of four. (In a heterogeneous class, Ss from the same country might find it easier to work together.) Give several ads to each group.

■ Explain the situation: Six unexpected guests are coming to dinner and Ss must plan a quick menu using only the items in the ads. Write these dinner courses on the board:

Appetizers
Soup
Salad
Entree
Vegetables
Dessert
Drinks

■ Model how to use the ads to plan a menu:

T: Let's make an appetizer with . . .
S1: OK! Great idea! And let's have . . . soup.
S2: Yeah, that's good. And I think we'll cook . . . for an entree. Does that sound good?
S3: Yes. But what about dessert?
S4: . . .

■ Now groups look over the items in their ads and plan dinner menus. Set a time limit of about 10 minutes. Go around the class and give help as needed.

■ Groups take turns reading their menus to the class:

For an appetizer, we're having . . .
Then we'll have chicken soup.
For our main dish, we're cooking . . .
We want to have . . . and . . . for vegetables.
And for dessert, we'll have . . .
We are serving . . . and . . . for drinks.

---

## 8 GRAMMAR FOCUS:
Modal verbs *would* and *will*

This exercise introduces the modal verbs *would* and *will* for requests. *Will* is often incorrectly referred to as a future tense; *will* is not a tense in English but is part of the modal system and behaves like other modal verbs. It can also be used to refer to future time (e.g., "There'll be a concert on Friday"), as can the present simple or present continuous. Both *would* and *will* refer to intention here.

■ Use the tape to present the questions and statements in the box. Point out that requests with *would* and *will* are usually considered more polite than more direct questions (e.g., "What would you like to drink?" is more polite than "What do you want to drink?").

■ Ask Ss to write two more questions like the ones in the box using *would* and *will*. Compare Ss' questions around the class.

## 1 and 2

This exercise is in two parts. In part 1, Ss complete the missing words; in part 2, they match the waiter's questions and the customer's responses to make a conversation.

■ Ss complete the missing words and then number the sentences.

## 3

■ Ss compare answers. Check Ss' answers.

Possible answers:

| *Waiter* | *Customer* |
|---|---|
| [1] What <u>would</u> you like to <u>order</u>? | [10] I'll <u>have</u> chocolate chip. |
| [9] What flavor <u>would</u> you like? | [12] I guess I <u>would</u> like coffee. |
| [11] <u>OK</u>. And what will you <u>have</u> to drink? | [8] Yes, I <u>will</u> have ice cream, please. |
| [13] Would you <u>like</u> anything <u>else</u>? | [6] I <u>will</u> have french fries, please. |
| [7] <u>Would (Will)</u> you <u>like (have)</u> dessert? | [14] No, that'll be all, thanks. |
| [5] What kind of potatoes <u>would</u> <u>(will)</u> you <u>like</u> <u>(have)</u>, mashed, <u>baked</u>, or french fries? | [4] I <u>will</u> have potatoes. |
| | [2] I <u>would</u> like fried <u>chicken</u>, please. |
| [3] <u>Would</u> you like <u>rice</u> or potatoes? | |

■ Ss practice the conversation.

## 9 ROLE PLAY:
## In a coffee shop

This exercise provides the communicative follow-up to this cycle of activities.

■ Set the scene and explain the task: Ss should cover the conversation in Exercise 8 when doing the role play. Call on two Ss to model the task. Ss can go beyond the cues and should be as creative as possible.

■ Ss practice the role play in pairs. Then Ss change roles and do the role play again.

■ Call on Ss to act out the role play in front of the class.

## Optional activity

Make photocopies of some real restaurant menus in English or ask Ss to bring some to class. Ss work in groups of four and role play ordering from the menus. Alternatively, Ss in pairs or groups prepare restaurant menus in English. Give Ss categories to include in their menus (e.g., appetizers, entrees, side orders, desserts, beverages). For unusual dishes, provide short descriptions of the dish (e.g., Nasi Goreng = a fried rice dish topped with egg and chicken). Ss then use each other's menus for role plays.

## 10 CONVERSATION:
## Thanks and goodbye

This exercise presents expressions and gambits used to thank someone for a meal and to say goodbye.

## 1

■ Books closed. Set the scene: People are saying goodbye at the end of a meal.

■ Books open. Play the tape. Ss repeat.

■ Present the conversations. Model the correct intonation in the expressions.

■ Ss practice the conversations.

## 2 Pair work

■ Ss cover the conversation in part 1 and practice the conversations again using the cues.

## 11 WRITING:
## Restaurant reviews

This task practices describing a restaurant and a menu, and reviews the past tense.

**1**

■ Explain the task. Ss read the model composition. Explain any unfamiliar vocabulary. Ask Ss to think of the information they need to write a restaurant review. Elicit Ss' suggestions and write them on the board:

*Description:*

Name of restaurant:
Type of restaurant:
Size:
Location:
Other information:

*Evaluation:*

Food:
Service:
Other (e.g., waiter, waitress, atmosphere, music):

■ Either in class or for homework, Ss make notes using the topics on the board.

■ Ss write a first draft, one paragraph for the description and one paragraph for the evaluation. Remind them to use the past tense where needed.

■ Ss check for content, organization, and grammar, and revise their drafts. Give feedback as necessary.

**2**

■ Ss put their reviews on the class bulletin board and read each other's reviews. Find out which restaurants Ss would like to try.

## Optional activity: *Restaurant guide*

Ss work in groups. Each group chooses an area of the town or city (e.g., near your school, downtown, in the shopping mall) and writes a local restaurant guide for it. The guide can also include inexpensive or fast food restaurants or coffee shops. The task is to make a list of five interesting restaurants and coffee shops, and then the Ss visit each one and write a brief description of them, like the following:

Name: Coffee Cantina
Address: 3443 Western Ave.
Telephone: 575-9880
Hours: 7 A.M. to 8 P.M., Monday–Saturday

The Coffee Cantina is a European coffee shop. It has excellent espresso, capuccino, and tea. It's a small, low-priced cafe where you can get a drink and a snack, and the music is very good . . .

■ Ss either put their guides on the board or bulletin board, or they combine all of the groups'

guides into a "Restaurant Guide" and make photocopies for everyone in the class.

---

## 12 READING: To tip or not to tip?

This exercise practices reading for main ideas and scanning for key words.

**1**

■ Present the pre-reading discussion questions and elicit answers from Ss. Discuss the concept of tipping and why people tip in some countries.

■ Before Ss read the passage, explain these words: *porter, bellhop, parking valet, maid, service charge.*

■ Ss read the passage. Remind Ss to try to guess meanings of any words they may not know.

■ Check Ss' comprehension and answer any questions.

## 2 and 3

■ Ss work in pairs and answer the follow-up questions.

■ Check Ss' answers around the class.

Answers to part 2:

*How much should you tip someone who:*
takes your bag at an airport?                     $1
parks your car at a hotel or
    restaurant?                                   $1
serves you in a fast food restaurant?     Nothing

Answers to part 3:

*What tip should you leave for the following checks:*
a $27 haircut?              $4.00–$5.40
a $50 restaurant check?     $7.50–$10.00
a $14 taxi fare?            $2.10–$2.80

■ Optional: Discuss tipping customs in other countries you or your students have visited:

Which countries don't have tipping?
Is it better not to have tipping at all?

---

## INTERCHANGE 13:
## Are you ready to order?

This role play practices ordering from a menu and negotiation skills.

■ Explain the situation: Ss work in groups of four. One S is the waiter or waitress, and the other three Ss are customers.

■ Assign roles: Students A (waiters/waitresses) look at page 119, and Ss B–D (customers) at page 122.

■ Ask Ss to read their cues silently for comprehension. Point out that there are four stages to the activity.

■ Clarify the waiter's/waitress's task and the customers' task.

■ Model the pronunciation of the items on the menu.

**Alternative presentation**

■ Ss listen again to Exercise 7 on page 84, which will help them prepare for the role play.

■ Remind Ss to be creative, to improvise, and to use their own language. Ss should not look at each other's cues during the role play.

■ Now groups act out the role play. Go around the class and give help as needed. Set a time limit of 10 or 15 minutes.

■ Ask several groups to perform in front of the class.

# 14 It's the greatest!

This unit has two cycles and practices comparing cities and talking about world geography. It introduces comparative and superlative adjectives.

## UNIT PLAN

### Cycle 1

**1** Conversation: *Introduces making comparisons with adjectives*

**2** Pronunciation: *Presents intonation for questions of choice with* or

**3** Grammar Focus: *Practices comparative adjectives with* -er *and* more

**4** True or False?: *A game involving comparisons of cities and places*

**5** Listening: *Practices listening for comparisons*

**6** Writing: *Practices comparing and contrasting two cities*

### Cycle 2

**7** Word Power: *Introduces the vocabulary for talking about world geography (e.g.,* ocean, mountain*)*

**8** Snapshot: *Introduces superlative adjectives with* -est

**9** Conversation: *Introduces Wh-questions with the superlative*

**10** Listening: *Practices listening for key words*

**11** World Knowledge Quiz: *A game involving comparative and superlative adjectives*

**12** Reading: *Practices scanning and inferencing*

Interchange 14: *An extended practice involving world knowledge and comparative and superlative adjectives*

## 1 CONVERSATION:
## Making comparisons

This exercise introduces comparisons with adjectives.

■ Books closed. Introduce the topic of comparisons by asking Ss to compare Los Angeles and New York City. Ss probably know something about these cities even if they have not visited them. Elicit information with these questions:

Which is nicer, New York or Los Angeles?
Is New York warmer than L.A.?
Where would you like to live, New York or L.A.?

■ Point out that some places are called by their initials (e.g., Los Angeles = L.A., Washington, D.C. = D.C.), but New York isn't.

■ Set the scene and play the tape. Ss listen only.

■ Books open. Play the tape again. Point out that the two people are just having a "friendly argument" (i.e., this is not a serious disagreement between friends). Present the conversation line by line. Explain "Come on!" = I don't agree, and "You can have New York!" = I don't like it even if you do.

■ Ss practice the conversation.

## 2 PRONUNCIATION:
## Intonation – questions of choice

This exercise presents intonation for questions that give a choice. Usually these questions have the word *or*.

**1**

■ Play the tape and present the questions. Point out the rising and falling intonation patterns.

**2**

■ Play the tape again and Ss practice the questions.

■ Write other questions of choice on the board for Ss to practice:

Which is older, Tokyo or Kyoto?

Which is closer to Vancouver, San Francisco or Seattle?

Which is colder in winter, London or Berlin?

## 3 GRAMMAR FOCUS:
## Comparisons with adjectives

This exercise presents the two patterns used for comparisons with adjectives: adjective + *er*, and *more* + adjective. Guidelines:

1. One-syllable adjectives, add *-er*:   small – small*er*
2. Adjectives ending in a single consonant, double the consonant:   big – big*ger*
3. One- or two-syllable adjectives ending in *y*, change *y* to *i* and add *-er*:   dry – dr*ier*
   friendly – friendl*ier*
4. For other adjectives of two or more syllables, add *more*:   expensive – *more* expensive

■ Use the tape to present the questions and statements in the box. Point out that in expressions with *more*, the adjective is stressed (e.g., "Is New York more ex**pen**sive than L.A.?"). Give examples with *much* as an intensifier (e.g., "Alaska is **much** colder than Florida").

■ Refer Ss to the list of comparative forms of adjectives on page 133 in the Student's Book and ask additional questions using information about places Ss know. Use other adjectives (e.g., *older, nicer, safer, colder in winter, wetter in winter, more exciting, more expensive, more dangerous*). Ss provide answers.

**1**

■ Ss complete the conversations and then compare with a partner. Ss should check their answers with the list of comparative forms of adjectives on page 133.

Answers:

A: Is Vancouver <u>cooler</u> in winter <u>than</u> Toronto?
B: No, Toronto is <u>much</u> <u>colder</u>. It's great for skiing.

A: Which city is <u>more</u> interesting, London or Paris?
B: I think London is <u>more</u> <u>exciting</u> <u>than</u> Paris. It has great shopping <u>and</u> good nightlife. But I love Paris in the spring.

A: Is Singapore <u>larger</u> <u>than</u> Hong Kong?
B: No, it isn't. Hong Kong is <u>bigger</u> and <u>more</u> <u>crowded</u>. But you know, they are both <u>fascinating</u> places.

A:  Which is cheaper, Tokyo or Taipei?
B:  Taipei is much cheaper than Tokyo.

■ Ss practice the conversations in pairs.

## 2

■ Ss write six questions and then practice with a partner. Go around the class and check that Ss are using the correct comparative forms.

■ Optional: Ss write their questions on the board or take turns asking them around the class.

---

## 4  TRUE OR FALSE?

This is a game that provides a follow-up to Exercise 3.

### 1  Group work

■ Explain the task: Ss use the comparative form in making statements about places, and they should write about places their classmates are likely to know about. Their statements must be facts rather than opinions (e.g., "Munich is nicer than Budapest" is an opinion and would not work here).

■ Groups write their statements. Allow 5 or 10 minutes for this activity. Go around the class and check Ss' statements.

### 2

■ Groups take turns reading their statements. Each time a statement is read, Ss in other groups decide if the statement is true or false. Then they give their group's answer. Do not give the correct answer till each group has called out an answer. Record group scores on the board. The group with the most correct answers is the winner.

### Optional activity: *That's not right!*

This is an extended activity that practices describing a country. Time: 15–20 minutes.

■ Explain the task: Ss think of a country and write six statements about it – five true and one false. They should be factual statements, not opinions. Write this model on the board:

Holland is a small country.
It is in northern Europe.
It is also known as the Netherlands.
The people in Holland speak French.
The capital city is Amsterdam.
There are a lot of windmills in Holland.

(The false statement is that people in Holland speak French. They speak Dutch.)

■ Ss work in pairs and do the task.

■ Now groups of four (two pairs each) work together. One pair reads their statements. The other pair tries to find the false statement and correct the false information in it.

---

## 5  LISTENING: Radio quiz show

This exercise involves listening for comparisons.

■ Set the scene and explain the task.

■ Play the tape once or twice. Ss check their answers and then compare with a partner. Check answers around the class.

Answers:

| | |
|---|---|
| 1. Statue of Liberty | 6. Moscow |
| 2. 747 | 7. mile |
| 3. neither (this is a "trick" question) | 8. Australia |
| 4. Canada | 9. Nile |
| 5. horse | 10. Pacific |

**Alternative presentation**

■ Before Ss listen to the tape, read the questions to the class and let the Ss check their own answers. Here are the questions:

1.  Which is older, the Statue of Liberty or the Eiffel Tower?
2.  Which is bigger, a 747 or the Concorde?
3.  Which is heavier, a pound of gold or a pound of butter?
4.  Which is larger, Canada or the U.S.?
5.  Which lives longer, a cat or a horse?
6.  Which is bigger, Moscow or New York?
7.  Which is longer, a mile or a kilometer?
8.  Which is smaller, Australia or Brazil?
9.  Which is longer, the Amazon or the Nile?
10. Which is bigger, the Pacific or the Atlantic?

■ Play the tape. Ss compare their answers with the correct answers.

■ Find out who got the most answers correct.

---

## 6  WRITING: Comparison of places

This exercise practices comparing and contrasting two cities.

## 1

■ Each S chooses two cities to write about. Ss brainstorm by making notes on the following categories:

|                      | *City A* | *City B* |
|----------------------|----------|----------|
| Location             |          |          |
| Physical description |          |          |
| Size                 |          |          |
| Climate              |          |          |
| Main attractions     |          |          |
| Other                |          |          |

■ Ss use their notes to write two paragraphs – one on each city. Point out how to start a paragraph with a main idea or topic sentence. Write these examples on the board:

Tokyo and Kyoto are very different cities.
There are many similarities between Hong Kong and Singapore.
Sydney and San Francisco are my two favorite cities.

■ When Ss finish their drafts, remind them to check grammar, spelling, and comparative forms. Go around the class and give help as needed.

## 2

■ Ss exchange papers in pairs or groups.

■ Ask for volunteers to read their compositions to the class.

---

## 7 WORD POWER: Geography

This exercise introduces the theme of the second cycle – world geography – and some of the vocabulary Ss will need.

## 1

■ Model the pronunciation of the words in the lists and the stress in "**a**venue," "**can**yon," and "**de**sert."

■ Ss complete the task individually, using a dictionary if necessary.

■ Ss compare answers with a partner. Check Ss' answers.

Answers:

a) avenue (this is a road; the others are natural – not built by people)
b) path (this is built by someone or made by animals)
c) hill (this is a land formation; the others are water)

d) desert (this is a land formation; the others are associated with water)

## 2

■ Ss make their own lists. They should stay on the theme of geography by recombining the words presented in part 1 into a new list (e.g., *mountain, hill, volcano, beach*), or they can use their dictionaries to find other words on related topics (e.g., *weather, nature, flora, fauna*).

■ Ss exchange lists with a partner and circle the word that doesn't belong. They should try to say why it does not fit.

■ Ss take turns reading their lists to the class or writing them on the board for everyone to guess.

## 3

■ Ss complete the task and then compare answers. Elicit answers from Ss around the class.

Possible answers:

*Mountains*
Mount Fuji
Mount St. Helens
Mount Vesuvius
the Matterhorn

*Waterfalls*
Niagara Falls
Yosemite Falls
Iguazu Falls
Victoria Falls

*Continents*
Africa
Asia
North America
South America

*Oceans*
the Pacific Ocean
the Indian Ocean
the Atlantic Ocean
the Arctic Ocean

Optional activity: *Guess the word*

This game practices giving definitions and descriptions. Time: 10–15 minutes.

*Preparation:* Make a set of vocabulary cards (about 20) with one word on each card. The words should be from the Word Power (Exercise 7).

■ Divide the class into groups of five and place the cards face down on a desk at the front of the class.

■ Explain the activity: Groups take turns. One S from a group comes to the front of the class and picks up a card. That S gives clues (i.e., short definitions or descriptions, synonyms) to his or her group. The group tries to guess the word.

■ Model the task with *countryside* and suggest cues for the word:

*Countryside*

It's away from the city.
It's a nice place for a picnic.
It has birds and trees.
It's the opposite of "city."

■ Now start the activity. Allow 30 seconds for each S. If a group cannot guess the word, the S gives the answer. Then a S from another group takes a turn. The group that guesses the most answers wins.

---

## 8 SNAPSHOT: World geography

This exercise continues the theme of world geography and introduces the superlative form of adjectives. For this activity, it would be helpful to have a world map. Don't worry if your Ss know more about geography than you do!

■ Books closed. Before Ss read the Snapshot, ask questions about some of the topics, but do not give the correct answers yet. Let Ss argue and talk about the possible answers:

What's the largest island in the world?
What's the longest river in the world?
What's the largest lake in the world?

■ Books open. Ss read the information in the Snapshot. Explain that the answers here are ranked in order (e.g., Greenland is the largest island in the world, with New Guinea as second largest, and Borneo as third).

■ Ss do the task and then compare with a partner. Check answers around the class.

■ Explain or illustrate how to form the superlative and how it is used when comparing three or more things. Present these spelling guidelines. Ss should use adjectives they learned earlier in the unit to practice spelling their superlative forms. (Ss don't need to memorize these rules.)

*Spelling check: The superlative*

1. Adjectives ending in two
   consonants, add -*est*:                     long – long*est*

2. Adjectives ending in -*e*, add
   -*st*:                                       large – large*st*
3. Adjectives ending in a
   single consonant, double
   the consonant and add -*est*:   big – big*gest*
4. For most adjectives of two
   or more syllables (except
   those ending in -*y*), add
   *most* + adjective:                 unusual – *most
   unusual*

■ Model the correct pronunciation of "**long**est" /'lɔŋgist/ and "**high**est" /'hɑyest/.

## Optional activity: *Question and answer*

This activity practices asking Wh-questions about world geography or your country and reviews comparative and superlative adjectives. Time: 10 minutes.

*Preparation:* Make a set of Wh-questions on cards and corresponding answers on different cards – write only one question or one answer on each card (see Figure 14.1). Half of the Ss have one question card each, and the other half have one answer card each. (For small classes, make additional sets of questions and answers.) The questions should be about local geography, your country, or the world, and they should be easy for Ss to answer.

| | |
|---|---|
| What's the capital of France? | Paris |
| What country is south of Canada? | The U.S. |
| What's the longest river in the world? | The Nile |
| What's the biggest country in South America? | Brazil |
| What's the highest mountain in Japan? | Mount Fuji |

Figure 14.1

■ Give either a question card or an answer card to each S. (Give more than one question or answer card to Ss in small classes.)

■ Explain the task: Ss move around the class and try to match their questions and answers. To do this, they can either read their questions and answers aloud or they can use these phrases:

S1: What's your question?
S2: . . .
S1: No, my answer doesn't match.   *(or)*   Yes, my answer matches.

■ Set a time limit of about five minutes. When two Ss find a question and answer that match, they sit down.

■ Check answers: Ss read their questions and answers.

## 9 CONVERSATION

This exercise practices the superlative in Wh-questions.

■ Books open. Set the scene and play the tape. Ss listen.

■ Present the conversation line by line. Point out that in the superlative, the noun following the adjective is stressed (e.g., the largest **con**tinent, the highest **moun**tain).

■ Ss practice the conversation.

## 10 LISTENING

This exercise practices listening for key words.

■ Ss read the True/False statements first and then circle their answers. Explain that *Monaco* is pronounced "**Mon**aco" or "Mo**na**co" in American English.

■ Set the scene and play the tape. Ss listen and check their answers.

Answers:

a)  T (Shanghai is given as the correct answer, though some reference sources may give a different city, depending on how city boundaries are defined.)
b)  T
c)  F (The Amazon is the longest river in South America.)
d)  F (Vatican City is the country with the smallest population.)

## Optional activity: *Word association*

This activity reviews vocabulary. Time: 10 minutes.

■ Write six words from the unit on the board (e.g., *Canada, Australia, city, island, mountain, river*). Explain the task: Ss think of as many word associations as they can for each word.

■ Model the task by eliciting word associations for *Canada* and writing them on the board:

*Canada*

snow
Air Canada
mountains
Toronto
skiing
French

■ Ss work in groups of four. Go around the class and give help as needed.

■ Find out which group made the most associations for each word.

## 11 WORLD KNOWLEDGE QUIZ

This exercise practices both the comparative and superlative forms.

### 1 Group work

■ Ss could prepare their questions either for homework or in class. Where necessary, they should consult an atlas or other reference sources. If possible, bring in a world map or a map of your country for Ss to use when preparing questions. Encourage Ss to be creative in their questions (e.g., "Which is nearer the Sun, Mars or Mercury?"). However, it is important that the questions are not opinions (e.g., "Is Paris more beautiful than Bucharest?"), which would not work here.

### 2 Class activity

■ Groups take turns reading their questions. Ss in other groups discuss a question quickly and then call out their group's answers. When each group has given an answer, ask the S who read the question to say the correct answer. Record the group scores on the board. The group with the most correct answers is the winner.

## 12 READING:
### Nations of the world

This exercise practices scanning and inferencing, and using world knowledge.

**1**

■ Go through the list of countries and tell where they are located. Model the pronunciation of each country: /ˈbəldʒem/, /ˈkænedə/, /ˈtʃɪliy/, /ˈiydʒɪpt/, /ˈfræns/, /ˈɪtəliy/, /məˈleyʒə/, /ˈmɛksɪkow/, /ˈswɪtserlənd/, /ˈtɑylænd/.

■ Go over any new vocabulary.

■ Ss complete the task individually and then compare with a partner. They may use a dictionary if necessary. (The information on area and population varies slightly in different reference sources.)

■ Check Ss' answers around the class.

Answers:

| | |
|---|---|
| Chile | Egypt |
| Canada | Malaysia |
| Belgium | Switzerland |

**2**

■ Ss do the task individually. Check answers around the class.

Answers:

Canada is the biggest in area; Belgium is the smallest.
Egypt has the largest population.
Canada, Belgium, Malaysia, and Switzerland use more than one language.
Canada has the coldest winter.
There are three basic forms: military, parliamentary monarchy, and republic.

## INTERCHANGE 14:
### How much do you know?

This is a lighthearted wind-up to the unit.

### Pair work

■ Before Ss begin the task, present each question on page 120 and go over any new vocabulary or pronunciation problems.

■ Ss do the task in pairs, using the "Look Up and Say" technique. Tell Ss to check their answers on page 134 of their book.

Answers:

1. A giraffe
2. No
3. A hexagon
4. The liver (liver = 3.1 pounds; brain = 3.0 pounds; heart = 9.8 ounces)
5. No (Japan = 120 million; Pakistan = 97 million)
6. Rotterdam
7. Middle Ages
8. Beer (beer = 150 calories; Coke = 145 calories; wine = 85 calories)
9. No (a banana = 100 calories; an orange = 65 calories)
10. Coffee
11. Yes (an egg = 80 calories; a teaspoon of sugar = 18 calories)
12. Gold
13. Yes, Venus is closer.
14. The Earth
15. No (Paris dates from the 5th century B.C.; London dates from the 1st century B.C.)

■ Go over the "score" box at the bottom of the page. Take a class poll and find out who got the most correct answers.

# 15 What are you doing Friday night?

This unit has two cycles and presents giving and accepting invitations. It introduces requests with *tell* and *ask,* and the present continuous with future meaning.

## UNIT PLAN

### Cycle 1

**1** Conversation: *Introduces* tell *and* ask *when relaying messages*

**2** Listening: *Practices listening to telephone messages*

**3** Pronunciation: *Introduces reduced forms for* could you *and* would you

**4** Grammar Focus: *Practices relaying messages with* tell *and* ask

Interchange 15: *A fluency activity that practices taking and leaving phone messages*

### Cycle 2

**5** Snapshot: *Introduces more vocabulary for leisure activities*

**6** Conversation: *Introduces the present continuous with future meaning and practices making invitations*

**7** Grammar Focus: *Practices the present continuous with future meaning*

**8** Word Power: *Practices categorizing leisure activities*

**9** Role Play: *A fluency activity that practices making, accepting, and declining invitations*

**10** Reading: *Practices skimming, scanning, and inferencing*

**11** Listening: *Practices listening and making inferences*

**12** Writing: *Practices writing invitations and responses*

**13** What an Invitation! What an Excuse!: *A follow-up activity to Exercise 12 that involves making invitations*

## 1 CONVERSATION: Telephone messages

This exercise introduces *tell* and *ask* for relaying telephone messages.

■ Books closed. Set the scene and write these questions on the board:

Who is the man calling?
What's his name?
What's he calling about?
What's his phone number?

■ Play the tape. Ss listen and then compare answers.

■ Books open. Use the tape to present the conversation. Point out the stressed words and the rhythm:

Please **tell** her the **meet**ing is on **Fri**day.
**Would** you **ask** her to **phone** me this after**noon?**

■ Ss practice the conversation in pairs.

## 2 LISTENING: Listening to telephone messages

This exercise practices listening to telephone messages and writing them down.

■ Books closed. Set the scene and play the tape. Ss listen.

■ Books open. Play the tape again. Ss write down the messages and then compare answers with a partner. Check Ss' answers.

Answers:

*While you were out*
*Date*: [today's date]
*To*: Mr. Kawachi
*From*: Mrs. Sato
*Phone*: 554-3290
*Message:* Call Mrs. Sato before 3:30 this afternoon. Very important.

*While you were out*
*Date*: [today's date]
*To*: Ms. Wendy Carson
*From*: Sandy
*Phone*: 462-1187  *Ext.:* 313
*Message:* Call Sandy at the First National Bank.

## 3 PRONUNCIATION: Reduced forms of *could you* and *would you*

This exercise practices reductions in questions with *could* and *would*.

### 1

■ Play the tape. Model how *you* is reduced in "couldya" /kʊdjə/ and "wouldya" /wʊdjə/ and how the *d + y* = /djə/. Ss practice.

### 2

■ Play the tape. Ss practice.

■ Give additional sentences for Ss to practice:

Would you tell John to see me?
Could you ask Maria to help me?
Would you tell Carlos there's a call for him?
Could you tell Sally there's a message for her?

## 4 GRAMMAR FOCUS: Requests with *tell* and *ask*

This exercise practices using *tell* and *ask* to relay messages and reviews object pronouns.

With a message based on a statement (e.g., "The meeting is on Friday."), the statement remains intact (e.g., "Please tell Ann *the meeting is on Friday.*" or "Would you tell Ann *the meeting is on Friday?*"). However, with a message containing an imperative (e.g., "Phone me this afternoon."), the imperative becomes an infinitive (e.g., "Please ask him *to phone* me this afternoon.").

■ Use the tape to present the sentences in the box. Explain the differences between requests made with statements and imperatives. Point out that the verb *ask* is used with messages in the imperative.

■ Give Ss additional examples to change into requests. Ss practice making requests from statements first. Either dictate messages to the class or write messages on the board:

The picnic is on Saturday at 2 P.M.
The movie starts at 8 o'clock.
The video store is having a sale on Friday.
Chen is not coming to school today.

■ Then Ss practice making requests from imperatives:

Call me tonight.
See me after class today.
Return my dictionary.
Bring roller skates on Saturday.

### 1

■ Remind Ss to check whether the messages are based on statements or imperatives, and then to use the appropriate patterns.

■ Ss write requests and then compare with a partner. Check Ss' answers.

Possible answers:

a) Please tell Kim the movie is at 7 P.M.
b) Would you tell Jan there's a class party at the Blue Moon tonight?
c) Could you tell/ask Kay to come over for dinner on Friday at 6:30?
d) Would you tell Antonio the concert on Saturday is canceled?
e) Please tell/ask Sue to meet us in front of the cafeteria at 6:15.

## 2 Pair work

This activity gives Ss practice in writing real requests to classmates and in relaying them to each other. This activity can be fun if Ss are creative and imaginative.

■ Model the task by writing a message to a S on the board. Then ask another S to relay it for you:

T: *(Writes on board)* Please ask Mary to see me after class today.
S1: Mary, see the teacher after class today.
T: *(Writes on board)* Would you tell John the movie starts at eight?
S2: John, the movie starts at eight.

■ Ss do the task. Encourage them to write interesting messages for their partners to relay. Go around the class and give help as needed.

## INTERCHANGE 15: Would you like to leave a message?

This activity practices making telephone calls and leaving messages. There are four tasks in the Interchange.

### Pair work

■ Divide the class into A/B pairs. Explain the task: One student calls and asks for someone on the phone; the other student answers the phone. The person the caller wants to speak to is out. The caller leaves a message. The information for the message is provided, but Ss should provide additional information of their own.

■ Model the beginning of the telephone call:

B: Hello?
A: Hello. Could I speak to Carol, please?
B: Sorry. Carol's not here right now. I think she went to the library. Would you like to leave a message?
A: ...

Explain that when leaving a message, Ss use their own words based on the cues on the page.

■ Call on two Ss to try the first phone call. Ask them to sit back to back at the front of the class. Either elicit Ss' help or give suggestions as needed.

■ Ss practice tasks 1 and 2, sitting back to back. Remind Ss not to look at their partner's information.

■ Stop Ss after 5 or 10 minutes. Ss change partners and do tasks 3 and 4.

■ Ask volunteers to perform one of the tasks in front of the class; alternatively, ask several Ss to make up new messages and take turns relaying them to each other (with the whole class writing the messages down).

## 5 SNAPSHOT: Free time

This exercise introduces the topic of leisure activities and presents language Ss will use later to practice making invitations.

■ Books closed. Introduce the vocabulary by asking questions around the class about the leisure activities mentioned:

T: How often do you visit a museum, Terry?
S1: About twice a year.
T: How often do you go to a concert, Jan?
S2: About once a month.

■ Books open. Ss read the Snapshot and complete the task.

■ Ss compare with a partner. Check answers around the class.

■ Find out the class average for the four activities. (The easiest way to do this is to call on each S by name and ask the S to give his or her information. Add the Ss' data and write the class total on the board. Finally, divide the total by the number of Ss in the class.)

## 6 CONVERSATION: Inviting someone out

This exercise introduces present continuous with future meaning and reviews making invitations.

### 1

■ Books open. Set the scene and play the tape. Ss listen.

■ Use the tape to present the conversation. Model the reduction of *are* in "How're you doing?" and "What're you doing on Friday night?"

- Ss practice the conversation in pairs.
- Optional: Books closed. Ss try the conversation again using their own words.

## 2

- Play the second part of the conversation and have Ss write down the answers. Check Ss' answers.

Answers:

They are seeing *Cats.*
They are meeting at 6:45 P.M. on Saturday.
They are meeting in front of Pizza Hut on State Street.
They are having pizza.

---

## 7 GRAMMAR FOCUS: 🔲
### Present continuous with future meaning

This exercise practices the present continuous with future meaning. The form of the present continuous is not new (it was introduced in Unit 9); however, its use to describe future events is new. The present continuous is a common form for describing future events. When contrasted with the present simple (e.g., "Does your sister work on Sundays?" "Is your sister working on Sunday?"), we see that the present simple describes a regular, unchanging event, and the present continuous describes an event that is not regular or typical. *Going to* + verb can also be used to refer to the future (e.g., "Are you going to work on Sunday?"). This adds the notion of intention. Only the present continuous is practiced in this unit.

- Use the tape to present the sentences in the box.
- Elicit additional Wh- and Yes/No questions using the present continuous, and ask other Ss to answer them. Make sure they have future meaning (e.g., "What are you doing after class today?" "Are you going out tonight?").
- Ss complete the two-part task and then compare answers.

Answers:

*A*
a) What are you <u>doing</u> on Fri<u>day</u>? <u>Would</u> you like to go to a disco?
b) <u>Are</u> you <u>doing</u> anything on Saturday night?

*B*
[c] Well, my mother is <u>going</u> away for the weekend. But my father and I <u>are</u> not <u>doing</u> anything special. We'd love to come.

Do you want to see a movie?
c) We <u>are</u> <u>having</u> friends over for a barbecue on Sunday. Would you and your parents like to come?

[a] Sorry, I can't. I <u>am</u> working overtime. But how about Saturday?
[b] I <u>am working</u> till 7 P.M., but I <u>am</u> not <u>doing</u> anything after that. Can we go to a late show?

- Explain these expressions: "We're not doing anything special" = We have nothing planned; "I'm working overtime" = I'm working extra hours, for which I get extra pay.
- Ss practice the conversations.
- Optional: Books closed. Ss practice the conversations again using their own words.

---

### Optional activity: *A fantastic weekend!*

This activity practices planning weekend activities for visiting guests. Time: 15–20 minutes.

- Explain the situation: Two wealthy friends are coming to visit you this weekend. They have very expensive tastes and like to enjoy the best of everything. Of course, they will pay all expenses, including yours, for the weekend.
- Ss work in groups of four. If Ss live in a large city, they should plan the weekend activities for that city. However, if Ss live in a small town, they should plan to spend the weekend in the nearest big city or in the capital. Write these ideas and an outline for weekend plans on the board:

*Ideas for the weekend*

| | |
|---|---|
| Transportation | Shopping |
| Hotel | Sightseeing |
| Restaurants | Entertainment |

*Weekend plans*

Friday evening (guests arrive at 6 P.M.):
Saturday morning:
Saturday afternoon:
Saturday evening:
Sunday morning:
Sunday afternoon (guests leave at 6 P.M.):

- Groups plan their weekends. Go around and give help as needed.
- Groups report their weekend plans to the class:

Here are the plans for our weekend guests.
On Friday evening, we're going to . . . (name of restaurant) for dinner.

On Saturday morning, we're . . .
On Sunday, we're . . .

■ Ss decide which group had the most expensive
weekend plans.

## 8 WORD POWER:
Leisure activities

This exercise reviews and expands the vocabulary
of leisure activities.

### 1

■ Model the pronunciation of the words and
categories. Explain any new vocabulary:

| | | |
|---|---|---|
| craft fair | = | a public event where people (usually amateurs) sell homemade crafts (e.g., pottery, jewelry) |
| exhibition | = | a place where there are displays of things |
| live performances | = | events where a singer, a dancer, a musician, or an actor/actress performs before an audience |
| spectator sports | = | sports events with audience |

■ Ss do the task either individually or in pairs.

Answers:

*Exhibitions*

art show
car show
craft fair

*Gatherings with friends*

barbecue
beach party
picnic

*Live performances*

concert
opera
play

*Spectator sports*

baseball game
hockey game
tennis tournament

### 2

■ Ss can work individually, in small groups, or as
a whole class.

Possible answers:

*Exhibitions*

cat or dog show
photo exhibition
science fair

*Gatherings with friends*

board game (e.g., Scrabble)
card game (e.g., poker)
dinner party
party

*Live performances*

ballet
piano recital
poetry reading
reggae concert

*Spectator sports*

basketball
football
ice hockey
the Olympics

### Optional activity

■ Ss work in pairs and make a list of four words
with one word that does not fit (e.g., concert, play,
opera, soccer). Tell them to use the vocabulary in
Exercise 8 and other words related to leisure
activities.

■ Pairs exchange lists and try to guess which word
does not fit. If possible, they should tell why it's
wrong (e.g., "Soccer is a sport. The other words are
live performances.").

■ Pairs take turns reading their lists to the class.
Other Ss try to guess the answer. The S who gives
the most correct answers is the winner.

## 9 ROLE PLAY

This exercise is an extension of Exercise 6. Ss
improvise and make up information about an
event and then make invitations to each other.

■ Ss work in pairs. Explain the task. Encourage Ss
to elaborate and to use their own words.

■ Write these cues on the board to guide Ss:

Event
Location
Date
Time
Place to meet

■ Model the task:

T: Hey, Antonio, there's a great concert this weekend. Are you doing anything on Saturday night?
S: Um, no. What kind of concert is it?
T: It's a terrific rock group from Argentina.
S: Yeah? Gee, that sounds interesting. Sure! I'd like to go. Where is it?
T: It's at the Concert Hall downtown.
S: And what time is it?
T: . . .

Elicit Ss' suggestions on how to accept and politely decline invitations.

■ Pairs practice the role play. Go around the class and give help as needed.

■ Call on several pairs to perform the role play in front of the class. Give comments on how the role plays are good and suggestions on how they could be improved.

■ Ss change roles and do the activity again.

## Optional activity

This role play practices making, accepting, and declining invitations.

*Preparation:* Ss bring information from English language newspapers about local events (e.g., movies, concerts, sports events, fairs).

■ Explain the activity: Ss work in pairs (or groups) and practice inviting each other to real events in the city or town. One S tells a partner about an event that he or she would like to see and then invites the partner to it. The partner either accepts or declines the invitation. If necessary, explain that this activity is just a role play – that is, Ss should not feel obliged to go out with one another.

## 10 READING: Is that an invitation?

This exercise practices reading for information, skimming, scanning, and inferencing.

■ Ss read the passage and try to guess words they do not understand. Ss should circle any words they cannot guess from context and which they think are important.

■ Ask which words Ss circled and explain them to the class.

## 1

■ To check Ss' general comprehension, tell them to cover the passage and then elicit answers to the first question from the class.

Answer:

Real invitations mention a special time and date.

## 2

■ Ss do the task and then compare answers with a partner. Check Ss' answers.

Answers:

a) F    b) I    c) F    d) F    e) I

■ Optional: Lead a class discussion on invitations. Focus on any cross-cultural similarities and differences in customs between North America and the Ss' countries.

## 11 LISTENING

This exercise practices listening and making inferences. It is also a follow-up on the topic in Exercise 10.

■ Explain the task: Ss listen and decide if people are making real invitations or just being friendly. Play the tape. Ss listen only.

■ Play the tape again. Ss do the task and then compare answers. Check Ss' answers.

Answers:

a) I    b) F    c) F    d) I    e) I    f) F

## 12 WRITING

This exercise practices writing invitations and responses. (These will be used in Exercise 13.)

Each S will need six blank cards for this task.

## 1

■ Explain the first part of the task. Go over the examples in the book. Elicit suggestions from Ss for similar kinds of invitations. Encourage Ss to think up invitations to interesting, funny, or unusual events.

■ Ss write out their three invitation cards (one invitation per card). Move around the class and give help as needed.

## 2

■ Before Ss prepare three response cards, go over the examples. Explain that they have to write one acceptance card and two refusal cards. Again elicit suggestions for other ways of accepting an invitation. Point out that there should be both an expression of interest or a direct acceptance along with a question about a time or place to meet.

■ Go over the refusal cards in the same way. Encourage Ss to suggest funny reasons for refusing.

■ Ss write their three response cards. Move around again and give help as needed.

## 3

■ Ss are now ready for Exercise 13.

---

## 13 WHAT AN INVITATION! WHAT AN EXCUSE!

This is a fun activity for the whole class and is a follow-up to the writing task in Exercise 12.

### Class activity

■ Go over the directions and explain the activity.

■ Model the task with one S.

■ Give each S a total of six cards: three invitation cards and three response cards. Tell Ss to get up and move around the room. Encourage them to get as many acceptances as they can with their invitations. Set a time limit of 10 or 15 minutes.

■ Find out which S got the most invitations accepted.

### Optional activity: *Class party*

This activity practices describing plans for a class party, and it is a fun way to end Book 1 and the course. Time: 15–20 minutes.

■ Explain the task: Ss plan a class party including a menu, activities, and entertainment. Write these topics on the board:

Date
Place
Menu (food and drinks)
Activities
Entertainment
Responsibilities (who brings what, and who does what)
Cost per student

■ Ss work in groups of four using the topics to plan their party:

S1: Let's have the party on . . .
S2: OK. And let's bring . . .
S3: I think we should have . . .

■ Set a time limit of about 10 minutes. Go around the class and give help as needed.

■ Groups report their plans to the class. Who has the best plan? How many Ss really want to have a class party? Take it from there.

# Review of Units 13–15

This unit reviews describing food and restaurants, talking about places using comparative and superlative adjectives, and telephoning and inviting someone out.

## UNIT PLAN

**1** Favorite Restaurant: *Reviews describing a restaurant*

**2** Listening: *Practices listening to questions and choosing the correct response*

**3** The Biggest and the Best: *Reviews comparative and superlative adjectives in describing places*

**4** Listening: *Practices listening for key words and comparisons*

**5** Inviting a Friend: *Reviews telephoning and making invitations*

## 1 FAVORITE RESTAURANT

This exercise practices describing a restaurant.

### 1 Group work

■ Explain the task. Go over some of the words used to describe "atmosphere" (e.g., *quiet, noisy, elegant, nice, relaxed*) and "service" (e.g., *excellent, very good, good, fair, poor, terrible*).

■ Model the task with the class:

T: My favorite place to eat is the Hard Rock Cafe.
S1: Oh? Where is it?
T: It's on the corner of First Street and Jones Avenue.
S2: What kind of food do they serve?
T: Well, they serve delicious hamburgers and french fries, and they have great chicken and rib dishes, too.
S3: Does it have a nice atmosphere?
T: Yes, it does. There are lots of interesting pictures and things on the wall, and the music is really good.
S4: ...

■ Form groups of four. Ss take turns talking about their favorite restaurants. Give help as needed.

### 2

■ Groups take turns describing the most interesting place they heard about. Find out which place everyone in the class would like to go to.

## 2 LISTENING

This exercise reviews listening to questions and statements, and choosing the correct responses.

■ Explain the task: Ss listen to each question or statement and then check the correct response.

■ Play the tape once or twice. Ss check their responses.

■ Ss compare answers. Check Ss' answers.

Answers:

a) Yes, this way, please.
b) Yes, I'll have tea, please.
c) I'd like a steak, please.
d) Thousand Island, please.
e) Carrots, please.
f) No, I don't think so.
g) I'm glad you enjoyed it.
h) Bye! See you soon.

## 3 THE BIGGEST AND THE BEST

This exercise reviews comparative and superlative adjectives used to describe places in cities.

### 1 Pair work

■ Explain the task and go over the model dialog.

■ Ss work in pairs and take turns asking questions. Tell Ss to write down their answers. Go around the class and give help as needed.

### 2 Class activity

■ Compare Ss' answers around the class and write them on the board for a class poll.

## 4 LISTENING

This exercise reviews listening for key words and making comparisons.

■ Set the scene: Ss will hear radio commercials for three used car dealers. Explain that the word *financing* = the rate of interest on a loan. It is expressed as a percentage (e.g., the price of a car is $1,000 + 10% financing for one year, so $1,100 is the total amount the buyer will pay at the end of the year).

■ Play the tape. Ss listen.

■ Play the tape again once or twice. Ss complete the chart.

■ Ss compare answers. Check Ss' answers.

Answers:

| | The no. of cars on sale | Prices |
|---|---|---|
| Ajax Motors | over 500 | $500 and up |
| Nixon Autos | over 1,000 | $800 and up |
| Bob's Used Cars | over 400 | $1,000 |

| | Min. from downtown | Financing |
|---|---|---|
| Ajax Motors | 25 | 5% |
| Nixon Autos | 0 | 8% |
| Bob's Used Cars | 10 | 0% |

■ Read each follow-up question and elicit Ss'

answers. Tell Ss to use the information in their charts. Check Ss' answers.

Answers:

Which company has the biggest selection of cars? Nixon Autos
Which has the cheapest cars? Ajax Motors
Which is closer to downtown, Ajax Motors or Nixon Autos? Nixon Autos
Which has the best financing? Bob's Used Cars

## 5 INVITING A FRIEND

This exercise reviews telephoning and asking someone out.

### 1 Pair work

■ Explain the task: One S phones a friend and invites him or her to go out. Model the task:

S: Hello?
T: Hi, Chen. This is George Jones. How's everything?
S: Fine, thanks.
T: Say, are you doing anything on Friday?
S: Well, yes. I'm working on Friday.
T: Oh. Well, how about on Saturday? Would you like to go out to dinner or a movie?
S: . . .

■ Pairs sit back to back and practice the phone conversation. Go around the class and give help as needed.

### 2

■ Pairs change partners and roles, and try the conversation again.

■ Optional: Pairs perform the dialog in front of the class. Point out how the conversations were good and realistic, and ask Ss how they might have been improved.

### Test 5

See page 151 for general instructions on using the tests. Test 5 covers Units 13–15. Photocopy the test (p. 166–169) and distribute it in class. Allow 45–60 minutes for the test. Listening material for tests is on Side 4 of the Class Cassette, and the test answer key and tape transcripts are at the back of the Teacher's Manual.

# Tape Transcripts

## 1 Please call me Dave

### 2 NAMES IN ENGLISH [p. 2]

2  Now listen to people greet Mr. Kenji Ota, Mrs. Francine Dupont, and Ms. Susan Taylor. Do they use names and titles correctly or incorrectly?

**a)**
MR. KENJI OTA:  Good afternoon.
WOMAN:  Good afternoon, Mr. Kenji. Please sit down.

**b)**
MR. KENJI OTA:  Good afternoon.
WOMAN:  Hello, Kenji. Nice to see you.

**c)**
MRS. FRANCINE DUPONT:  Hello.
MAN:  Hello, Mrs. Francine.

**d)**
MRS. FRANCINE DUPONT:  Good morning!
MAN:  Oh, good morning, Mrs. Dupont.

**e)**
MS. SUSAN TAYLOR:  Good morning!
MAN:  Oh, good morning, Mrs. Taylor.

**f)**
MS. SUSAN TAYLOR:  Hi! How are you?
MAN:  Oh, hello, Ms. Susan.

### 7 SPELLING [p. 5]

1  Listen to people talk to a bank clerk. How do they spell their names? Check the correct answer.

**a)**
CLERK:  Louis Jones. Your first name is spelled L-E-W-I-S. Is that right?
MAN:  No. My name's L-O-U-I-S, Louis.
CLERK:  Oh, sorry.
MAN:  That's OK.

**b)**
WOMAN:  My name is Helen Lee.
CLERK:  Ellen Lee . . .
WOMAN:  No, *Helen*, with an *H*.
CLERK:  Oops. Sorry. *Helen* Lee.

**c)**
CLERK:  OK. Thank you, Mr. Brown. Here you are.
MAN:  Oh, my first name's spelled wrong here. It's Roger without a "d." R-O-G-E-R.
CLERK:  Oh, I'm sorry. Let me correct that.

**d)**
CLERK:  All right. And your name's Kathryn Simpson, correct?
WOMAN:  Yes, that's right.
CLERK:  And how do you spell your first name, Ms. Simpson?

WOMAN:  It's K-A-T-H-R-Y-N.
CLERK:  OK. Thank you very much.
WOMAN:  You're welcome.

### 9 CONVERSATION [p. 6]

2  Now listen to the rest of the conversation. Who says these things? Write **V** for Vera and **G** for Giovanni.

GIOVANNI:  And are you here with your family? With your husband?
VERA:  Husband? Oh, no, no, I'm not married.
GIOVANNI:  Oh, good.
VERA:  Huh?
GIOVANNI:  Oh, nothing. Uh, so are you living at the school dormitory?
VERA:  No, I'm staying with friends. How about you?
GIOVANNI:  Oh, well, we're living in an apartment.
VERA:  In an apartment? How nice! With your wife?
GIOVANNI:  Wife? No, no, my sister. I'm here with my sister.
VERA:  Oh . . .
GIOVANNI:  By the way, Vera, are you busy tonight?
VERA:  Oh, I'm sorry. I'm not free tonight. Oh! This is my stop.
GIOVANNI:  Well, how about tomorrow? Let's see a movie, huh?
VERA:  Uh, thank you, but I'm going out with my boyfriend . . . Well, Giovanni, nice talking to you. Bye!
GIOVANNI:  Bye, Vera.

## 2 It's a great job!

### 2 LISTENING [p. 8]

Listen to greetings and choose the correct responses.

**a)**
WOMAN:  Good morning!

**b)**
MAN:  Hi! How's everything today?

**c)**
MAN:  Good evening! How are you?

**d)**
WOMAN:  Oh, hi! How are you doing?

### 6 ALL IN A DAY'S WORK [p. 9]

Listen to five people at work. What is each person's job?

**Job Number 1**
RECEPTIONIST:  Good morning. General Motors. Can I help you?

**Job Number 2**

PHOTOGRAPHER: OK, now sit still . . . and don't move! Ready? Now say "cheese."

MODEL: Cheeessse.

PHOTOGRAPHER: Good!

**Job Number 3**

TAXI DRIVER: OK, here we are . . . City Airport. That will be twenty-five dollars, please.

**Job Number 4**

TYPIST: Oh, darn it! Not again! This typewriter keeps breaking down, and this report is due in twenty minutes! I'll never get it done in time!

**Job Number 5**

TEACHER: Could we have some quiet, please? Quiet, please! Open your books to page twenty-one!

## 10 LISTENING [p. 11]

Listen to three people talk about their jobs. Number the jobs from 1 to 3 in the order you hear them.

**Number 1**

DOCTOR: I work for the city hospital. My patients are mothers and babies. I work with nurses and other medical professionals. I also teach at the University Medical School. I like my job, but I work long hours.

**Number 2**

BUSINESSWOMAN: I love my job! I travel a lot. I buy clothes in Hong Kong and Taiwan, and then I sell them in my shop in downtown San Francisco. Business is really great this year!

**Number 3**

OFFICE WORKER: I work in a big office. I hate my job! It's boring, boring, *boring!* Every day, it's the same thing. I type letters and I answer the phone. I go to the post office for the mail. I make coffee for the boss, too! And I only get . . . seven hundred dollars a month!

## 11 NUMBERS [p. 12]

3 Now listen and write down the numbers you hear. Then practice them.

**a)** sixteen

**b)** fifty

**c)** thirty

**d)** nineteen

**e)** ninety

**f)** fourteen

**g)** seventeen

**h)** eighty

## 12 CONVERSATION: Names and addresses [p. 13]

2 Now listen to the clerk talking to two more people and complete the information.

CLERK: Good morning, sir. What's your name, please?

MAN: John Foster.

CLERK: John . . . Foster. Is that F-O-S-T-E-R?

MAN: Yes, that's right.

CLERK: And, uh, what's your address, Mr. Foster?

MAN: Nineteen fifty-nine Bank Street.

CLERK: Nineteen . . . fifty-nine . . . Bank Street.

MAN: Yes. Apartment eight-eleven.

CLERK: Apartment eight . . . one . . . one.

MAN: Uh-huh. Miami, Florida.

CLERK: Mi . . . am . . . i . . . Flor . . . i . . . da. OK. And what's your phone number, please?

MAN: It's four-six-eight . . . three-five-oh-three.

CLERK: Four . . . six . . . eight . . . three . . . five . . . oh . . . three. Thank you.

MAN: You're welcome.

CLERK: All right, Mr. Foster, here is your room key.

CLERK: Good afternoon, ma'am. What's your name, please?

WOMAN: Pat Phillips.

CLERK: Pat . . . Phillips. Is that with one "ell" or two?

WOMAN: Two. It's P-H-I-L-L-I-P-S.

CLERK: OK. And what's your address, please, Ms. Phillips?

WOMAN: Twenty-seven fifty-one Cook Street.

CLERK: Two . . . seven . . . five . . . one Cook Street.

WOMAN: Yes, and it's apartment three-oh-one.

CLERK: Apartment three-oh-one.

WOMAN: Uh-huh. And that's Dallas, Texas.

CLERK: Dallas . . . Texas. OK. And what's your phone number?

WOMAN: It's five-two-four . . . three-eight-nine-one.

CLERK: Five . . . two . . . four . . . three . . . eight . . . nine . . . one. All right, Ms. Phillips. Thank you very much. I'll call someone to help you with all those suitcases.

# 3 I'm just looking, thanks

## 3 LISTENING [p. 15]

Listen to people compare prices in three cities. Complete the information.

MAN: Ann, you're from Honolulu, right?

ANN: Yes, I am.

MARIA: Honolulu is a very expensive place to live, isn't it?

ANN: Well, yes, I guess so. It's probably more expensive than Mexico City. That's your hometown, isn't it, Maria?

MARIA: Yes.

MAN: Yeah, but it costs more to live in Tokyo than in Mexico City *or* Honolulu.

ANN: Oh, I'm not sure about that. Why don't we compare some prices and find out?

MAN: OK. Like what?

ANN: Well, how about gas? How much does a gallon of gas cost in Tokyo?

MAN: A gallon of gas costs about three dollars and seventy cents in Tokyo.

MARIA: In Mexico City, it only costs seventy cents a gallon!

ANN: And in Honolulu, gas costs about a dollar thirty a gallon.

MARIA: How about public transportation . . . like taking the bus?

ANN: Bus fare is very cheap in Honolulu. It costs only sixty cents to go anywhere on the island.

MAN: In Tokyo, it costs about a dollar-thirty to take the bus.

MARIA: And it's much cheaper in Mexico City. It's only three pesos – about one cent.

MAN: Well, how about going out for dinner? Um, it costs about eighty dollars for two to go to a nice restaurant in Tokyo. It *can* cost a lot more, of course.

ANN: In Honolulu, it costs about fifty dollars for dinner for two.

MARIA: Well, it's *very* cheap to eat out with my husband. Only twelve dollars for us to go to a restaurant in Mexico City.

ANN: Gee, I'd say that Mexico City . . .

MAN: Yeah, Mexico City seems . . .

MARIA: *I* think . . .

## 7 CONVERSATION: Prices [p. 16]

2   Now listen to the rest of the conversation. What else do Sally and Carlos ask about?

CARLOS: Come on, Sally . . . Oh! Look at this jacket! It's on sale! It's fifty percent off! It's only . . . ninety-nine dollars.

SALLY: Ninety-nine . . . for a jacket?

CARLOS: OK, OK . . .

SALLY: Oh, say, Carlos! What a beautiful camera! It's a new Konica!

CARLOS: Sally! You don't need another camera!

SALLY: I know, but it's on sale for only seventy-nine fifty!

CARLOS: *Only* seventy-nine fifty?

SALLY: Never mind . . . Oh, just a minute, Carlos. Look at these ballpoint pens. They're just a dollar forty-nine each. Where's the clerk?

CARLOS: Over there.

SALLY: Oh, I'd like to buy this pen, please.

CLERK: OK. One forty-nine plus nine cents tax. That'll be one dollar and fifty-eight cents. *(Sound of cash register)* And here's your change.

SALLY: Thanks.

CARLOS: Well, a dollar fifty-eight. Mmm . . . well, we still have plenty of money for my jacket.

SALLY: Your jacket? What about my camera?!

## 11 LISTENING [p. 18]

Three people are calling about things for sale. Complete the missing information.

### Number 1

WOMAN: *(Phone rings)* Hello?

CALLER: Hello. I'm calling about the piano for sale.

WOMAN: Yes! What do you want to know?

CALLER: Well, it's a Baldwin, right?

WOMAN: That's right.

CALLER: And how old is it?

WOMAN: Well, I guess it's about fifty years old.

CALLER: Fifty years?

WOMAN: Yes, but it's in *really* good condition.

CALLER: And how much is it?

WOMAN: Nine hundred dollars.

CALLER: Nine hundred. Oh, well, I don't know.

WOMAN: Hey! Just a minute. I have an idea. Listen to this . . . *(Plays out-of-tune piano)* Well, what do you think? Hello? Hello? Oh, darn! *(Hangs up)*

### Number 2

WOMAN: *(Phone rings)* Hello?

CALLER: Hello. Do you have a TV for sale?

WOMAN: Yes, we do!

CALLER: What kind of TV is it?

WOMAN: It's an RCA.

CALLER: An R . . . C . . . A . . . , huh. OK. How much is it?

WOMAN: Only fifty dollars.

CALLER: Only fifty dollars? Well, how old is it?

WOMAN: Um, I think it's about fifteen years old.

CALLER: Well, that sounds pretty good. I'd like to take a look at it if I could . . .

### Number 3

MAN: *(Phone rings)* Hello?

CALLER: Hello. I'm calling about your car for sale.

MAN: Yeah? What do you want to know?

CALLER: Well, what kind of car is it?

MAN: Oh, it's a classic Volkswagen.

CALLER: Mmm, well, how old is it?

MAN: About twenty years old.

CALLER: Twenty years old!

MAN: Yeah, but it's a great car! Really!

CALLER: Mmm, how much is it?

MAN: Well, I'm asking three thousand six hundred dollars.

CALLER: Three thousand . . . six hundred! Wow, that's a lot! Well, I'll think about it. Thanks for the information.

MAN: OK. Bye. *(Hangs up)*

# Review of Units 1–3

## 4 LISTENING [p. 21]

Listen to one side of a conversation and choose the correct answers.

**a)**
WOMAN: Where do you work, Tom?

**b)**
WOMAN: Oh, yeah? Where's that?

**c)**
WOMAN: Uh-huh. And what do you do there? Are you a salesperson?

**d)**
WOMAN: Do you have CD players and VCRs there?

**e)**
WOMAN: By the way, how much are typewriters?

**f)**

WOMAN: Are you at the store on Saturday afternoon?

**g)**

WOMAN: Great! I'll come by on Saturday afternoon.

## 4 What kind of music do you like?

### 7 LISTENING: TV game show [p. 25]

Four people are playing *Who's My Date?* Three men want to invite Linda on a date. What kinds of things do they like?

HOSTESS: *(Music and clapping)* Welcome to *Who's My Date?* Today Linda is going to meet Bill, John, and Tony. So, let's start with the first question . . . on music. Bill, what kind of music do you like?
BILL: Oh, classical music.
HOSTESS: Classical, OK. And how about you, John?
JOHN: Well, I like jazz.
HOSTESS: And you, Tony?
TONY: My favorite music is rock. *(Audience laughs)*
HOSTESS: How about you, Linda?
LINDA: Well, I like pop music. I don't like jazz or classical music very much. *(Clapping)*
HOSTESS: OK. Now let's talk about movies. Bill, what kind of movies do you like?
BILL: I like thrillers.
HOSTESS: And how about you, John?
JOHN: Oh, I like westerns.
HOSTESS: Westerns are good. And how about you, Tony?
TONY: I love horror films.
HOSTESS: And what about you, Linda?
LINDA: I *really* like horror films, too! *(Audience laughs)*
HOSTESS: And now for question number three. Let's talk about TV programs. Bill, what kind of TV programs do you like?
BILL: Well, I like to watch TV news programs.
HOSTESS: John?
JOHN: Uh, well, you know, I really like TV talk shows.
HOSTESS: And Tony, how about you?
TONY: I like TV game shows a lot.
HOSTESS: And Linda, what do you like?
LINDA: Well, I like TV talk shows *and* game shows. *(Clapping)*
HOSTESS: OK! Now who do you think is the best date for Linda?

### 10 LISTENING [p. 26]

Listen to the recorded telephone announcements on the "film information number." Complete the information below. Then compare with a partner.

ANNOUNCER: Thank you for calling the film information number. The following classic films are playing at the Screening Room this week. *Kramer versus Kramer* is playing on Monday and Tuesday at two, four, six, eight, and ten P.M. . . . The classic *Gone With the Wind*, in its *original* color version, can be seen on Wednesday and Thursday at twelve, four, and eight P.M. . . . For the weekend, the horror classic *Dracula* can be seen at three, five, seven, nine, and eleven P.M. on Friday, Saturday, and Sunday.

## 5 Tell me about your family

### 5 LISTENING: Hollywood lives [p. 29]

Listen to some facts about these famous people. What do you learn about each person's family? Take notes. Then compare with a partner.

MAN: Jane Fonda is a famous American actress, political activist, and physical fitness expert. Jane is the daughter of the famous American actor Henry Fonda. She is the sister of Peter Fonda, who is also an actor. In nineteen seventy-three, she married Tom Hayden, a California state politician. They have a son named Troy. Jane also has a daughter, Vanessa, from her first marriage. Jane lives in Southern California near Hollywood.

MAN: Thank you, thank you, very much! Good evening and welcome to the show! Tonight our special guest is the very successful . . . Madonna! That's right. Now she comes from a very large family, and she is the oldest daughter. She also has two sisters and three brothers. And did you know that in nineteen eighty-five she married the famous young American actor Sean Penn? He was her first husband. Well, she's with us tonight! Give a big hand to . . . Madonna!

### [9] LISTENING [p. 31]

Listen to Dick and Jane playing "Twenty Questions." Can you guess who they are describing?

DICK: Do you want to play "Twenty Questions," Jane?
JANE: What's that?
DICK: I'm going to think of a famous person, and you have to guess who I'm thinking of. OK?
JANE: OK! It sounds like fun!
DICK: All right, I'll start.
JANE: Is it a man?
DICK: Yes.
JANE: OK. Is he a famous singer?
DICK: Yes.
JANE: Yeah? Good! Does he live in the United States?
DICK: Yes.
JANE: Mmm. Is he in his twenties?
DICK: No.
JANE: Oh. OK, then, is he in his thirties?
DICK: Yes! That's five questions, Jane. You have fifteen more.
JANE: OK, OK. Is he a rock singer?
DICK: Yes.
JANE: Is he also an actor?
DICK: No. Do you give up?
JANE: No, not yet. Mmm, does he make music videos?
DICK: Yes!
JANE: Uh, and is he black?
DICK: Yeah, he is. That's nine questions.
JANE: Oh! Is it Stevie Wonder?

DICK: No!
JANE: OK, did he have a hit album called *Thriller?*
DICK: Yes!
JANE: Oh, I know! I know! Is it . . .

## 12 CONVERSATION [p. 32]

2   Now cover the expressions above. Listen to people talking to friends and choose the correct responses.

**a)**
MAN: Well, nice talking to you.

**b)**
WOMAN: How's the family?

**c)**
WOMAN: How's everything?

**d)**
MAN: How's school going?

# 6 Do you play tennis?

## 3 LISTENING [p. 35]

Listen to Mark, Sue, and Liz talk about what they do on their day off. Who likes to exercise? Who doesn't?

**Number 1   Mark**
MARK: Well, on my day off, I never get up before about noon. And then I just like to sit around at home and watch some videos. And maybe pick up a science fiction story . . . something like that.

**Number 2   Sue**
SUE: Well, on my day off, I like to go to the gym in the afternoon. And what I really like is lifting weights! Um, of course, that's partly because I want to lose five pounds by next month. And I also like to swim three times a week.

**Number 3   Liz**
LIZ: On my day off, I like to take long naps. And when I'm not sleeping, I like to watch old movies on TV and read magazines. I guess I just like to stay home, and I don't like to exercise much.

## 11 LISTENING [p. 38]

Listen to people asking questions about sports and exercise, and choose the correct responses.

**a)**
MAN: What do you usually do on Saturday?

**b)**
WOMAN: Do you go to the gym often?

**c)**
WOMAN: How often do you jog?

**d)**
MAN: Do you ever go skiing?

**e)**
MAN: What kinds of sports do you play?

**f)**
WOMAN: What other sports do you play?

# Review of Units 4–6

## 5 LISTENING [p. 41]

People are talking at a party. Listen to their questions. Are they polite or not polite?

**a)**
WOMAN: Nice to meet you, Mrs. Webster. And where do you work?

**b)**
MAN: I go to church every Sunday. Are you religious? Do you go to church?

**c)**
WOMAN: Tell me about your children, Mr. Johnson. Where do they go to school?

**d)**
WOMAN: What a beautiful watch! It looks *very* expensive! How much did you pay for it?

**e)**
MAN: Do you like sports, Debbie? What sports do you play?

**f)**
WOMAN: I guess you're about forty-five, Dr. Green. Am I right? . . . How old *are* you?

**g)**
WOMAN: And do you have any sisters or brothers, Peter?

**h)**
MAN: I *love* classical music! Do you?

# 7 It was terrific!

## 6 LISTENING [p. 44]

1   Three people are talking about their weekends. Listen and match each person with the correct newspaper headline.

**A.**
FRANK: Hi, Angela! How was your weekend in Toronto?
ANGELA: Oh, I didn't go.
FRANK: Really? Why not?
ANGELA: Well, because of the weather. I had a ticket for a flight on Friday, but the airport was closed because it was foggy.
FRANK: Oh, that's too bad!

**B.**
MARIA: Did you have a nice weekend, John?
JOHN: Yes, pretty good, thanks.
MARIA: What did you do?
JOHN: Well, I went to the Bruce Springsteen concert.
MARIA: Oh, lucky you! I wanted to go, but I couldn't get a ticket. What was it like?
JOHN: Oh, it was great, but the ticket cost me sixty dollars!
MARIA: Oh . . .

**C.**
HENRY: Hi, Gary! How's it going? How was your weekend?

GARY: Oh, hi Henry. Well, it was *very* interesting.

HENRY: Oh? What did you do?

GARY: Well, you know the electricity went out on Sunday afternoon ...

HENRY: Yeah.

GARY: Well, I was in the elevator of my apartment building when the power went off. I was stuck there for an hour!

HENRY: Mmm, that sounds terrible!

GARY: Ah, but guess who was in the elevator with me. That beautiful new neighbor who just moved into my building!

HENRY: Really? The woman from South America?

GARY: Yes! Her name is Sonya and she's really nice ...

2  Listen again. What happened to each person?

## 8  CONVERSATION: On vacation [p. 45]

2  Now listen to the rest of their conversation. Check the two photos they talk about. What did Celia say about each one?

MIKE: You really took a lot of pictures on your trip.

CELIA: Yeah, I know. And look at this picture of my friend from school. His name is Aki ...

MIKE: Ah, this is great!

CELIA: ... with his bride, Sashiko.

MIKE: Gee, what a beautiful bride and groom! How was the wedding?

CELIA: It was *very* nice! There were lots of guests and the food was delicious!

MIKE: Oh, and look at this picture! Where was this?

CELIA: That was Kyoto ... in a Japanese inn. (Oh, yeah.) It's like a small hotel. I stayed there for three days. Of course, I slept on the floor ... Japanese style ... (Oh.) and they gave me this Japanese robe ... called a *yukata* ... (Uh-huh.) to wear after my bath.

MIKE: Did you enjoy it?

CELIA: Yeah, sure! It was great! ... Oh! Look at this next picture.

# 8  You can't miss it!

## 3  LISTENING [p. 49]

1  Visitors to Vancouver are asking for information. Listen and mark these places on the map.

### a) the library

VISITOR: Excuse me ... excuse me, please.

MAN: Yes?

VISITOR: Um, I'm ... I'm a visitor here in Vancouver for the first time ...

MAN: Mm-hmm ...

VISITOR: And I want to go to the library ... the Main Public Library ... downtown.

MAN: Oh, yes, the library! Well, that's easy. Do you know Robson Street?

VISITOR: Uh, uh, yes, I ... I think I do ...

MAN: And do you know Burrard Street?

VISITOR: Yeah, but, uh ... Where is the library?

MAN: Well, it's ... it's very easy to find. The library is on the corner of Robson and Burrard.

VISITOR: Oh! Now I see. Thanks!

### b) Eaton's

VISITOR: Hello. Uh, do you know where Eaton's ... uh, Eaton's Department Store is, please?

MAN: Eaton's? It's on Granville Street Mall, and it's just across the street from the Castle Hotel.

### c) the Four Seasons Hotel

VISITOR: Uh, sorry to bother you, but where's the Four Seasons Hotel?

MAN: Oh, you're looking for the Four Seasons? Well, it's on Howe Street ... opposite the Mandarin Hotel. You can't miss it!

### d) the Orpheum Theatre

VISITOR: Hello. Um, I'm trying to find the Orpheum Theatre.

MAN: Well, let me think ... The Orpheum Theatre. It's on the corner of Smithe and Granville Street Mall. It's very easy to find.

VISITOR: Thanks a lot. I don't want to be late for the performance.

### e) the YMCA

VISITOR: Uh, excuse me. I'm looking for the YMCA.

MAN: Uh-huh, the YMCA. Mm-hmm ... it's opposite the B.C. Hydro Building. It's near the corner of Nelson and Burrard.

VISITOR: Oh, great! Uh, thanks!

### f) the Art Gallery

VISITOR: Excuse me ... I am new in town. Where is the Art Gallery, please?

MAN: Uh, let me see ... Oh, yes! The Art Gallery is on Robson Street ... opposite Robson Square. You can't miss it!

## 10  CONVERSATION [p. 52]

2  Now listen to the rest of the conversation. What does Dan say about his apartment?

KIM: And where do you live, Dan?

DAN: Well, I've got a place over on Seventh Street. It's a good location. (Uh-huh.) It's only a block away from the shopping center on Eighth Street.

KIM: Oh, that's good!

DAN: You bet! The rent's cheap ... only a hundred dollars a month.

KIM: Oh ...

DAN: It's pretty big for one person. It's got a large living room ... oh, and a good kitchen.

KIM: Uh-huh.

DAN: Although ... it's got a bedroom window next to a parking lot.

KIM: Oh, that's noisy, huh?

DAN: It sure is. And the apartment's only two blocks away from the airport. The planes are landing every two minutes.

KIM: Oh, no ...

DAN: I can't sleep at night ...

KIM: Hmm.

DAN: And ... it's got roaches!

KIM: Ah! Oh, no!

# 9 Which one is Judy?

## 2 CONVERSATION [p. 54]

2  Now listen to the rest of the conversation. Can you find Kevin, Michiko, Rosa, and John in the picture?

SARAH: Well, do you know Kevin Phillips? He's really nice.

RAOUL: No, I don't. Which one is he?

SARAH: Kevin's standing over there near the window. He's wearing white slacks and . . .

RAOUL: . . . and yellow polo shirt?

SARAH: That's right. And then there's Michiko Sasaki. She works with me at the office.

RAOUL: Oh? Which one is Michiko?

SARAH: Oh, Michiko's that *very* pretty looking woman who's wearing black pants and a green pullover sweater.

RAOUL: Oh, I see her. She's the one talking to Kevin, right?

SARAH: Uh-huh.

RAOUL: And who are those two people dancing?

SARAH: Oh, that's my best friend. Her name is Rosa, Rosa Ramirez. She's really nice.

RAOUL: Yeah, and she's *very* attractive in that . . . purple dress.

SARAH: Uh-huh. And (Huh.) she's dancing with John Dupont, her new boyfriend.

RAOUL: John is Rosa's boyfriend?

SARAH: Yeah, sorry, Raoul.

RAOUL: Huh! Gee, they're really good dancers, aren't they?

SARAH: Yeah, they are. Say, you promised to go over and talk to Judy.

RAOUL: Uh, Sarah. I'm sorry, but which one is Judy again? *(Laughs)*

## 4 WHAT'S GOING ON? [p. 56]

1  Listen to the sounds of five people doing different things. What is each person doing?

**Number 1**  Someone mixing a drink with ice cubes in a blender.

**Number 2**  Man taking a shower and singing.

**Number 3**  Someone vacuuming – wedding ring gets sucked into vacuum.

**Number 4**  Someone walking a dog.

**Number 5**  Someone snoring, waking up, turning over, and going back to sleep.

## 8 LISTENING: Missing person [p. 58]

1  Listen and take notes. Who is missing? What does the person look like? What is the person wearing?

POLICE OFFICER: Police Department. May I help you?

WOMAN: I'd like to report a missing person – my grandmother.

POLICE OFFICER: Your grandmother? OK.

WOMAN: Yes, she went out at three o'clock this afternoon. It's already past midnight and she hasn't come back.

POLICE OFFICER: Uh-huh. What's her name, please?

WOMAN: Mrs. Rose Baker.

POLICE OFFICER: And . . . how old is she?

WOMAN: She's seventy-eight.

POLICE OFFICER: OK. Now can you describe her?

WOMAN: Yes, she's about five feet tall.

POLICE OFFICER: Five feet, uh-huh.

WOMAN: She has curly gray hair and she wears glasses.

POLICE OFFICER: And what is she wearing?

WOMAN: Let me see. A red dress and a white jacket.

POLICE OFFICER: A red dress and a white jacket.

WOMAN: Oh, and a little hat with flowers on it.

POLICE OFFICER: All right. Now, just a few more questions . . .

2  Pair work: Compare your notes. Then listen to the rest of the conversation. What happened to the missing person?

WOMAN: [*Clock strikes three*] Oh, Grandma, it's you! I was so worried about you. It's three o'clock in the morning.

GRANDMA: Why were you worried? I was out on a date.

WOMAN: A date? With who?

GRANDMA: Mr. Franklin – my new boyfriend. He's only eighty-three!

# Review of Units 7–9

## 2 LISTENING [p. 60]

1  A thief robbed a hotel on Saturday. Inspector Dobbs is questioning Frankie. The pictures show what Frankie did on Saturday. Listen to their conversation. Are Frankie's answers true or false?

INSPECTOR DOBBS: [*Sound of knock on door*] Well, Frankie. How was your weekend?

FRANKIE: Oh, it's you, Inspector. My weekend? What do you want to know about it?

INSPECTOR DOBBS: Now just tell the truth. What did you do at one P.M. on Saturday?

FRANKIE: Uh . . . one P.M. . . . on Saturday? Well, oh, I remember! I watched a baseball game on TV. Yeah. The Expos won four to nothing. It was a great game!

INSPECTOR DOBBS: Ok . . . OK. What did you do at three P.M.?

FRANKIE: Uh . . . at three? Oh, yeah, I went to my karate class like I always do, every Saturday at three.

INSPECTOR DOBBS: Karate, huh? Well, well . . . OK. And what did you do on Saturday at five P.M.?

FRANKIE: Uh, oh yeah, uh, after karate, I visited some old friends of mine, Tom and Mary Kent, on Front Street.

INSPECTOR DOBBS: Yeah, Tom and Mary Kent. We'll talk to them. Now, Frankie, six o'clock. Where were you at six?

FRANKIE: Oooh! Gee, . . . at six? Well, I went home at six . . . yeah . . . to clean the house.

INSPECTOR DOBBS: Yeah, yeah, so you cleaned the house. Now listen carefully, Frankie. What did you do at eight on Saturday night?

FRANKIE: Jeez . . . at eight? Uh . . . oh, yeah . . . I remember now. I watched a terrific movie on TV. Yeah . . . it was great.

INSPECTOR DOBBS: Oh, you watched a movie on TV, did you? And what movie did you watch? What was the *name* of the movie, Frankie? Huh?

FRANKIE: The movie? The name of the movie? Uh, let me think a minute . . . it was a fantastic movie . . .

INSPECTOR DOBBS: Really?

FRANKIE: No, wait! I remember, it was a . . . a . . . well, it *was* exciting . . .

INSPECTOR DOBBS: OK, OK, Frankie . . .

FRANKIE: . . . and I clearly remember that I went to bed at ten-thirty, uh, exactly . . . Yeah, I watched the movie, and I went to bed right after . . . ahem . . . the movie. Yeah, boy, I was tired . . . a long day, like I said.

INSPECTOR DOBBS: Interesting. Very interesting, Frankie. Come on, Frankie, let's go down to the police station.

FRANKIE: The police station? Me? Why me? I was at home on Saturday night!

INSPECTOR DOBBS: Sure, Frankie, sure.

# 10 Guess what happened!

## 2 CONVERSATION [p. 62]

2    Now listen to the rest of the conversation. What happened?

JILL: I think I'll just move over into the left lane so we can get there even faster. OK?

TED: Well . . . But don't get a ticket!

JILL: I told you, I've never gotten a ticket.

TED: Have you ever been in a car accident?

JILL: Never!

TED: Uh-oh! It's a police car.

JILL: Oh, no! Can you see him?

TED: Yes. He's coming up right behind you . . . and his lights are flashing, too.

JILL: Yeah, you're right. Oooh! It's the first time this has ever happened to me!

POLICE OFFICER: Well, are you going to a fire? May I see your driver's license, please?

## 7 CONVERSATION: An embarrassing situation [p. 65]

1    Listen and practice.

BILL: Do you know what happened on Sunday?

ROSE: No, what?

BILL: I went downtown to do some shopping. Then I went to a restaurant for lunch. I ate lunch and asked for the check. (Uh-huh.) But I found I didn't have enough money!

ROSE: How embarrassing! So what did you do?

BILL: Well, first, I called my parents, but they were

out. After that, I tried my roommate, but he was out too. So, finally, I phoned my boss at home. He was very nice and brought me some money.

ROSE: Oh! That was lucky!

## 9 LISTENING: And *then* what happened? [p. 66]

1    Ken lost a bag with his passport, money, and airplane tickets while he was on vacation. What did he do? Number the phrases from 1 to 6.

WOMAN: So how was London, Ken?

KEN: Oh, good, bad.

WOMAN: Really? What happened?

KEN: Well, one day I parked my car, and I went to get something to eat. And when I came back, my bag was gone from the trunk! Stolen!

WOMAN: Oh, no!

KEN: Oh, yeah! And I lost everything – my passport, money, airplane tickets.

WOMAN: That's terrible! What did you do?

KEN: Well, first I went to the American Embassy, but it was closed because it was a public holiday.

WOMAN: Oh, too bad.

KEN: So then I found a policeman and he took me to the police station. They were very nice, but there wasn't much they could do. And I felt so stupid. I had no money at all. But the policeman felt sorry for me and loaned me twenty pounds.

WOMAN: That was nice!

KEN: Yeah. So after that, I decided to give my mom and dad a call. Luckily, they were home and they promised to send me some money. But I needed money right away for my hotel and . . . and to buy some food.

WOMAN: Yeah. Well, what did you do next?

KEN: Well, I decided to sell my camera. I took it to a shop and . . . and they gave me thirty-five pounds for it.

WOMAN: Boy, that was smart!

KEN: Uh-huh. So, finally, I decided to move to a cheaper place and I found a youth hostel for only ten pounds a night.

WOMAN: Sounds like a bargain! But what did you do about your missing airline tickets?

KEN: Well, I phoned the airline and told them what happened. But then guess what happened the next day?

WOMAN: What?

KEN: Well, the police called and I got everything back! And then my parents' money arrived, so I really had a great time before I left London.

WOMAN: Oh, gee, Ken. What a vacation! And what a story, too!

# 11 It's an interesting place

## 3 CONVERSATION [p. 69]

2    Now listen to the rest of the conversation. What does Steve say about transportation and shopping in Toronto?

LINDA: Toronto sounds like a nice place. I've heard it has a good subway.
STEVE: Oh, yeah. It's excellent. And the buses are good, too.
LINDA: And what about shopping?
STEVE: There are some great shopping centers and department stores. Do you know the Eaton Centre?
LINDA: The Eaton Centre? No. What's that?
STEVE: Huh! It's one of the biggest shopping centers in the world. It has everything, and the prices are pretty good, too.
LINDA: Well, I hope some day I'll get a chance to go there.
STEVE: I hope so, too. If you ever go, I'll show you around the city . . .
LINDA: You will? Great! (Ha-ha!) Thanks!
STEVE: OK.

## 6 LISTENING [p. 70]

Listen to Joyce, Lou, and Nick talking about their hometowns. What do they say? Write **Y** for yes and **N** for no.

### Number 1: Joyce
WOMAN: So tell me about your hometown, Joyce.
JOYCE: Well, it's a real small town . . .
WOMAN: Really? What's it like there?
JOYCE: Oh, I think it's a very boring place.
WOMAN: Why?
JOYCE: Well, there's nothing exciting to do. No good restaurants. No nightlife of any kind. I really get bored there.
WOMAN: Oh, that's too bad.
JOYCE: Yeah, but lots of people love it there because it's so pretty.
WOMAN: Yeah?
JOYCE: Uh-huh. It has lovely scenery – lots of mountains, rivers, lakes, trees . . .
WOMAN: Well, I don't know, Joyce, it sounds like a nice place!
JOYCE: Well, yeah, if you like to go hiking in the summer and skiing in the winter. But, you know, I'm not the outdoors type! I'm a real city person!

### Number 2: Lou
WOMAN: Do you come from a big city, Lou?
LOU: Oh, yeah, I do. It's pretty big.
WOMAN: What's it like there?
LOU: Oh, it's a really great place! It has some fantastic art museums, and wonderful theaters, and terrific restaurants of all kinds . . . like Greek, Russian, French, Thai, Japanese . . .
WOMAN: Ah . . . really? And how are the prices? Is it expensive?
LOU: Yeah, yeah, I guess so. Food costs a lot . . . both in the supermarket and in restaurants. And apartments! They're so hard to find . . . and the rents are pretty high.
WOMAN: Yeah, I guess it's expensive everywhere these days.

### Number 3: Nick
MAN: Hey, Nick. Are you going home for the holidays?
NICK: No way!

MAN: Oh, why not?
NICK: I don't like my hometown. Too many people, too many buildings, too many factories. It's big and it's ugly! I like places that are small and quiet. Like here!
MAN: Is your hometown as bad as that?
NICK: Yes, it's pretty bad. It doesn't even have any good restaurants.
MAN: No, c'mon, Nick! No interesting theaters or nightlife?
NICK: No, not really.
MAN: It sounds like a terrible place.
NICK: Yeah, it really is.

## 10 LISTENING [p. 72]

1  Listen to three lectures about Japan, Argentina, and Italy. Take notes.

### Number 1: Japan
WOMAN: Today, I'm going to speak of Japan. Japan has several major islands, and a lot of smaller islands. The capital city is called Tokyo. The highest mountain in Japan is known as Mount Everest. There are many many beautiful Buddhist temples and Shinto shrines in the country. Visitors should try Japanese food, especially "sashimi," which is raw fish.

### Number 2: Argentina
MAN: Let me tell you about Argentina. Argentina is a country located in southeastern South America. It's a very large country, and the capital city is Buenos Aires. The people all speak French. Argentina's neighbors include Chile, Bolivia, Paraguay, Brazil, and Uruguay.

### Number 3: Italy
MAN: Italy is a country in southern Europe and it is on the Mediterranean Sea. Now, the country is shaped like a boot. And it's famous for its excellent food, especially pasta. Now, Italy is also famous for its art, old buildings, and several beautiful cities; for example, Venice, Florence, Rome, Naples. The capital city is Madrid.

2  Listen again. One thing about each country is incorrect. What is it?

# 12 It really works!

## 5 LISTENING [p. 76]

Listen to three people complaining. What are their problems? What advice do they get?

### Number 1
FIRST MAN: Oh, oh, I feel awful. I've got the most terrible hangover.
SECOND MAN: Oh, a hangover, eh?
FIRST MAN: Mmm . . .
SECOND MAN: That's too bad! So, what was the party like?
FIRST MAN: The party was great, thanks very much, but I had far too much to drink.

SECOND MAN: Huh! What were you drinking?

FIRST MAN: Um, I mixed my drinks, actually. I had some beer, some wine, and then some whiskey. I didn't have that much of any of them, though.

SECOND MAN: Ha-ha-ha-ha!

FIRST MAN: Say, haven't you got any advice for somebody with a hangover?

SECOND MAN: Well, you know what you should do is eat four raw eggs and then drink a bottle of warm beer.

FIRST MAN: Thanks very much! I think I'd rather have the hangover!

SECOND MAN: Ha-ha-ha!

### Number 2

WOMAN: Oh, gee! How did you get that black eye?

MAN: Oh! I walked into a lamppost.

WOMAN: Huh! You're kidding!

MAN: What do you think I ought to do about it?

WOMAN: I've heard you should put raw steak on it . . . Yeah, for at least an hour.

MAN: You're kidding?!

WOMAN: Mm-hmm.

### Number 3

WOMAN: [*Sneezes*]

MAN: Oh! What's wrong?

WOMAN: Uuuh! I have hay fever.

MAN: Hay fever? Hmm. You know what you should do? You should take Contac 500. It's a decongestant.

WOMAN: Uuuh, I don't know. Those decongestants make me sleepy.

## 11 LISTENING [p. 78]

Listen to people asking questions and choose the correct responses.

**a)**

WOMAN: Is hot chicken soup good for a cold?

**b)**

MAN: What do you usually take for a sore throat?

**c)**

MAN: Could I have something for a headache?

**d)**

MAN: Can I have a box of Kleenex?

**e)**

MAN: I'd like a large bottle of vitamin C tablets, please.

**f)**

WOMAN: I'm having terrible trouble getting to sleep these days. Are these pills any good for insomnia?

# Review of Units 10–12

## 2 LISTENING [p. 80]

1   Listen to Max and Doris talking about unusual things that happened to them on Saturday. Take notes. Where were they? What happened? What did they do?

DORIS: Hi, Max! How was your dinner party last Saturday?

MAX: Oh, it was *terrible*, Doris!

DORIS: What happened?

MAX: Well, I went out around five P.M. . . . And then I came home and . . . I couldn't get in because I forgot my keys!

DORIS: So what did you do?

MAX: Well, I broke a window and climbed in.

DORIS: Really?

MAX: Yeah. And after I finally got in, I started to cook dinner . . . *fast*. And then around seven o'clock, a few people came. But then, do you know what happened next?

DORIS: No, what?

MAX: My new stove caught on fire!

DORIS: Oh, no!

MAX: It was terrible! So we all went out for a pizza. So enough about me . . . How was your weekend?

DORIS: Well, I had trouble Saturday, too. I was just walking downtown, doing a little shopping, you know, when suddenly someone ran into me . . .

MAX: Yeah?

DORIS: . . . and he grabbed my handbag!

MAX: Oh, no! What did you do?

DORIS: Well, I shouted, "Thief! Stop him! He stole my bag!" and things like that, but nobody helped me! Oh, it was *awful*, Max.

MAX: Gee, that's too bad. I'm sorry. What did you finally do?

DORIS: Well, I went to the nearest police station. And I filled out forms and described what the thief looked like. But the police haven't caught him yet . . .

MAX: Gee, I guess your weekend was worse than mine. But at least you missed my *terrible* dinner party!

# 13 May I take your order, please?

## 2 CONVERSATION: Reservations [p. 82]

2   Now listen to another call and complete the reservation form.

HOST: [*Phone rings*] Hard Rock Cafe. Can I help you?

MS. PARKER: Yes, I want to make a reservation for Saturday night.

HOST: For *this* Saturday, the sixteenth?

MS. PARKER: That's right.

HOST: And for what time, please?

MS. PARKER: Six-thirty. We need to be at the theater by eight o'clock.

HOST: Oh? Just a moment, please. Hello? I'm very sorry, but we don't have a table available for six-thirty.

MS. PARKER: Oh, no!

HOST: Well, we *could* seat you at seven.

MS. PARKER: Hmm. That won't give us enough time. How about six-forty-five?

HOST: How many are in your party?

MS. PARKER: Four.

HOST: Let me see . . . Six-forty-five . . . Yes, I think we can manage that.

MS. PARKER: Oh, great!

HOST: Now, could I have your name and phone number?

MS. PARKER: It's Parker, P-A-R-K-E-R, and the number's five-four-nine, two-two-three-seven.

HOST: Five-four-nine, two-two-three-seven. All right, Ms. Parker . . . That'll be a party of four for Saturday the sixteenth, at six-forty-five.

MS. PARKER: Right. And one more thing . . . Could I make a special request?

HOST: Yes?

MS. PARKER: Can you guarantee quick service, so that we can get to the theater on time?

HOST: Yes, that's no problem. We have a special pre-theater menu that guarantees quick service.

MS. PARKER: Oh, that's wonderful! Thank you very much.

HOST: You're welcome. We look forward to seeing you this Saturday, Ms. Parker.

MS. PARKER: Yes, and thank you again. Bye.

HOST: Goodbye. [*Hangs up*]

## 7 LISTENING [p. 84]

1 Listen to Tom and Tina ordering in a restaurant. What did each of them order?

WAITER: May I take your order now?

TOM: Yes, I'll have a cup of coffee.

WAITER: Cream and sugar?

TOM: Oh, yes, please.

WAITER: And you?

TINA: I'd like a chicken sandwich. And I'll have some chips . . . uh, oh, you call them french fries here. (Hah!) Uh, right, I'll have some french fries, please.

WAITER: All right. One coffee with cream and sugar and a chicken sandwich with french fries. Uh, anything else?

TINA: Yes, I'd like an iced tea, too, please.

WAITER: One iced tea. Thank you.

TOM: Oh, w . . . wait a minute. What kind of desserts do you have?

WAITER: Well, we have pie, cake, ice cream, chocolate mousse . . .

TOM: Oh, oh, oh! What kind of pie do you have?

WAITER: Today we have apple, cherry, lemon . . .

TOM: Hmm . . . I think I'd like a piece of apple pie with my coffee. How about you, Tina?

TINA: Oh, uh, maybe I'll have a piece later . . . or . . . I'll have some of yours . . . Ha-ha-ha!

WAITER: Then it's one coffee, one apple pie, one chicken sandwich, an order of french fries, and an iced tea. Right?

TOM: Yes, thank you.

TINA: Thanks.

2 Now listen to the rest of the conversation. What happened?

TINA: Oh, here comes our waiter!

TOM: Yeah, I wonder what took so long . . .

WAITER: Whew! Here you are!

TINA: Uh, well, I ordered *french fries* with my chicken sandwich and . . . you brought me . . . ugh! . . . mashed potatoes with gravy.

WAITER: Oh, you ordered french fries?

TINA: Yes!

WAITER: Well, then, OK.

TOM: Uh, excuse me. And could you bring me the apple pie I ordered?

WAITER: What apple pie? Did you order apple pie?

TOM: Uh-huh. Yeah, I did . . . with my coffee. Remember?

WAITER: Really? Gee, how did I forget that?

TINA: Uh, c . . . can I ask you a question?

WAITER: Yeah?

TINA: How long have you been working here as a waiter?

WAITER: Who me? Uh, oh, today is my *first* day. Well, I . . . I'll get your apple pie and the french fries right away. Sorry about that.

TOM: Oh, that's OK.

TINA: Yeah, thanks. Good luck!

# 14 It's the greatest!

## 5 LISTENING: Radio quiz show [p. 90]

Listen to the radio quiz show. Listen to each question and check the correct answer.

HOSTESS: Our contestants this evening are Jack, Jonathan, and Sue. And now, contestants, let's get right to our first question. Question number one: Which is older, the Statue of Liberty or the Eiffel Tower? [*Buzzer*] Jack.

JACK: The Statue of Liberty is older. It was built in 1886 and the Eiffel Tower wasn't built until 1889.

HOSTESS: That's correct! Question number two: Is a seven-forty-seven bigger than the Concorde? [*Buzzer*] Sue.

SUE: Yes, a seven-forty-seven is bigger. It carries up to five hundred people; the Concorde only carries about . . . a hundred passengers.

HOSTESS: That's right! Question number three: Which is heavier, a pound of gold or a pound of butter? [*Buzzer*] Jonathan.

JONATHAN: They both weigh the same.

HOSTESS: That's correct! Question number four: Which is larger, Canada or the U.S.? [*Buzzer*] Jack.

JACK: Uh . . . the U.S. is larger? [*Gong*]

HOSTESS: No, sorry! Canada is larger. Question number five: Which lives longer, a cat or a horse? [*Buzzer*] Sue.

SUE: Horses live longer. They live about twice as long as cats.

HOSTESS: Absolutely right! Question number six: Which is bigger, Moscow or New York? [*Buzzer*] Jack.

JACK: Moscow is bigger. It has more then eight million people and New York has around seven point one million.

HOSTESS: Correct! Question number seven: Which is longer, a mile or a kilometer? [*Buzzer*] Jack.

JACK: A kilometer. [*Gong*]

HOSTESS: No, a mile is longer.

JACK: Oh, shoot!

HOSTESS: Question number eight: Which is smaller, Australia or Brazil? [*Buzzer*] Jonathan.

JONATHAN: Australia is smaller?

HOSTESS: That's right! Question number nine: Which river is longer, the Amazon or the Nile? . . . Nobody knows? Does anybody want to guess? [*Buzzer*] Sue.

SUE: The Amazon? [*Gong*]

HOSTESS: No, it's the Nile.

SUE: Oooh!

HOSTESS: Question number ten: Which is bigger, the Pacific Ocean or the Atlantic? [*Buzzer*] Yes, Jack.

JACK: The Pacific Ocean is bigger. It's about twice the size of the Atlantic Ocean.

HOSTESS: Correct! OK, contestants, the winner is . . .

## 10 LISTENING [p. 92]

Listen to people talking about different places in the world. Circle **T** (true) or **F** (false).

JOHN: OK, Mary, what's your next trivia question on world geography?

MARY: OK, John. What's the largest city in the world?

JOHN: Uh, the largest city . . .? Do you mean the city that has the most people?

MARY: Yeah, that's right. Do you know?

JOHN: Uhmm, is it Seoul?

MARY: No, it isn't Seoul.

JOHN: OK, I give up!

MARY: Shanghai is the biggest city.

JOHN: Oh, Shanghai, of course! OK, what's the world's largest ocean?

MARY: Oh! That's simple! The Atlantic Ocean.

JOHN: Ha-ha! No, you're wrong, Mary. The Pacific Ocean is the largest ocean in the world.

MARY: Oh, no, I didn't know that. OK, my turn again. I've got a hard one for you. Which is the longest river in South America, the Amazon River in Brazil and Peru, the Paraná River in Argentina, or the São Francisco River in Brazil?

JOHN: Uh, the longest river in South America? Well, I've never heard of the other two, so I guess it's the Amazon.

MARY: Right! OK, your turn.

JOHN: OK, which country has the smallest population in the world, Monaco, Luxembourg, or Vatican City?

MARY: Mmm . . . gee, I don't know, John.

JOHN: This'll surprise you. Vatican City has the smallest population in the world . . . only eight hundred people live there!

MARY: Only eight hundred! That's really interesting! OK, now it's my turn again . . .

# 15 What are you doing Friday night?

## 2 LISTENING: Listening to telephone messages [p. 94]

Listen to telephone calls to Mr. Kawachi and Ms. Carson and write down the messages.

RECEPTIONIST: [*Phone rings*] Good afternoon. IBM. May I help you?

MRS. SATO: Hello. I want to speak to Mr. Kawachi, please.

RECEPTIONIST: I'm sorry. Mr. Kawachi is in a meeting right now. Would you like to leave a message?

MRS. SATO: Yes, please. This is Mrs. Sato . . . of City Car Center . . .

RECEPTIONIST: Mrs. Sato of City Car Center . . .

MRS. SATO: Please ask him to call me before three-thirty this afternoon. It's very important.

RECEPTIONIST: All right. And your number, please?

MRS. SATO: Five-five-four, three-two-nine-zero.

RECEPTIONIST: Five-five-four, three-two-nine-oh.

MRS. SATO: Yes.

RECEPTIONIST: I'll give Mr. Kawachi your message, Mrs. Sato.

MRS. SATO: Thank you. Goodbye.

RECEPTIONIST: Goodbye. [*Hangs up*]

RECEPTIONIST: [*Phone rings*] This is Software Systems. Good morning.

SANDY: Good morning. May I speak to Ms. Carson, please?

RECEPTIONIST: Mmm . . . Do you mean Mrs. Carter?

SANDY: No, Carson, Ms. Wendy Carson. She's new there.

RECEPTIONIST: Let me check. Oh, yes, I'll ring her . . . I'm sorry. There's no answer. May I take a message?

SANDY: Yes. Would you please ask her to call Sandy at the First National Bank . . .

RECEPTIONIST: Sandy . . . at the First National Bank . . .

SANDY: The number is four-six-two, one-one-eight-seven, extension three-one-three.

RECEPTIONIST: Four-six-two, eleven eighty-seven . . . extension three-one-three.

SANDY: That's right.

RECEPTIONIST: OK. I'll give her the message.

SANDY: Thanks so much. Goodbye.

RECEPTIONIST: Goodbye. [*Hangs up*]

## 6 CONVERSATION: Inviting someone out [p. 96]

2 Listen to the rest of the conversation. What musical are they seeing? What time are they meeting? Where are they meeting? What are they doing before the musical?

TONY: So, Anna, what musical do you want to see? There's *A Chorus Line* . . .

ANNA: Well, I've already seen that.

TONY: OK, then, would you like to see *Cats*? It's at the Plaza Theater.

ANNA: I'd love to see *Cats*! What time is the show?

TONY: Well, it starts at eight. Maybe we can have a pizza before it starts.

ANNA: Terrific!

TONY: Shall I pick you up at your house?

ANNA: Well, I'll be in the city on Saturday afternoon, so let's meet there.

TONY: OK, do you want to meet in front of the Pizza Hut on State Street? At a quarter to seven?

ANNA: OK, great. See you Saturday.

## 11 LISTENING [p. 99]

Listen to people talking. Are they giving an invitation or are they just being friendly?

**a)**

WOMAN: There's a great movie on TV tonight. Would you like to come over and watch it?

**b)**

MAN: Hey! It was nice to see you again. Let's get together again soon.

**c)**

WOMAN: I'd like you to meet my husband. You must come over for dinner sometime.

**d)**

MAN: I'm having friends over on Sunday night. Would you like to join us for dinner?

**e)**

WOMAN: Are you doing anything tomorrow afternoon? Would you like to go downtown?

**f)**

MAN: Well, it's been great talking to you. We must do this more often.

# Review of Units 13–15

## 2 LISTENING [p. 100]

Listen and check the best responses.

**a)**

MAN: Could I have a table for two, please?

**b)**

WOMAN: Can I get you anything to drink?

**c)**

WOMAN: What would you like to eat?

**d)**

MAN: What kind of dressing would you like?

**e)**

WOMAN: What vegetable will you have?

**f)**

MAN: Would you like dessert?

**g)**

MAN: Thanks for dinner. It was delicious.

**h)**

WOMAN: Bye now. Take care.

## 4 LISTENING [p. 101]

Listen to radio commercials for three used car dealers and complete the information below.

**Commercial number 1**

WOMAN: Announcing the biggest sale of the year at Ajax Motors, your friendly car dealer! Come and visit us today. We have over five hundred used cars to choose from. We have them all, Cadillacs, Toyotas, Fords. You name it, we have it! And compare our prices: We have cars priced from five hundred dollars and up. Yes! I said five hundred dollars! And we'll make it easy for you with only five percent financing. Yes, that's right! I said only five percent! So why not drive out and see for yourself? We're only twenty-five minutes from downtown. Come and talk to us today at Ajax Motors, the place for a friendly deal.

**Commercial number 2**

MAN: Here's a name you can _really_ trust in used cars: Nixon! The biggest used car dealer in town! We have over one thousand cars in our lot today. And . . . they are all in excellent condition. All our cars are at prices you can afford, with some as low as only eight hundred dollars! And you can't find better financing anywhere – only eight percent financing on any car you choose. So come on by and have a look today! We're easy to find. We're downtown on Ford Street. Hurry down today while these prices last! And get the best car deal in town . . . a Nixon deal!

**Commercial number 3**

WOMAN: Did you know Bob's Used Cars is having another sale?

MAN: Oh, great! Tell me more about it.

WOMAN: Well, Bob's has over four hundred cars today.

MAN: Is that right? Over four hundred cars? But what about their prices?

WOMAN: Their prices are great! I've seen cars at Bob's that look brand new and they're only a thousand dollars!

MAN: A thousand dollars! But what about financing? I suppose I'll have to pay ten percent or more.

WOMAN: No, that's the best part about it. They have no financing charges!

MAN: Did you say _no_ financing charges?

WOMAN: That's right.

MAN: Well, where is it?

WOMAN: It's only ten minutes from downtown at 2950 Pacific Drive.

MAN: Hey, excuse me. I'm going right now! [_Sound of car speeding off_]

# Tests

The following sets of five tests may be used to assess students' mastery of the material presented in Book 1. Each test covers three units. Not only will these tests allow you to determine how successfully the students have mastered the material, but the tests will also give the students a sense of accomplishment. For general information about these tests and about testing, see "Testing Students' Progress" on page 7.

**When to give a test**

■ Give the appropriate test after Ss complete each cycle of three units and the accompanying review unit in the Student Book.

**Before giving a test**

■ Photocopy the test for the Ss to take in class.

■ Schedule a class period of about 45 minutes to one hour for each test.

■ Locate the taped passage for the test listening section on the Class Cassette. The tests are at the end of the cassette set (side 4).

■ Tell the Ss that they are going to have a "pencil and paper" test (i.e., oral production will not be tested) and suggest that they prepare for the test by reviewing the appropriate units. In studying for the test, Ss should pay particular attention to the grammar, conversations, and Word Power exercises. Remind Ss that the test will also contain short listening and reading sections.

**How to give a test**

■ Explain that the point of the test is not to have Ss competing with each other for the highest grade; rather, the test will inform each S (and the teacher) how well the material was learned and what material may need extra review and practice.

■ Hand out one photocopy of the test to each S.

■ Allow about five minutes for the Ss to look through the test first, without answering any of the test items. Make sure Ss understand how to complete each section (e.g., fill in the blank, circle *T* for true or *F* for false, check the correct response). Tell Ss that they should allow the last five minutes of the test time for the listening section at the end of the test.

■ Remind Ss not to use their Student's Books or dictionaries during the test.

■ To help Ss use their time efficiently and to finish on time, write the total time for the test on the board before beginning the test:

45 minutes

■ After the test begins, revise the time remaining every five or ten minutes to show Ss how much time is left.

■ Stop Ss after about 40 minutes for the listening section of the test.

■ Play the tape twice. Ss only listen the first time, and then listen and mark their answers during the second playing.

■ Alternatively, if you do not wish to use the class time for the test, tell Ss to complete everything at home except the last section (i.e., the listening test item). Remind them to complete the test at home in 40 minutes and not to use the Student's Book or dictionary. In class, play the taped section and then score the tests.

**How to score a test**

■ Either collect the tests and use the Answer Keys to score them, or go over the test with the class. Alternatively, tell the Ss to exchange tests and correct each other's answers as you read the answers aloud.

■ Each test is worth a total of 100 points. If you wish to give a grade, use this scoring system:

90–100 points  =  A or Excellent
 80–89 points  =  B or Very Good
 70–79 points  =  C or Fair
  69 or below  =  Need to review the units

# Test 1: Units 1-3

1. Fill in the missing words with **am, is,** or **are.**

John and I _____ from Australia. John _____ from Sydney, and I _____ from Melbourne.
He _____ twenty, and I _____ nineteen. We _____ students. John _____ a graduate
student in Japanese. I _____ studying architecture. We _____ in the U.S. on vacation. We
_____ visiting John's sister. She _____ a teacher in Portland. Her husband _____ a chef.
They _____ very nice, and Portland _____ a great city. I love it here, and the food _____
good, too.

2. Complete the questions or answers. Use the correct form of **be.**

a)  A: Is this your bag?
    B: Yes, _____

b)  A: _____?
    B: Yes, Mr. West is a writer.

c)  A: Are you in English 202?
    B: No, _____

d)  A: _____?
    B: No, Mr. and Mrs. Simpson aren't Canadian. They are American.

e)  A: Is Ms. Lopez in your class?
    B: No, _____

f)  A: _____?
    B: Yes, that's John's book.

3. Fill in the missing prepositions with **at, for, from, in,** or **to.**

a)  Pierre and Marie are Canadian. They are _____ New Brunswick. They work _____ a
    hospital.

b)  Miami is _____ Florida. It's about 175 miles _____ Cuba.

c)  Do you work _____ General Motors or _____ Toyota?

d)  I work _____ a department store. I'm _____ the toy department.

e)  Celia is _____ my Spanish class. She is _____ Seattle.

f)  Where do you go _____ school? Are you _____ UCLA?

4. Write suitable responses for these expressions.

a) Nice to meet you. _____

b) What do you do? _____

c) How are you doing? _____

d) Thank you very much. _____

e) Have a nice evening. _____

f) See you tomorrow. _____

5. Circle the incorrect word in each passage. Write the correct word or words in the blank.

a) I am a clerk. I work in a restaurant. I serve the meals. The restaurant is on Elm.

_____

b) My name is Cathy Brooks. I am from Houston, Texas. My address is 348-7630.

_____

c) Nice to meet you, Mrs. Kennedy. And what is your family name again, please? Is it Jane or Jean?

_____

d) I work for Pacific Travel. I am a receptionist. I take people on tours.

_____

6. Complete these questions.

a) A: What _____ name?          B: My name is Gloria Santos.

b) A: Where _____ from?          B: I'm from Chile.

c) A: Where _____ from?          B: Keiko and Noriko are from Japan.

d) A: What _____ name?          B: His name is Bob Jones.

e) A: Where _____ work?          B: I work in a restaurant.

f) A: What _____?          B: I'm a cashier.

g) A: Where _____ to school?          B: I go to UC–Berkeley.

h) A: What _____ phone number?          B: My number is 971-3422.

7. Circle the correct answers.

a) What's Mrs. Sato's first name?   (Her / She / His) name's Naomi.

b) Where are you and your wife from? (They / We / Our) are from Rome.

c) Excuse me. Is this your pen? No, it's not (mine's / my / mine).

d) I think this is Sue's backpack. Yes, that's (her / hers / Sue).

e) These shoes are nice. Yes, (they are / that is / it is).

f) How much is that ring? (It's / Its / That) only $60.

g) How much are these sunglasses? (That is / They are / It's) $25.

8. Read and then circle **T** (true) or **F** (false).

*Names*

In English-speaking countries, many people have three names – a first name, a middle name, and a last or family name (e.g., John Fitzgerald Kennedy). Many people use a short name (Dan for Daniel, Liz for Elizabeth). People use a title (Ms., Mr.) with a first and last name (Ms. Mary Murphy) or with a last name (Ms. Murphy). Many Americans and Canadians use first names at work or at school. In colleges and universities, teachers often call their students by their first names.

a) T F Many people have a middle name in English-speaking countries.

b) T F Dan is a short name for Daniel.

c) T F People use a title with a first name, such as Ms. Mary.

d) T F American and Canadian teachers don't call their students by their first names.

9. Listen to Ken and Rosemary talking. Check (✓) the correct answers. 📼

a) Ken works
   __ in a hotel.
   __ at an airport.
   __ downtown.

b) He works in a
   __ travel office.
   __ bank.
   __ law office.

c) He is a
   __ lawyer.
   __ secretary.
   __ clerk.

d) Their lunch appointment is at
   __ 1:00 on Wednesday.
   __ 12:00 on Thursday.
   __ 1:00 on Thursday.

e) His office phone number is
   __ 503–4650.
   __ 513–4650.
   __ 513–4690.

# Test 2: Units 4-6

1. Complete these sentences with **it, she, her, he, him, they** or **them.**

a)   Cher is my favorite actress. I like _____ a lot. _____ is great.

b)   I don't like music videos. _____ aren't very interesting. Do you like _____ ?

c)   I can't stand the actor Sly Stallone. I think _____ is a terrible actor. Do you like
      _____ ?

d)   "Dallas" is great. _____ is my favorite TV program. Do you watch _____ ?

e)   I love horror films. _____ are great. Do you like _____ ?

f)   I love country music. _____ is terrific! Do you like _____ ?


2. Circle the correct verbs.

A: (Do / Does) you go to school here?

B: No, I (do / don't). I'm on vacation with my family.

A: Really? (Do / Does) you like it here?

B: Yes, I (do / does). But my parents (don't / doesn't) like the weather. It's too hot.

A: Oh. (Do / Does) your parents come here often?

B: Yes, they (do / does).

A: By the way, what (do / does) your parents do?

B: Well, my mother (manage / manages) a restaurant, and my father (work / works) for
   Toshiba.

A: How interesting. And do your parents (speak / speaks) English?

B: Well, my mother (do / does), but my father (don't / doesn't).


3. Put the adverb in the correct place in each sentence.

a)   I have eggs for breakfast.   (always)

b)   Do you eat lunch at the cafeteria?   (every day)

c)   What do you do on Saturday night?   (usually)

d)   I catch the train at 7:15.   (always)

e)   I go to the dentist.   (twice a year)

4. Circle the correct prepositions.

a) There's a jazz concert (on / at / in) Tuesday night (for / to / at) the Town Hall.

b) The movie is (on / in / at) 7:45 (in / on / for) Friday evening.

c) I like to play tennis (for / on / at) my day off.

d) Do you work out (at / in / to) home or (on / to / in) a gym?


5. Circle the correct words to complete each passage.

a) I usually get up at 6 A.M. and eat a big (breakfast / lunch / dinner). I (start / have / get) work at 8 A.M. and finish at 4:30 P.M. After work, I usually go to the gym and (sleep / read / work out).

b) This Saturday, there is a sports (day / time / week) at Kennedy High School. There is swimming and tennis in the (midnight / month / morning). In the afternoon, there is a baseball (sport / game / class) from one to four o'clock. On Saturday night, there is a rock (concert / exercise / game) with a rock band in the school hall. It's at 8 P.M.


6. Complete these questions.

a) What _____ usually _____?
   I always stay home on my day off.

b) Do _____?
   No, I don't drive to school. I take the bus.

c) What _____?
   My favorite day is Sunday.

d) How _____?
   I play tennis every Saturday afternoon.

e) Do _____?
   No, I don't like baseball, but I like football.

f) What kind _____?
   I like swimming, bicycling, and hiking.


7. Answer these questions. Write complete sentences.

*Example:* Who is your favorite singer?  *My favorite singer is Madonna.*

a) What kind of music do you like?  _____

b) What do you think of rock music?  _____

c) What kinds of TV programs do you like?  _____

d) What do you usually do on your day off? _____

e) Do you get much exercise? _____

f) How often do you play sports? _____

g) How many people are in your family? _____


8. Read Rosa's letter to Susan. Circle **T** (true) or **F** (false).

Dear Susan,

Berkeley is an interesting city. I really like it here. There's always
a lot to do. After school, I often go downtown for coffee. I usually
go to my favorite coffee shop and meet friends there. In the
evening, there is always something interesting at the Student
Center, such as a movie, a concert, or a dance.

On Saturday, my friends and I usually take the bus to San
Francisco for the day. San Francisco is a beautiful place. I love
the shops and restaurants, and it's a great city for music and
movies. My friends and I often go to Chinatown for good Chinese
food, and then we see a movie in the afternoon.

On Sunday, I sometimes play tennis with friends from school
or watch a football game. American football is very exciting.

Love,<br>Rosa

a) T F Rosa doesn't like Berkeley.

b) T F She always studies after school.

c) T F She lives in San Francisco.

d) T F She spends the weekend in San Francisco.

e) T F She likes football.


9. Listen to people talking. Circle **T** (true) or **F** (false). 🔳

a) T F John doesn't like music very much.

b) T F The movie is tomorrow night at 7:00.

c) T F Peggy comes from a big family.

d) T F Peter's wife usually cooks dinner.

# Test 3: Units 7–9

1. Complete this story with the past tense (e.g., **did, talked**).

I _____ (have) a fantastic weekend! My friend from college _____ (come) to visit me. On Saturday morning, we _____ (take) a helicopter ride and _____ (see) the city. Then we _____ (walk) to the beach and _____ (eat) lunch at a wonderful seafood restaurant. In the afternoon, we _____ (go) water skiing. It _____ (be) great fun! That night, some friends _____ (come) over, and I _____ (cook) dinner for everybody. On Sunday morning, we _____ (watch) a soccer match on TV. We _____ (see) England play West Germany. My friend _____ (stay) until eight o'clock on Sunday night. We both really _____ (enjoy) our weekend together.

2. Answer these questions. Write complete sentences.

a)  What did you do on Saturday?  _____

_____

b)  Where did you go on Sunday?  _____

_____

c)  What did you wear yesterday?  _____

_____

d)  What did you do last night?  _____

_____

e)  What time did you get up this morning?  _____

_____

f)  Where did you go on your vacation last year?  _____

_____

3. Look at the map and circle the correct prepositions.

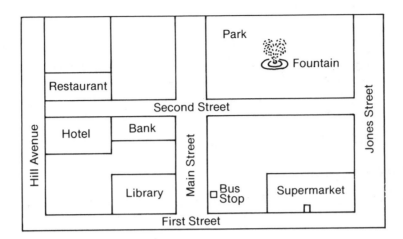

a)  The hotel is (next to / opposite) the bank.

b)  The supermarket is (on / near) First Street.

c)  The fountain is (in / near) the park.

d)  The restaurant is (across from / next to) the hotel.

e)  The bus stop is (opposite / next to) the library.

f)  The library is (near / on) the corner.


4. Circle the correct words.

a)  My sister is (in / on / at) her thirties. She (does / has / is) blond hair, and she (has / is / does) medium height. She (is / has / are) a flight attendant.

b)  My brother (has / is / are) pretty tall, and he (does / is / has) a beard and a moustache. He (is / has / are) his own business.


5. Circle three incorrect words in each passage. Then write the correct words in the blanks.

a)  On Saturday, I always take my clothes to the drugstore and wash them. After that I go to the library and borrow a bed for the weekend. Then I go to the market and buy medicine for the week.

_____

_____

_____

b)  My apartment has four bedrooms: a living room, a dining room, a kitchen, and two bathrooms. It's a very small apartment. There's a new stove in the living room. The neighborhood is nice. But there is a school opposite my apartment and it is very quiet sometimes.

_____

_____

_____

6. Use the map and write complete answers.

*Example:* Is there a police station near here?

*Yes, there's one on Fox Street near the post office.*

a)  Is there a bank near here?

_____

b)  Are there any hotels near the school?

_____

c)  Are there any shops in this neighborhood?

_____

d)  Is there a grocery store around here?

_____

e)  Are there any coffee shops near here?

_____

f)  Is there a pay phone nearby?

_____

7. Complete the passage using the present continuous (e.g., **is playing, are playing**).

I am looking out my window. Some children _____ (play) in the park opposite

my house. A man and a woman _____ (sit) on the grass. The man

_____ (eat) a hamburger, and the woman _____ (drink) a

soda. An old man _____ (walk) his dog on the street. Some construction

workers _____ (work) on the road. They _____ (dig) a big

hole in the road. One of the workmen _____ (wear) a helmet. Two of them

_____ (wear) gloves. A police officer _____ (talk) to two

boys on a motorcycle. The boys _____ (answer) the police officer's questions.

8. The police are looking for two people. Read the descriptions and check (✓) the correct people.

"The man was very tall. He was in his twenties. He had long dark hair and a moustache. He was wearing glasses. He was wearing a long black coat and jeans. He was carrying a small suitcase."

"The woman was short and in her forties. She had curly blond hair. She was wearing a cap, a white T-shirt, and dark pants. She wasn't wearing glasses. She was carrying a camera."

9. Listen to people talking and check (✓) the correct information. 📼

a) __ She went to the baseball game.

__ She went out.

__ She stayed home

b) __ He lives with his parents.

__ He lives in a dormitory near the school.

__ He has an apartment with a friend.

c) __ She is short and in her thirties.

__ She is medium height and in her twenties.

__ She is fairly short and in her twenties.

d) __ He liked the people and the hotels.

__ He liked the people, but he didn't like the hotels.

__ He didn't like the people, but he liked the hotels.

e) __ The Italian restaurant is near the school.

__ The good restaurants are near the school.

__ There are no good restaurants near the school.

# Test 4: Units 10–12

## 1. Complete the questions or answers. Use the present perfect.

*Example:* A: _Have you been to San Diego?_
    B: No, I haven't been to San Diego.

a) A: Has Carol's brother arrived?

   B: Yes, _____.

b) A: _____?
   B: No, the movie hasn't started.

c) A: Have the children eaten?

   B: Yes, _____.

d) A: _____?
   B: No, I have never studied French.

e) A: Has your mother called you today?

   B: No, _____.

## 2. Circle the correct word.

a) a (box / tube) of matches

b) a (bottle / jar) of soda

c) a (tube / jar) of jam

d) a (box / package) of gum

e) a (can / tube) of hairspray

## 3. Check (✓) if these sentences need **a** or **an**. Then write **a** or **an** in the correct place.

a) ___ Los Angeles is very exciting city.

b) ___ Food is cheap in my hometown.

c) ___ Mexico is great place for a vacation.

d) __ Toronto is cold in the winter.

e) __ The Peninsula Hotel is expensive place to stay.

f) __ Paris is very beautiful city.

g) __ Washington, D.C., is crowded in the summer.

h) __ My hometown is not interesting place to visit.

4. Circle the incorrect word in each passage. Then write the correct word in the blank.

a) I feel terrible today. I have the flu and a bad headache. I should get some lotion from the drugstore for it.      _____

b) I have a really bad cold. I have a bad cough and my knee hurts when I eat.      _____

c) I picked up a heavy suitcase yesterday, and now I have a terrible backache. I should go to the dentist today.      _____

d) I should get some glasses. When I read, I get a bad headache, and my ears are always red and sore.      _____

e) I should see the doctor about my hand. It's really sore when I walk or run. And when I'm wearing shoes it's terrible.      _____

5. Check (✓) the correct response.

a) A: I feel terrible today.
   B: __ Oh, that's too bad.   __ Gee, that's great.   __ Here you are.

b) A: Gee, what's the matter?
   B: __ All right.   __ I have a toothache.   __ Try this lotion.

c) A: What's your class like?
   B: __ No, I hate it.   __ Yes, I do.   __ It's pretty interesting.

d) A: I forgot Bob's birthday party.
   B: __ How interesting!   __ That was lucky!   __ How embarrassing!

e) A: Does Paris have nice weather in the fall?
   B: __ Yes, it is.   __ It's not bad.   __ Yes, thanks.

6. Answer these questions. Use complete sentences.

a) What's your hometown like?   _____

b) What's the weather like in the winter?   _____

c) What's the best time to visit?   _____

d)   Are there any museums?   _____

e)   What places should a visitor see?   _____

f)   What's shopping like there?   _____

g)   Is it an interesting place?   _____


## 7.  Choose the correct adjectives.

a)   Bill's car is never clean. Why does he drive a _____ car?
     (boring / dirty / noisy)

b)   It's not safe to walk around this neighborhood at night. The streets are very

     _____ .   (interesting / quiet / dangerous)

c)   It's not cheap to stay at the Plaza Hotel. The rooms are very _____ .
     (small / old / expensive)

d)   Rome is not a modern city. The buildings are very _____ .
     (old / noisy / boring)

e)   The movie was not interesting. I thought it was very _____ , and I left after
     thirty minutes.   (exciting / beautiful / boring)

f)   Washington state is very wet in the winter. It's not _____ like Texas.
     (dry / cold / clean)


## 8.  Read Sue's composition and circle **T** (true) or **F** (false).

*Mexico*

One of my favorite places for a vacation is Mexico. I really like
the climate because it never gets cold there. The people are very
nice, too. They never laugh at my bad Spanish! And the food is
wonderful.

Mexico City is a very interesting place to visit. It has some great
museums and lots of fascinating old buildings. And the hotels are
not expensive. But you shouldn't stay only in Mexico City. You
should also go to some of the beach resorts, like Acapulco. And
you shouldn't miss the Mayan temples near Mérida.

a)   T   F   Sue's Spanish is very good.

b)   T   F   She likes warm weather.

c)   T   F   She thinks there is lots to see and do in Mexico.

d)   T   F   The hotels in Mexico City are pretty expensive.

e)   T   F   The Mayan temples are in Mexico City.

9. Listen to people talking. Circle **T** (true) or **F** (false). 🔲

a)  T  F  Bob and his friends went to the party.
   T  F  The party was pretty boring.

b)  T  F  He doesn't usually get bad backaches.
   T  F  He hasn't done anything for it.

c)  T  F  It's not a very nice place.
   T  F  You shouldn't go there in the winter.

# Test 5: Units 13–15

## 1. Circle the correct word.

a) What (would / will) you like to eat?

b) I (will / would) have chocolate ice cream, please.

c) What kind of dressing (would / will) you like?

d) (Will / May) I take your order?

e) (Would / Will) you like anything else?

f) (Will / Could) I have your name, please?


## 2. Check (✓) the correct response.

a) Good night. Drive carefully.

— I'm glad you enjoyed it.

— See you soon.

— I'd love to.

b) Thank you for a lovely evening.

— I'm glad you enjoyed it.

— That sounds good.

— Thanks. I'd like to.

c) Thanks for a wonderful dinner.

— Sure. I'd love to.

— You too.

— You're welcome.

d) Do you want to go to the play?

— No, I'm not doing anything.

— I'm sorry, I can't.

— You're very welcome.


## 3. Circle the correct word.

a) There are lots of beautiful trees in the (pond / forest / volcano).

b) A (desert / continent / hill) is a very hot and dry place.

c) I always swim in the (waterfall / countryside / ocean) because I don't like swimming in a pool.

d) Take that little (lake / path / mountain) over there. It goes to the beach.

e) Spain is my favorite (climate / country / countryside). The weather and the food are great there.


## 4. Complete these sentences with the comparative form of the adjective (e.g., **smaller, more exciting**).

a) Is Rio _____ (crowded) than Buenos Aires?

b) Which is _____ (cheap), a Cadillac or a Mercedes?

c) Are apartments in Tokyo _____ (expensive) than in Los Angeles?

d) California is _____ (large) than France.

e) The weather here is _____ (nice) in the summer.

f) Is your French class _____ (interesting) than your Spanish class?

5. Circle the correct word or phrase.

a) Please (tell / to tell) Mary there's a school party on Saturday.

b) Would you ask John (phone / to phone) me?

c) Please (ask / tell) Bill the meeting is on Thursday.

d) Would you like (leave / to leave) a message?

e) Could you (tell / ask) her the movie starts at eight?

6. Use the present continuous to complete these questions (e.g., What **is** she **doing** tonight?).

a) A: Are _____ on Sunday afternoon?
   B: No, I'm not doing anything.

b) A: Where _____ on vacation?
   B: My parents are going to Europe.

c) A: Is _____ to the barbecue?
   B: Yes, my sister is coming.

d) A: When _____ this week?
   B: I'm playing tennis on Friday morning.

e) A: What kind of food _____ for dinner tonight?
   B: He's cooking Chinese food.

7. Write a request for each sentence. Use your classmates' names.

a) The test on Thursday is at 1:00 P.M.

   Please tell Maria _____.

b) Meet me after class today.

   Would you ask _____?

c) There's a meeting tonight at six.

Could you tell _____?

d) Come to the meeting on Saturday.

Please ask _____.

e) The telephone isn't working.

Would you tell _____?

f) Phone me tonight at seven o'clock.

Could you ask _____?

8. Complete each conversation with a question or a statement.

a) A: _____?
   B: Yes, I'd like some coffee, please.

b) A: _____.
   B: I'm glad you enjoyed the meal. Please come again.

c) A: _____?
   B: I think San Francisco is more interesting. I don't like L.A.

d) A: _____?
   B: No, Africa is not the biggest continent in the world. The biggest continent is Asia.

e) A: _____?
   B: I'm sorry, Ms. Clark is not in. Can I take a message?

9. Read Joanna's restaurant reviews. Circle **T** (true) or **F** (false).

This week I tried two new restaurants – Michelle's and Anton's.
They are both French restaurants downtown. Michelle's is a
small place with about twenty tables. The waiters and waitresses
are very friendly, and the service is excellent. I ordered chicken
with orange sauce, with rice and a salad. Then I had chocolate
cake and coffee. The chicken was delicious, but the cake was very
dry. The meal cost twenty dollars.

Anton's is a much bigger restaurant, and it was very crowded. I
waited twenty minutes for a table. Anton's is noisier than
Michelle's. The waiter was very slow with my meal. I ordered
soup and a steak with fried potatoes and vegetables. The soup
wasn't very hot. The steak was OK, but the vegetables weren't
very good. For dessert, I had ice cream. The meal was expensive –
forty-five dollars. I would go to Michelle's again, but not to
Anton's.

a)  T  F  Michelle's is smaller than Anton's.

b)  T  F  Joanna didn't have dessert at Michelle's.

c)  T  F  She liked Michelle's.

d)  T  F  The service was very good at Anton's.

e)  T  F  She thought the meal was excellent at Anton's.

f)  T  F  Anton's is more expensive than Michelle's.

10.  Listening  ▭

a)  Listen to a waiter take an order in a restaurant. Fill in the restaurant check.

**RESTAURANT CHECK**

1 ...........................................

1 large order of

...........................................

to drink:...........................

...........................................

b)  Listen to this telephone conversation. Complete the message form.

*Message*

*Donna called*

*The* ...........................

*is on* ........................... *at* ...........

*It's in* ...........................

*Bring your* ...........................

...........................................

# Tape Transcripts for Tests

## Test 1: Units 1–3

9  Listen to Ken and Rosemary talking. Check the correct answers.

ROSEMARY:  So what do you do now, Ken? Are you still working at the Hilton Hotel?
KEN:  No, I'm not. Now I'm working in an office downtown.
ROSEMARY:  Oh, really?
KEN:  Yes, I work for Smith and Thomas. It's a law office on King Street.
ROSEMARY:  And what do you do there?
KEN:  Well, I'm a secretary for a lawyer.
ROSEMARY:  Oh, that sounds interesting. By the way, let's have lunch this week.
KEN:  Sure. How about Wednesday? Are you free on Wednesday?
ROSEMARY:  No, I'm not, but Thursday is OK with me. How about you?
KEN:  Yes, that's fine.
ROSEMARY:  Is twelve o'clock OK?
KEN:  Mmm . . . yeah, that's fine.
ROSEMARY:  By the way, what's your office telephone number?
KEN:  It's five-one-three, four-six-nine-oh.
ROSEMARY:  Five-one-three, four-six-nine-oh. OK. See you on Thursday. Bye!
KEN:  Bye!

## Test 2: Units 4–6

9  Listen to people talking. Circle **T** for true and **F** for false.

**a)**
WOMAN:  What kind of music do you like, John? Do you like classical music?
JOHN:  Well, I don't like classical music very much, but I really like rock music.
WOMAN:  Really? Who's your favorite singer?
JOHN:  Well, I like Madonna a lot.

**b)**
FIRST WOMAN:  What time is the movie tonight? Is it at six-thirty or seven?
SECOND WOMAN:  Oh, it's at seven o'clock. But it's not tonight! It's tomorrow night!

**c)**
MAN:  So tell me about your family, Peggy. How many brothers and sisters do you have?
PEGGY:  Well, I have four sisters – Mary, Liz, Debbie, and Sue.
MAN:  Oh, that's nice! And do you have any brothers?
PEGGY:  Yes, I have four brothers – Dick, Ted, Sam, and Harry.

**d)**
WOMAN:  What time do you usually get home, Peter?
PETER:  Oh, about six o'clock.
WOMAN:  And do you have dinner at home?
PETER:  Yes, I love to cook. I usually cook dinner for my wife and me. My wife works at the hospital and she doesn't usually get home until eight o'clock.
WOMAN:  Uh-huh.
PETER:  We usually have dinner around eight or eight-thirty.

## Test 3: Units 7–9

9  Listen to people talking and check the correct information.

**a)**
MAN:  How was your weekend? Did you go to the baseball game on Sunday or did you stay home?
WOMAN:  I didn't go to the game, but I had a good time anyway. I went out for lunch with my sister. Then we went to her house and watched a video.

**b)**
WOMAN:  Are you still living in the dormitory or did you move to an apartment with your friend?
MAN:  No, I didn't move to an apartment because my friend got married. So, guess what! I'm living with mom and dad. (Hah!) It's great! And my mom's such a good cook, you know.

**c)**
FIRST MAN:  Hey, I think I just saw the new manager, Ms. Collins! Is she pretty short, and is she about twenty-five?
SECOND MAN:  Well, mmm, she is fairly short, and she's about twenty-five, I guess. She's really nice!

**d)**
WOMAN:  Did you enjoy your trip to Europe?
MAN:  Well, yes and no. Everyone I met was very friendly. But the hotels were not so good. They were very expensive and the rooms were very small.

**e)**
MAN:  Are there any good restaurants near the school?
WOMAN:  No, there aren't. But there are some good ones downtown. My favorite is an Italian restaurant called Luigi's.

## Test 4: Units 10–12

9  Listen to people talking. Circle **T** for true or **F** for false.

**a)**
WOMAN:  Why didn't you come to the party, Bob?
BOB:  Oh, some friends came to visit me and they didn't leave until eleven P.M.
WOMAN:  Oh, really? Well, it was a great party. The music was terrific and the food was good, too!

**b)**

DOCTOR: Have you ever had a backache like this before, Mr. Brown?

PATIENT: No, I haven't doctor. I get a lot of exercise and I play lots of sports, but I've never had such a terrible backache like this one.

DOCTOR: Uh-huh, I see. Have you tried anything for it?

PATIENT: I took some aspirin, but it didn't help.

DOCTOR: Well, let's have a look at it.

PATIENT: OK.

**c)**

MAN: What's your hometown like?

WOMAN: It's a great little place! It has a very beautiful beach. And the restaurants are pretty good, and the shopping is, too.

MAN: And what's the weather like there?

WOMAN: Well, I don't like the winter very much. It's cold and wet every day. But the spring and summer are great! The weather is really nice then.

# Test 5: Units 13–15

**10**

a) Listen to a waiter take an order in a restaurant. Fill in the restaurant check.

WAITER: What would you like to eat? How about a hot dog or a hamburger? They're very good here.

CUSTOMER: That sounds good. I think I'll have a hot dog.

WAITER: Would you like french fries with that?

CUSTOMER: Yes, please. Give me a large order of french fries.

b) Listen to this telephone conversation. Complete the message form.

MAN: Hello?

DONNA: Hello. Could I speak to David, please?

MAN: Sorry. He's out. Would you like to leave a message?

DONNA: Yes. This is Donna. I'm calling about the meeting. Would you tell him the meeting's on Friday evening at eight o'clock?

MAN: Sure.

DONNA: It's in room two-five-one.

MAN: Room two-five-one, mm-hmm.

DONNA: And please ask him to bring his cassette recorder.

MAN: OK, I'll give him the message.

# Test Answer Keys

## Answers to Test 1

**1.**
are; is; am; is; am; are; is; am; are; are; is; is; are; is; is.
$$[15 \times 1 = 15]$$

**2.**
a)  B: Yes, <u>it is</u>.
b)  A: Is Mr. <u>West</u> a writer?
c)  B: No, <u>I'm not</u>.
d)  A: Are <u>Mr.</u> and Mrs. Simpson Canadian?
e)  B: No, <u>she isn't</u>.
f)  A: Is that <u>John's</u> book? (*or* Is this John's book?)
$$[6 \times 2 = 12]$$

**3.**
a)  from; in (*or* at)      d)  in (*or* at); in
b)  in; from               e)  in; from
c)  for (*or* at); for (*or* at)    f)  to; at
$$[12 \times 1 = 12]$$

**4.**
Any logical and grammatically correct answer is acceptable. Suggested answers:
a)  Nice to meet you, too.
b)  I'm a student. (*or* I'm a salesclerk.)
c)  Fine, thanks. (*or* Not bad, thanks.)
d)  You're welcome.
e)  Thanks. You, too!
f)  See you. Take it easy. (*or* Yeah, bye!)
$$[6 \times 2 = 12]$$

**5.**
a)  *incorrect:* clerk; *correct:* waiter (*or* waitress)
b)  *incorrect:* address; *correct:* phone number (*or* number)
c)  *incorrect:* family; *correct:* first
d)  *incorrect:* receptionist; *correct:* tour guide
$$[14 \times 2 = 8]$$

**6.**
a)  What <u>is</u> your name?
b)  Where <u>are</u> you from?
c)  Where <u>are</u> <u>Keiko</u> and <u>Noriko</u> from?
d)  What <u>is</u> <u>his</u> name?
e)  Where <u>do you</u> work?
f)  What <u>do you</u> do?
g)  Where <u>do you go</u> to school?
h)  What <u>is</u> your phone number?
$$[8 \times 2 = 16]$$

**7.**
a)  Her        d)  hers       f)  It's
b)  We         e)  they are   g)  They are
c)  mine
$$[7 \times 1 = 7]$$

**8.**
a) T      b) T      c) F      d) F
$$[4 \times 2 = 8]$$

**9**
a) downtown      b) law office      c) secretary
d) 12:00 on Thursday      e) 513-4690
$$[5 \times 2 = 10]$$

## Test 2

**1.**
a)  her; She      c)  he; him      e)  They; them
b)  They; them    d)  It; it       f)  It; it
$$[6 \times 2 = 12]$$

**2.**
A: Do you go to school here?
B: <u>No</u>, I <u>don't</u>. I'm on vacation with my family.
A: Really? <u>Do</u> you like it here?
B: Yes, I <u>do</u>. But my parents <u>don't</u> like the weather. It's too <u>hot</u>.
A: Oh. <u>Do</u> your parents come here often?
B: Yes, <u>they</u> <u>do</u>.
A: By the way, what <u>do</u> your parents do?
B: Well, my mother <u>manages</u> a restaurant, and my father <u>works</u> for Toshiba.
A: How interesting. And do your parents <u>speak</u> English?
B: Well, my mother <u>does</u>, but my father <u>doesn't</u>.
$$[13 \times 1 = 13]$$

**3.**
a)  I <u>always</u> have eggs for breakfast.
b)  Do you eat lunch at the cafeteria <u>every</u> <u>day</u>?
c)  What do you <u>usually</u> do on Saturday night?
d)  I <u>always</u> catch the train at 7:15.
e)  I go to the dentist <u>twice</u> <u>a</u> <u>year</u>
$$[5 \times 2 = 10]$$

**4.**
a)  on; at      b)  at; on      c)  on      d)  at; in
$$[7 \times 1 = 7]$$

**5.**
a)  breakfast; start; work out
b)  day; morning; game; concert
$$[7 \times 2 = 14]$$

**6.**
a)  What <u>do you</u> usually <u>do on</u> your <u>day off</u>?
b)  Do <u>you</u> <u>drive</u> to <u>school</u>?
c)  What <u>is</u> your <u>favorite</u> <u>day</u>?
d)  How <u>often do you play</u> <u>tennis</u>?
e)  Do <u>you like</u> <u>baseball</u>?
f)  What <u>kind of</u> <u>sports</u> <u>do you</u> <u>like</u>?
$$[6 \times 2 = 12]$$

**7.**
Any logical and grammatically correct sentence is acceptable. Suggested answers:
a)  I like pop music.

b)   Well, I don't like it very much. (*or* It's OK.)
c)   I like game shows and news programs.
d)   Well, I always get up early. (*or* Nothing much. I often sleep until noon.)
e)   Yes, I do. (*or* No, I don't.)
f)   I play sports twice a week. (*or* I don't play sports very much.)
g)   There are five in my family. (*or* There are four in my family. We have two daughters.)

**[7 × 2 = 14]**

**8.**
a) F     b) F     c) F     d) F     e) T

**[5 × 2 = 10]**

**9.**
a) F     b) T     c) T     d) F

**[4 × 2 = 8]**

# Test 3

**1.**
had;   came;   took;   saw;   walked;   ate;   went;   was;   came;   cooked;   watched;   saw;   stayed;   enjoyed

**[14 × 1 = 14]**

**2.**
Any logical and grammatically correct sentence is acceptable. Suggested answers:
a)   I watched the ballgame.
b)   I went to a disco.
c)   I wore jeans and a sweater.
d)   I stayed home and studied.
e)   I got up at 6:30. (*or* I got up very early.)
f)   I went to Europe.

**[6 × 2 = 12]**

**3.**
a)   next to     c)   in          e)   opposite
b)   on          d)   across from  f)   on

**[6 × 2 = 12]**

**4.**
a)   in; has; is; is     b)   is; has; has

**[7 × 1 = 7]**

**5.**
Any logical answer is acceptable. Suggested answers:
a)   *incorrect:* drugstore; *correct:* laundromat
     *incorrect:* bed; *correct:* book
     *incorrect:* medicine; *correct:* food
b)   *incorrect:* small; *correct:* large
     *incorrect:* living room; *correct:* kitchen
     *incorrect:* quiet; *correct:* noisy

**[6 × 2 = 12]**

**6.**
Any logical and grammatically correct sentence is acceptable. Suggested answers:
a)   Yes, there's one on the corner of Elm and Fox.
b)   No, there aren't.
c)   Yes, there are some (shops) on Fox Street.
d)   No, there isn't.
e)   Yes, there's one on Maple Avenue.
f)   Yes, there's one near the bank on Elm.

**[6 × 2 = 12]**

**7.**
are playing;   are sitting;   is eating;   is drinking;   is walking;   are working;   are digging;   is wearing;   are wearing;   is talking;   are answering

**[11 × 1 = 11]**

**8.**
Man in Picture #1; Woman in Picture #4

**[2 × 5 = 10]**

**9.**
a)   She went out.
b)   He lives with his parents.
c)   She is fairly short and in her twenties.
d)   He liked the people, but he didn't like the hotels.
e)   There are no good restaurants near the school.

**[5 × 2 = 10]**

# Test 4

**1.**
Both short answers and long answers are acceptable.
a)   B: Yes, he has (arrived).
b)   A: Has the movie started (yet)?
c)   B: Yes, they have (eaten). (*or* Yes, the children have eaten.)
d)   A: Have you (ever) studied French?
e)   B: No, she hasn't (called me today). (*or* No, my mother hasn't called me today.)

**[5 × 2 = 10]**

**2.**
a) box     b) bottle     c) jar     d) package     e) can

**[5 × 1 = 5]**

**3.**
a)   ✓   Los Angeles is a very exciting city.
b)   ___  Food is cheap in my hometown.
c)   ✓   Mexico is a great place for a vacation.
d)   ___  Toronto is cold in the winter.
e)   ✓   The Peninsula Hotel is an expensive place to stay.
f)   ✓   Paris is a very beautiful city.
g)   ___  Washington, D.C., is crowded in the summer.
h)   ✓   My hometown is not an interesting place to visit.

**[8 × 2 = 16]**

**4.**
Any logical answer is acceptable. Suggested answers:
a)   *incorrect:* lotion; *correct:* medicine, aspirin, *or* tablets
b)   *incorrect:* knee; *correct:* throat
c)   *incorrect:* dentist; *correct:* doctor
d)   *incorrect:* ears; *correct:* eyes
e)   *incorrect:* hand; *correct:* foot, toe, *or* ankle

**[5 × 2 = 10]**

**5.**
a)   Oh, that's too bad.
b)   I have a toothache.
c)   It's pretty interesting.
d)   How embarrassing!
e)   It's not bad.

**[5 × 2 = 10]**

**6.**
Any logical and grammatically correct sentence is acceptable. Possible answers:
a) It's pretty nice.
b) It's very cold.
c) You should go in the spring.
d) Yes, there are two museums.
e) A visitor should see the zoo.
f) It's terrible.
g) Yes, it's an interesting place.

[7 × 3 = 21]

**7.**
a) dirty          d) old
b) dangerous      e) boring
c) expensive      f) dry

[6 × 1 = 6]

**8.**
a) F    b) T    c) T    d) F    e) F

[5 × 2 = 10]

**9.**
a) F; F    b) T; F    c) F; T

[6 × 2 = 12]

# Test 5

**1.**
a) would    c) would    e) Would
b) will     d) May      f) Could

[6 × 2 = 12]

**2.**
a) See you soon.              c) You're welcome.
b) I'm glad you enjoyed it.   d) I'm sorry, I can't.

[4 × 2 = 8]

**3.**
a) forest    c) ocean    e) country
b) desert    d) path

[5 × 2 = 10]

**4.**
a) more crowded    d) larger
b) cheaper         e) nicer
c) more expensive  f) more interesting

[6 × 1 = 6]

**5.**
a) tell        c) tell      e) tell
b) to phone    d) to leave

[5 × 2 = 10]

**6.**
a) A: Are <u>you</u> <u>doing</u> <u>anything</u> on Sunday afternoon?
b) A: Where <u>are</u> <u>your</u> <u>parents</u> <u>going</u> on vacation?
c) A: Is <u>your</u> <u>sister</u> <u>coming</u> to the barbecue?
d) A: When <u>are</u> <u>you</u> <u>playing</u> tennis this week?
e) A: What <u>kind</u> of <u>food</u> <u>is</u> <u>he</u> <u>cooking</u> for dinner tonight?

[5 × 2 = 10]

**7.**
a) Please tell Maria <u>the test</u> <u>is</u> <u>on</u> <u>Thursday</u> <u>at</u> <u>1:00 P.M.</u>
b) Would you ask <u>(Maria)</u> <u>to</u> <u>meet</u> <u>me</u> <u>after</u> <u>class</u> today?
c) <u>Could</u> you tell <u>(Maria)</u> <u>there's</u> <u>a</u> <u>meeting</u> <u>tonight</u> <u>at six</u>?
d) <u>Please ask</u> <u>(Maria)</u> <u>to</u> <u>come</u> <u>to</u> <u>the</u> <u>meeting</u> <u>on Saturday</u>.
e) Would you tell <u>(Maria)</u> <u>the</u> <u>telephone</u> <u>isn't working</u>?
f) <u>Could</u> you ask <u>(Maria)</u> <u>to</u> <u>phone</u> <u>me</u> <u>tonight</u> <u>at seven o'clock</u>?

[6 × 2 = 12]

**8.**
Any logical and grammatically correct answer is acceptable. Suggested answers:
a) Would you like anything to drink? (*or* Would you like anything else?)
b) The dinner was delicious. (*or* That was a wonderful meal!)
c) Which is more interesting, San Francisco or L.A.? (*or* Which is more interesting, Los Angeles or San Francisco?)
d) Is Africa the biggest continent in the world?
e) May I speak to Ms. Clark, please? (*or* Hello. Could I please speak to Ms. Clark?)

[5 × 2 = 10]

**9.**
a) T    b) F    c) T    d) F    e) F    f) T

[6 × 1 = 6]

**10.**
a) 1 hot dog
   1 <u>large</u> order of <u>french fries</u>
   to drink: <u>water</u>
b) Donna called. The <u>meeting</u> is on <u>Friday (evening)</u> at <u>8 (o'clock)</u>. It's in <u>room 251</u>. Bring your <u>cassette recorder</u>.

[8 × 2 = 16]

# Workbook Answer Key

## 1 Please call me Dave

**1.**
Answers will vary.

**2.**
1. a) F   b) M   c) F   d) M   e) F
   f) M   g) M   h) F   i) M   j) F
2. Bob (g);   Cathy (c);   Jenny (j);   Dave (f);
   Jim (b);   Liz (e);   Maggie (a);   Mike (d);
   Sue (h);   Tom (i)

**3.**
c) Michael Charles Kennedy
e) P. W. C.
d) Smith
b) Cathy
a) Ms. Celia Frances Jones

**4.**
A: Hi! I am Jack Jones. What is your name?
B: I am Marie.
A: And what is your last name?
B: My last name is Dupont.
A: Are you from the United States, Marie?
B: No, I am from Canada.
A: Oh? What city are you from?
B: I am from Montreal.
A: Really? What do you do?
B: I'm a journalist. How about you?
A: I'm an engineer.

**5.**
d) No, I'm not. I'm a high school teacher. And how about you?
e) Oh, really? How interesting!
a) I'm Jane Thomas. Nice to meet you.
b) It's Thomas. Jane Thomas.
c) Washington. But I live in Toronto now.

**6.**
b) lawyer   c) manager   d) doctor   e) teacher
f) clerk   g) engineer   h) secretary

**7.**
a) What is your first name?
b) What is your last name?
c) How do you spell it? (*or* How do you spell your last name?)
d) What do you do?
e) Where is your wife from?
f) What is her name? (*or* What is your wife's name?)

**8.**
a) Their   c) your   e) me
b) Our   d) He   f) Her

**9.**
SA Brazil
SA Chile
A China
AF, ME Egypt

E France
E Italy
E Japan
A, ME Jordan
AF Kenya
A Korea
A, ME Kuwait

AF Nigeria
SA Peru
E Portugal
A, ME Saudi Arabia
E Spain
A Taiwan
A, ME Turkey

Japan – Japanese
Chile – Chilean
China – Chinese
Egypt – Egyptian
France – French
Italy – Italian
Jordan – Jordanian
Kenya – Kenyan
Korea – Korean

Kuwait – Kuwaiti
Nigeria – Nigerian
Peru – Peruvian
Portugal – Portuguese
Saudi Arabia – Saudi Arabian
Spain – Spanish
Taiwan – Taiwanese
Turkey – Turkish

**10.**
a) Are you on vacation?
b) Are you from Spain?
c) Are you staying in a dormitory?
d) Are you in English 101?
e) Is your teacher Mr. Brown?
f) Is Ms. West Australian? (*or* Is she Australian?)

**11.**
a) Oh, hello.
b) Thanks. You, too. Bye!
c) Yes, I am.
d) OK. See you.
e) I'm a student.

## 2 It's a great job!

**1.**
a) salesperson   b) waitress   c) reporter   d) factory worker

**2.**
apartment
Argentina
college
department
factory
hotel
Japanese

Monday
photographer
receptionist
seventy
sixteen
tomorrow
Wednesday

**3.**
A: Where do you work?
A: What do you do there?
A: Where do you live?
B: And what do you do?
B: Where do you go to school?
B: What do you sell?

**4.**
1. a) I'm a driver. I work for a travel company. I drive a bus and I take people on tours.
b) I'm a nurse. I work in a public hospital. I have an interesting job.
c) I'm a waitress. I work in an Italian restaurant. I'm also taking an English course at night.
d) I'm a counselor. I work in an elementary school. It's a great job.
2. Answers will vary.

**5.**
A: Do you still work for the bus company?
B: No. I work at Macy's now. I work in the toy department.

A: I hate my job! I work for the government. I'm in the tax department. It's really boring. How about you?
B: Oh, I work in a gym downtown. I teach aerobics. Come by sometime!

A: Do you work in a high school?
B: No, I work at Honolulu Community College. I teach in the sports department. I teach surfing from nine to five at the beach. It's a tough job!

A: Where do you go to school?
B: I'm studying at City College. I'm in the Asian languages department. I'm majoring in Japanese.

**6.**
a) You're welcome.
b) Pretty good, thanks.
c) That sounds interesting.
d) Oh, really?
e) That's right.

**7.**

|   | ¹S | ²T | A | R | ³T |   |
|---|----|----|---|---|----|---|
|   |    | A  |   |   | Y  |   |
|   | ⁴G |    |   |   |    |   |
| ⁵W | O | R | K |   | P |   |
| R |   | E |   | ⁶G | E | T |
| I |   |   |   |   |   |   |
| T |   | ⁷S | T | ⁸U | D | Y |
| ⁹S | E | R | V | E |   |   |
|   |   | L |   | S |   |   |
|   | ¹⁰H | E | L | P |   |   |

**8.**
Lab Technician. Part-time job for college student majoring in science. $6.50 an hour. Start in July. No experience necessary. Call Dr. Ladd at 879-1005 for an appointment.

Food and beverage manager needed for Mexican restaurant. Work afternoons and evenings. Free meals and good salary. 872-9135.

Full-time salesperson wanted for telephone company. Good English and Spanish needed. Interviews Wednesday, Sept. 23, 9–noon, 321 First St.

# 3 I'm just looking, thanks

**1.**
1. £672;  F1,199;  Ptas2,048,000;  ¥15,750
2. five hundred (and) nineteen pounds
one hundred (and) fourteen thousand (and) sixty-seven francs
one thousand (and) eighty-nine pesetas
twelve thousand (and) three hundred yen

**2.**
1. Answers will vary.
2. Answers will vary.

**3.**
a) bracelet   b) shorts   c) road   d) briefcase
e) notebook

**4.**
A: Excuse me, Mary. Are these socks yours?
B: No, those are not mine. My socks are red.

A: I think that's Jane's new racquet.
B: No, that's not hers.

A: Is this Pat Hill's watch?
B: No, it's not hers.

A: Betty and Jean, are these your bags?
B: Yes, those are ours.

**5.**
a) banks
b) buses
c) cities
d) clerks
e) houses
f) dishes
g) offices
h) secretaries
i) shirts
j) shoes
k) sweaters
l) taxes

**6.**
*Words ending with /z/*
cities
secretaries
shoes
sweaters

*Words ending with /s/*
banks
clerks
shirts

*Words ending with /ɪz/*
buses
houses
dishes
offices
taxes

**7.**
B: Yes, how much is this watch?
B: Oh. How much is that one?
A: It's $220.

A: Excuse me. How much are <u>those</u> shoes?
B: <u>They're</u> on sale for $135.

A: Are <u>these</u> stereos on sale?
B: Yes, <u>they</u> are.
A: And <u>how</u> much is <u>this</u> Sony?
B: <u>It's</u> $350.
A: <u>And</u> how much are <u>these</u> portable stereos?
B: <u>They're</u> only $99 each.

**8.**
1. a) I have a color TV for sale. It's an RCA. It's 6 months old. I'm asking $250 for it.
b) I have a camera for sale. It's a Kodak. It's 4 years old. I'm asking $95 for it.
c) I have two stereo speakers for sale. They are Sonys. They are 2 years old. I'm asking $100 each.
d) I have a car for sale. It's a Volkswagen. It's 20 years old. I'm asking $1,700 for it.
2. Answers will vary.

**9.**
a) Electronic Word Check   b) Friend Finder
c) Currency Converter and Calculator   d) Pocket TV

# 4 What kind of music do you like?

**1.**
Answers will vary.

**2.**
1. a) Now and Then   b) A Question of $1 Million   c) The Best Man Wins
2. a) science fiction film   b) thriller   c) western

**3.**
Answers will vary.

**4.**
A: Let's go <u>to</u> a movie <u>on</u> Friday or Saturday.
B: OK. There's a new <u>T</u>om Cruise movie <u>at</u> the Elmwood Theater.
A: Great! Let's go <u>on</u> Saturday night. What time is the movie?
B: It's <u>at</u> 8 and 10. Would you like to go <u>to</u> dinner before the movie?
A: Sure. There's a new Italian restaurant on Vine Street.
B: All right. Let's meet <u>at</u> the restaurant <u>on</u> Saturday at 6 P.M.
A: <u>O</u>K. And then we'll go <u>to</u> the 8 o'clock show.

**5.**
a) That sounds good.   b) I can't stand them.   c) Great! Let's go and see it.   d) She's terrific.

**6.**
b) There's a Chinese movie at the Century Cinema on Friday, July 22, at 8:00 P.M. The movie is called *Shanghai Story*.
c) There's a Canadian movie at the Star Theater on Saturday, July 23, at 6:30 P.M. The movie is called *Love in Winter*.
d) There's a Japanese movie at the Star Theater on Saturday, July 23, at 8:15 P.M. The movie is called *Autumn Colors*.

e) There's an American movie at the Varsity Theater on Sunday, July 24, at 5:45 P.M. The movie is called *Star Wars*.
f) There's a Brazilian movie at the Varsity Theater on Sunday, July 24, at 7:00 P.M. The movie is called *Black Orpheus*.

**7.**

| | | | | | | ¹W | | ²N |
|---|---|---|---|---|---|---|---|---|
| | | ³S | ⁴C | I | E | N | C | E |
| | ⁵T | | L | | S | | | W |
| ⁶S | H | O | W | | ⁷A | C | T | R | E | S | ⁸S |
| | R | | L | | S | E | | I |
| | ⁹V | I | D | E | O | S | R | | N |
| ¹⁰P | | L | | | C | | I | N | | G |
| O | | L | | | | | ¹¹R | E |
| | | E | | | ¹²A | C | T | O | R | R |
| ¹³P | R | O | G | R | A | M | L | | C |
| | | S | | | | | | K |

# 5 Tell me about your family

**1.**
a) uncle   b) son   c) father   d) nephew   e) brother
f) husband

**2.**
| children | people/persons |
|---|---|
| nieces | women |
| relatives | men |

**3.**
A: What do your children do?
A: What does your daughter study?
A: Do your sons live in a dormitory?
A: What do your parents do?
A: Do your parents live with you?
A: Does your wife speak English?

**4.**

| *With /z/* | *With /s/* | *With /ɪz/* |
|---|---|---|
| goes | asks | manages |
| lives | meets | practices |
| marries | thinks | relaxes |
| | writes | |

**5.**
b) Yes, <u>she does</u>.
c) Yes, <u>he is</u>.
d) No, <u>they don't</u>.
e) No, <u>they aren't</u>.
f) No, <u>he doesn't</u>.
g) Yes, <u>she is</u>.
h) <u>Yes</u>, <u>they do</u>. (*or* <u>No</u>, <u>they don't</u>.)

**6.**
a) Yeah, nice talking to you.
b) I've been just fine, thanks.

c) No kidding!
d) Oh, they're both OK.
e) Things are really busy now.
f) Thanks. You, too.

**7.**
a) Not polite   b) Polite   c) Not polite   d) Not polite   e) Polite   f) Polite   g) Not polite   h) Not polite

**8.**
American and Canadian families often <u>invite</u> (*or* <u>have</u>) friends and relatives over for dinner. The guests usually <u>bring</u> a small gift, like some flowers or a bottle of wine. Before dinner, the family and guests usually sit and <u>talk</u> together and <u>have</u> drinks. Then everyone <u>moves</u> to the dining table for dinner. At the end of the meal, everyone <u>has</u> dessert and coffee. After that, the family and the guests <u>go</u> back to the living room and <u>sit</u> and talk some more. The guests usually <u>leave</u> (*or* <u>go</u>) around 10:00 or 10:30 P.M.

**9.**
a) grandmother   b) retired   c) aunt   d) meet   e) help

**10.**
b) No, she doesn't drive a taxi. She drives a bus.
c) No, he doesn't work in a factory. He works in an office.
d) No, she doesn't study art. She studies music.
e) No, she doesn't sell computers. She sells videos.
f) No, he doesn't live in the United States. He lives in Canada.

# 6 Do you play tennis?

**1.**
a) What do you usually do on Saturday?
b) We usually don't get up early.
c) We often go downtown in the morning.
d) Sometimes my wife goes to the gym. (*or* My wife sometimes goes to the gym.)
e) I always go to my Spanish class.
f) We always meet for lunch.
g) We often do the shopping in the afternoon.
h) We never go out on Saturday night.

**2.**
A: What time do you get up <u>in</u> the morning?
B: I always get up <u>around</u> six o'clock and run for an hour. How about you?
A: Well, I usually wake up <u>at</u> seven and watch TV in bed until ten.
B: Oh, really? When do you go <u>to</u> work?
A: Twelve o'clock. I work <u>in</u> the afternoon.
B: What do you usually do <u>on</u> your day off?
A: I play basketball <u>in</u> the afternoon with some friends. How about you?
B: Oh, I usually go <u>to</u> the gym and work out.

**3.**
On Tuesday, he plays tennis after work. On Wednesday, he stays home and studies. On Thursday, he does the laundry in the morning. On Friday, he goes to the gym. On Saturday, he invites friends over for dinner. On Sunday, he works on the car.

**4.**
Answers will vary.

**5.**
Suggested answers:

*do:* aerobics, homework, housework, the laundry
*go:* hiking, roller skating, shopping, skiing
*listen to:* a ballgame, music, a play, the radio, sports, a talk show
*play:* music, the radio, sports, tennis
*watch:* a ballgame, a play, sports, a talk show, TV

**6.**
a)   YWCA/YMCA
b)   Hiking Club
c)   Adult Education Program or YWCA/YMCA
d)   YWCA/YMCA
e)   Adult Education Program or YMCA/YWCA
f)   Hiking Club

**7.**
B: Yes, I do.
B: About three times a week.
B: I usually go swimming and play racquetball.
B: I always go to the YWCA.
B: Thanks a lot.

**8.**

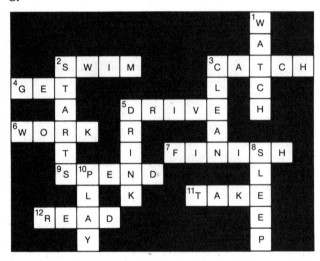

# 7 It was terrific!

**1.**
a)   added       e)   liked       i)   stayed
b)   carried     f)   listened    j)   tried
c)   danced      g)   married     h)   visited
d)   enjoyed     h)   phoned      i)   worked

**2.**
Dear Karen,
My vacation <u>was</u> great! I <u>visited</u> my friends in Puerto Rico. I <u>stayed</u> at a nice hotel near a beautiful beach. We <u>rented</u> a car and <u>traveled</u> around the island. I <u>tried</u> to learn windsurfing, but it <u>was</u> difficult. I <u>enjoyed</u> the food and really <u>liked</u> the fresh fruit. I <u>talked</u> to a lot of

local people there. I'm really glad I <u>studied</u> Spanish in high school. See you soon!

Love,
Ken

**3.**

| | | | | | |
|---|---|---|---|---|---|
| 5 | did | 9 | <u>did</u> | 12 | were |
| 1 | [was] | 11 | <u>were</u> | 10 | <u>didn't</u>, <u>didn't</u> |
| 3 | did | 4 | <u>was</u> | 2 | <u>was</u>, <u>was</u> |
| 7 | <u>Did</u> | 8 | <u>didn't</u> | 6 | <u>did</u> |

1 A: How was your trip to Europe?
2 B: The trip <u>was</u> pretty good, but the weather <u>was</u> a bit cool.
3 A: Where <u>did</u> you go?
4 B: We went to Spain. It <u>was</u> great.
5 A: Oh, good! And what <u>did</u> you do in Spain?
6 B: Oh, we <u>did</u> the usual sightseeing and shopping.
7 A: <u>Did</u> you see a bullfight in Spain?
8 B: No, we <u>didn't</u>. I don't like bullfights.
9 A: Oh, really? I enjoy them. And <u>did</u> you go to Portugal?
10 B: No, we <u>didn't</u>. We <u>didn't</u> have time, unfortunately.
11 A: So how long <u>were</u> you in Spain?
12 B: We <u>were</u> there for two weeks.

**4.**

A: How <u>was</u> your <u>weekend</u>?
A: What <u>did</u> <u>you</u> <u>do</u> <u>on</u> Saturday? (*or* What <u>did</u> <u>you</u> do?)
A: And what <u>did</u> you do <u>on</u> Sunday?
A: Did <u>you</u> <u>like</u> it? (*or* Did <u>you</u> <u>like</u> <u>the</u> <u>movie</u>? *or* Did you <u>enjoy</u> it? *or* Did you <u>enjoy</u> <u>the</u> <u>movie</u>?)
B: How <u>was</u> your <u>weekend</u>?
B: What <u>did</u> <u>you</u> <u>do</u>?

**5.**

In order of appearance: 3, 5, 7, 1, 4, 6, 2

1 We had a great vacation in California!
2 We started our trip in San Francisco.
3 We rode the cable car, saw Chinatown and Fisherman's Wharf, and took a cruise around San Francisco Bay.
4 After San Francisco, we went to Los Angeles. We loved Disneyland and Universal Studios, but I didn't much care for the city.
5 Then we rented a car and drove to Palm Springs. It's about three hours from Los Angeles. We played golf there and took a tour.
6 From Palm Springs, we went to San Diego. It's a beautiful city, and the zoo is really interesting.
7 Well, that's about all for now. I'll tell you about the rest of my trip when I get back.

**6.**

b) I met him in Japan.
c) I saw it on Thursday night.
d) I got them at Macy's.
e) I did it this afternoon.
f) I learned it in high school.
g) I visited them last summer.
h) I heard about it on the news.
i) I took her to an Italian restaurant.
j) I bought you something special.

**7.**
*Food:* buy, cook, drink, eat, make
*On Vacation:* fly, tour, travel, visit
*Sports and Exercise:* climb, jog, run, walk
*School:* learn, read, study, write

**8.**
There are seven differences:

| | *Tony's statement* | *Rita's statement* |
|---|---|---|
| 1 | after dinner, went for a walk | after dinner, drove around Chinatown |
| 2 | and did some shopping | and looked at the shops |
| 3 | I bought some magazines | — |
| 4 | and Rita bought some candy | — |
| 5 | then went for a drive along the lake | — |
| 6 | got home at 11 P.M. | came home at 10:30 P.M. |
| 7 | and went to bed | and watched TV until midnight |

# 8 You can't miss it!

**1.**
Suggested answers:

b) Yes, there's one on the corner of Ash and 3rd.
c) There's one across from (*or* opposite) the gas station on 2nd Street.
d) It's near 2nd Street.
e) Yes, there's one opposite (*or* across from) the YWCA on Ash.
f) There's one next to the YWCA.

**2.**
a) It's really nice.
b) It has five rooms.
c) It's very quiet.
d) Yes, just across the street.
e) Thanks. I really like it.

**3.**
Order of answers will vary. Suggested answers:

c) There is a school on the corner of Brown and 10th in A, but there isn't one in B. In B, there is a hospital.
d) There is a movie theater opposite the library in A, but there isn't one in B.
e) There is a restaurant across from some shops on 12th Street in A, but there isn't one in B. In B, there is a drugstore.
f) There is a post office next to the hotel in A, but there isn't one in B. In B, there's a movie theater.
g) There is a supermarket on the corner of White and 10th in A, but there isn't one in B.
h) There are some houses on 12th and 13th Streets, but there aren't any in B. In B, there are some apartment buildings.
i) There are some houses near the corner of White and 13th in B, but there aren't any in A.
j) There is a bank on the corner of Brown and 11th in A, but there isn't one in B. In B, there is a department store.

**4.**

a) For rent: Large house in <u>quiet location</u>. Near schools and public transportation. Good for family with children. <u>Right</u> <u>next</u> <u>to the</u> airport <u>and</u> <u>freeway</u>. Call Mr. Hill at 932-5570.

b) <u>Small</u> <u>studio</u> <u>apartment</u> available. <u>4</u> <u>bedrooms</u>. New carpet, bed, and stove. $350. Phone 442-8541.

c) <u>Unfurnished</u> <u>house</u> in quiet neighborhood. Available Nov. 1. Near schools and shops. <u>New</u> <u>carpets</u>, <u>sofa</u>, <u>beds</u>, <u>and</u> <u>refrigerator</u>. Call John at 437-9982.

d) <u>Room</u> (<u>200</u> <u>square feet</u>) available in comfortable home. Completely furnished with bed, TV, and carpet. No kitchen. Near the university. <u>Good</u> <u>for</u> <u>family</u> <u>with</u> <u>children</u>. Phone Mrs. Melrose mornings 389-4357.

e) Beautiful <u>new house</u> on Elm St. Only $500 month. 3 bedrooms, double garage, garden. <u>House</u> <u>only</u> <u>30</u> <u>years old</u> but in good condition. Riley Realtors.

f) Mobile home for rent. <u>Very</u> <u>cheap</u>. 1,200 square feet. 2 bedrooms, bath, and kitchen. $1,800/week. Furnished. Call 852-6103 now.

**5.**
Answers will vary.

**6.**

# 9  Which one is Judy?

**1.**
Suggested answers:

*Women only*
bikini      dress
blouse     miniskirt
bra

*Both men and women*

| | |
|---|---|
| belt | pants |
| bracelet | scarf |
| cap | shirt* |
| earrings | three-piece suit* |
| gloves | tie* |
| jeans | T-shirt |
| cufflinks* | |

*Men only*
boxer shorts

*These items are more often worn by men than women.

**2.**

| | | | |
|---|---|---|---|
| coming | having | running | swimming |
| doing | helping | selling | taking |
| getting | loving | smoking | working |

**3.**
e) bad    h) boring    g) curly    c) expensive    f) noisy
a) small    d) tall    b) young

**4.**

a) A woman <u>is walking</u> her dog. Two policemen <u>are</u> <u>talking</u> to a driver. A boy <u>is selling</u> newspapers. A girl <u>is riding</u> a skateboard. Some construction workers <u>are working</u> on a building. Some people <u>are</u> <u>waiting</u> at the bus stop. Two women <u>are jogging</u>. They <u>are listening</u> to music. A mail carrier <u>is</u> <u>collecting</u> the mail.

b) Dan and Cindy <u>are dancing</u>. Keiko <u>is serving</u> drinks. Angela <u>is sitting</u> on the sofa. She <u>is talking</u> to Kim. Marie and Joe <u>are playing</u> cards. Helmut <u>is eating</u> a pizza. Carlos <u>is standing</u> by the window. He <u>is</u> <u>smoking</u> a pipe.

**5.**

a) He's in his thirties. He's pretty tall. He has <u>straight</u> <u>black</u> <u>hair</u>. (He is bald.) He's wearing jeans and a <u>T-</u> <u>shirt</u>. (He's wearing jeans and a shirt.)

b) She's about <u>fifty</u>. (She's fifteen.) She's pretty tall. She has long hair. She's wearing jeans and boots. She's <u>standing</u> <u>next</u> <u>to</u> a motorcycle. (She's sitting on a motorcycle.)

c) She has <u>short</u> brown hair and she's <u>wearing glasses</u>. (She has long brown hair and she's not wearing glasses.) She's fairly short and she's about twenty-five. She's wearing a blouse and a skirt.

d) He's about ten. He has <u>curly</u> blond hair. (He has straight blond hair.) He's wearing shorts and a black and white shirt. He's carrying <u>some</u> <u>magazines</u>. (He's carrying a book.)

**6.**
A: What time <u>are you going to the party</u>?
A: How <u>are you going</u>? (*or* How <u>are you getting there</u>?
A: Who <u>are you going with</u>?
A: What <u>are you wearing</u>?
A: How long <u>are you staying</u>?
A: Where <u>are you going after the party</u>?

**7.**
Suggested answers:

Pierre du Pont is around twenty. He is medium height. He has long blond hair. He is wearing jeans, a T-shirt, and boots. He is carrying a backpack.

Diane Jones is about ten. She is fairly short. She has short curly hair. She is wearing a blouse, shorts, and sandals. She is carrying a doll.

**8.**
Answers will vary.

# 10 Guess what happened!

**1.**

| *Present* | *Past* | *Past Participle* |
|---|---|---|
| be | was | been |
| break | broke | broken |
| drive | drove | driven |
| forget | forgot | forgotten |
| go | went | gone |
| know | knew | known |
| see | saw | seen |
| take | took | taken |

**2.**
Answers will vary.

**3.**
A group of tourists on a tour of the Grand Canyon <u>had</u> a free helicopter ride on a recent vacation. The group <u>rented</u> a boat for a ride through the canyon, but the <u>boat ran</u> into a rock and sank. The tourists <u>swam</u> to the shore and <u>spent</u> the night in a cave. The next morning, a rescue team in a helicopter <u>saw</u> them and <u>lifted</u> them out of the canyon. "It <u>was</u> the best part of our tour," <u>said</u> one of the tourists.

A passenger traveling to California nearly <u>arrived</u> in New Zealand on Sunday. The passenger <u>took</u> a flight from Chicago. He <u>heard</u> an announcement and <u>got</u> on the plane. Two hours later, he <u>discovered</u> it was a flight to Auckland, New Zealand, and not Oakland, California. When the plane <u>stopped</u> (*or* <u>arrived</u>) in Honolulu, he <u>took</u> another flight back to California.

**4.**
a) That's terrible!   b) How embarrassing!   c) Lucky you!   d) Oh, that's terrific!

**5.**
In order of appearance: 6, 11, 1, 5, 12, 10, 2, 8, 3, 4, 7, 9

1 I had a terrible experience on Saturday.
2 I got a flat tire on the freeway.
3 I looked in the trunk for the spare tire, but it was flat, too.
4 Next, I stood by my car for thirty minutes, but no one stopped.
5 So then I walked for about two miles to a gas station.
6 The guy there drove me back to my car and fixed the tire.
7 Then I got in the car again and drove off.
8 But half an hour later, the car broke down.
9 This time, it was the engine.
10 I tried to get the engine to start, but nothing happened.
11 Then, luckily, someone stopped and helped me. He was a mechanic and he fixed the engine.
12 What a day! Next time, I'll take the bus!

**6.**
a) Have you ever been to Disneyland?
b) Have you ever been in a car accident?
c) Have you ever flown in a helicopter?
d) Have you ever gone to Europe? *or* Have you ever been to Europe?
e) Have you ever seen a Chinese opera?
f) Have you ever tried windsurfing?

**7.**
Suggested answers:

*drive:* a car, a truck, a taxi, a van
*have:* an accident, a bicycle, a car, a flat tire, a horse, a motorcycle, a taxi, a trip, a truck, a vacation, a van
*ride:* a bicycle, a bus, a horse, a motorcycle, a train
*take:* a bus, a flight, a taxi, a train, a trip, a vacation

**8.**

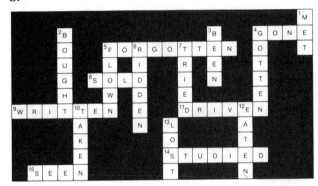

# 11 It's an interesting place

**1.**
B: Yes, it's beautiful and it has an excellent beach. (*or* Yes, it has an excellent beach and it's beautiful.)
B: It's very nice in the summer. (*or* In the summer, it's very nice.)
B: *Suggested answers:* It's very cold in the winter and it snows a lot. (*or* It snows a lot and it's very cold in the winter. *or* It snows a lot in the winter, and it's very cold.)
B: Yes, it's an interesting place with a good museum.
B: No, it's not too expensive and rents are cheap.

**2.**
a) expensive   b) boring   c) modern   d) safe   e) crowded

**3.**
Tokyo is Japan's most exciting city. It is a city where old Japan meets modern Japan, with beautiful new skyscrapers and fascinating old temples. It is a very <u>busy</u> city. The streets are always <u>empty</u> and the subways are crowded. It is also one of the most <u>expensive</u> cities in the world. A room in a good hotel <u>only</u> <u>costs</u> <u>a</u> <u>few</u> <u>dollars</u>.

Los Angeles is the biggest city in California. It is famous for its freeways, its movie stars, and its <u>smog</u>. It has excellent museums, universities, and shopping centers. Los Angeles is not far from Disneyland, which is only 1,500 miles away. Visitors like to go to the film studios and to drive along Hollywood Boulevard. Los Angeles has a warm climate, clean air, and good beaches nearby.

**4.**
c) You should go in the spring or the summer.
d) You shouldn't miss the National Museum.
e) You should see the new zoo.
f) You shouldn't walk alone late at night.
g) You should change your money at a bank.
h) You shouldn't change money on the street.
i) You shouldn't drink the tap water.

**5.**
b) London is an exciting city, and it has great nightclubs.
c) My hometown is a beautiful place, but the climate there is too cold for me in the winter.
d) Australia is a beautiful country, and it has a very good climate.
e) Tokyo is an exciting place for a vacation, and it is very good for shopping.
f) Washington, D.C., does not have a very good climate, but it is a very interesting place to visit.

**6.**
a) small   b) horrible   c) nice   d) ugly   e) excellent

**7.**
b) Copenhagen is a clean city.
d) Dallas has a big airport.
f) London is a crowded city in the summer.
h) Rio is an exciting place to visit.

**8.**
London is Britain's biggest city. It is a very old city and dates back to the Romans. It is a city of beautiful buildings and churches, and it has many beautiful parks. It also has some of the best museums in the world. London is very crowded in summer. It is a popular city with foreign tourists, and has more than eight million visitors a year. The city is famous for its shopping and has many excellent department stores. London has an excellent underground railway system, so it is easy for tourists to get around. There are plenty of good restaurants in London. You can get excellent British food, and London has lots of good Indian, Chinese, Japanese, French, Italian, and Greek restaurants.

# 12 It really works!

**1.**
d) a pain in your stomach after eating
c) an uncomfortable feeling after drinking too much alcohol
f) something you take to cure an illness
a) a place where you buy medicine
b) a hot feeling when you have a cold or the flu
i) difficulty going to sleep
g) a cream used mainly for burns and other skin problems

h) a liquid soap for washing your hair
e) a drink made from a fruit or vegetable

**2.**
Answers will vary.

**3.**
Suggested answers:

*a bottle of:* juice, milk, 7-Up, sunburn lotion, tablets
*a box of:* cookies, matches, tissues
*a can of:* juice, 7-Up, shaving cream
*a carton of:* juice, milk
*a jar of:* cookies, jam
*a package of:* butter, cookies, matches, tissues
*a tube of:* shaving cream, sunburn lotion, toothpaste

**4.**
b) For a headache, you should take aspirin.
c) For a cold, you should drink hot chicken soup.
d) For indigestion, you should drink water with baking soda.
e) For a sore throat, you should take some cough drops.
f) For insomnia, you should drink warm milk.
g) For a sunburn, you should use some lotion.

**5.**
a) F   b) F   c) T   d) T   e) F   f) T

**6.**
A: I need something for insomnia.
B: Try these tablets. Take two in the evening. And don't drink a lot of coffee.
A: OK, thank you.
B: And sometimes warm milk helps you go to sleep.
A: Really? I'll try it.
B: Anything else?
A: Yes, can I have a bottle of Valium tablets, please?
B: Oh, you should get a prescription from the doctor for those.

**7.**

# 13 May I take your order, please?

**1.**

A: May I take your order, please?
B: Yes, I'd like a steak, please. (*or* Yes, I'll have a steak, please.) I'd like it well done.
A: And would you like a salad?
B: Yes, please. (*or* Yes, I would.)
A: What kind of dressing would you like?
B: French, please.
A: Would you like anything to drink?
B: Yes, I'd like coffee, please. (*or* Yes, I'll have coffee, please.)
A: Anything else?
B: No, that'll be all, thanks.

**2.**

Suggested answers:

*Side Orders:* french fries, garlic bread, small salad
*Appetizers:* clam chowder, onion soup, shrimp cocktail
*Entrees:* baked fish, fried chicken, lobster, oysters, roast beef, spaghetti and meatballs, steak
*Desserts:* carrot cake, cheesecake, chocolate cake, ice cream, lemon meringue pie
*Vegetables:* beans, broccoli, carrots, fresh peas, sweet corn
*Drinks:* beer, coffee, soda, tea, wine

**3.**

In order of appearance: 7, 3, 11, 1, 8, 4, 6, 10, 5, 2, 9

1 The host or hostess greets you.
2 Someone takes you to a table and you sit down.
3 The waiter or waitress brings you a menu.
4 You look through the menu and decide what you want to eat and drink.
5 The waiter or waitress writes down your order.
6 Then he or she takes the order to the kitchen.
7 The cook prepares your meal.
8 The waiter or waitress then brings your meal.
9 You eat your meal, and then have dessert if you want.
10 When you are ready to leave, you ask for the check.
11 The waiter or waitress brings your check, and then you pay the bill and leave.

**4.**

A: Hello. Domino Pizza. May I help you?
A: Sure. Would you like a large one?
A: What kind of topping would you like? (*or* What kind of topping will you have?)
A: Fine. And would you like anything to drink?
A: Could I have your name, please?
A: And may I have your address?

**5.**

a) Not right now, thanks.
b) You're welcome.
c) Thanks. You, too.
d) I hope so. Bye.

**6.**

a) tips   b) salaries   c) order   d) flavor   e) a reservation   f) dressing   g) include   h) product

**7.**

a) YumYum
b) Giorgio's
c) YumYum
d) Cafe Athens
e) Dynasty, YumYum
f) Dynasty
g) YumYum, Giorgo's

# 14 It's the greatest!

**1.**

c) a dry sandy place where it doesn't rain
d) a large area of land covered with trees
b) the area where the ocean meets the land, usually with sand or rocks
f) an area of water with land all around it
i) the area of land between two rows of hills or mountains, often with a river running through it
j) a mountain with a hole at the top, which sometimes gives off hot gas and lava
g) a very high hill usually with trees at the top or covered with snow
a) a wide street in a city, or a road between two rows of trees
h) an area of salt water that covers a large part of the earth
e) a piece of land with water all around it

**2.**

a) bigger
b) busier
c) cooler
d) drier
e) friendlier
f) higher
g) larger
h) longer
i) noisier
j) safer
k) warmer
l) wetter

**3.**

c) bigger   d) cheaper   e) more exciting   f) more dangerous   g) more interesting   h) older   i) hotter

**4.**

a) better   b) worst   c) good   d) worse   e) best

**5.**

b) smallest   c) biggest   d) longest   e) highest
f) driest

**6.**

Australia is an island continent in the South Pacific. The capital is Canberra, but the city with the biggest population is Sydney, which has nearly four million. English is the first language of most people, but there are also many immigrants who speak other languages. Indonesia is one of Australia's nearest neighbors. It is only a short flight from the northern city of Darwin, Australia's biggest city.

Canada is the second largest country in land size. It stretches 3,223 miles from east to west, and from the North Pole to the U.S. border. Canada has a warm climate all year round. Both English and French are official languages. Many French-speaking people live in the province of Quebec, where Montreal is the biggest city. Canada has a cold winter, and many Canadians enjoy winter sports, such as skiing and ice skating.

Switzerland is a small country in central Europe. Its neighbors are France in the west, Italy in the south, Austria in the east, and West Germany in the north.

Sixty percent of the land is mountains. Switzerland is famous for its banks, tourism, and skiing. It's a very easy place to drive around because it's flat.

**7.**

# 15 What are you doing Friday night?

**1.**
A: Hello. Grant and Lee. Can/May I help you?
B: Yes, I'd like to speak to Mr. Ted Schmidt, please.
A: I'm sorry. He's out right now. Would you like to leave a message?
B: Yes, please. This is Ms. Curtis. Could you tell him I'm staying at the Clarion Hotel?
A: OK.
B: And would/could you ask him to phone me tonight? My room number is 605.

A: All right, Ms. Curtis. I'll give him the message.
B: Thank you very much. Goodbye.
A: Goodbye/Bye.

**2.**
a) OK. I'll tell her.
b) Sure. I'd love to.
c) Oh, sorry. I can't.
d) That'd be nice.

**3.**
A: Yes, thank you. Please tell her there is a birthday party for Fred on Sunday.
A: And could you tell her the party is at Jenny's apartment.
A: And one more thing. Please ask her to bring her guitar.

**4.**
*have:* a barbecue, a party, a picnic
*read:* a novel, a play
*see:* a movie, a musical, a play, a show
*take:* a cooking lesson, a driving test
*visit:* an art gallery, a museum
*watch:* a ballgame, a movie, a video

**5.**
Answers will vary.

**6.**
Answers will vary.

**7.**
1. a) Instant connections, clearer conversations, connections to central computers, fax machines
b) Making a phone call, doing banking, ordering videos for television, buying things, connecting home computers to computer information centers, sending letters and documents by fax, sending video pictures
c) Making phone calls from outside your home or office (e.g., from your car); also, same answers as in (b)
d) Along radio waves
2. Answers will vary.